West African Pop Roots

West African Pop Roots

John Collins

Temple University Press
Philadelphia

Temple University Press, Philadelphia 19122
Copyright © 1992 by Temple University Press. All rights reserved
Published 1992
Printed in the United States of America

An earlier version of this work was published in 1985 under the title *African Pop
Roots: The Inside Rhythms of Africa* by W. Foulsham & Co. Ltd., London.

The paper used in this publication meets the minimum requirements of
American National Standard for Information Sciences—Permanence of Paper
for Printed Library Materials, ANSI Z39.48-1984 ∞

Library of Congress Cataloging-in-Publication Data

Collins, John, 1944–
    West African pop roots / John Collins.
      p.   cm.
    Rev. ed. of: African pop roots. c1985.
    Includes index.
    ISBN 0-87722-793-4 (cloth). — ISBN 0-87722-916-3 (paper)
      1. Popular music—Africa, West—History and criticism. 2. Folk
music—Africa, West—History and criticism. 3. Musicians—Africa,
West—Biography. I. Collins, John, 1944–   African pop roots.
II. Title.
ML3503.A358C63   1992
781.63'0966—dc20
                                                              91-35089
                                                              CIP

Photographs: John Collins, Anton Corbijn, Flemming Harrev, Juliet Highet,
Jak Kilby, Sylvia Moore, Yemo Nunu, Ton van der Lee, Ian Watts

Contents

Section Four   Music Business

Section Five   Cross-Overs

Introduction

$\mathcal{W}$*est African Pop Roots* is the extraordinary and intimate story of the hidden roots of Africa's popular music. It traces the life and messages of Africa's body music—body music transported across the Atlantic to the New World, where it was transposed into myriads of time- and mind-bending styles. These styles reflect lifestyles generated from a common heritage, all pointing back to African roots.

This creative explosion crossed back to Africa, exposing Africans and blacks of the diaspora alike to a multitude of creative sources, from which new syntheses emerged. Cross-over music from Africa and the diaspora has spread to every part of the globe. For more than a hundred years dance music has been dominated by African and black-inspired rhythms.

What is the fascination of this pulsating force? The world has come to know it from the outside, back-to-front as it were. First there were the spirituals, the blues, jazz, and hot gospel, all based on the rhythms of Africa. Thelonius Monk thought of his piano as a drum. Then there was the emergence of African rhythms through modified white forms such as rock and roll, when Bill Haley cottoned on to the popular potential of black music—music that was driving young white Americans to tune in to illicit black radio stations, and to pace the wrong side of town to find out how to click their fingers, move their bodies, and talk in a language unknown in their homes.

Then West Africa's Osibisa burst onto the international music scene. Their "Afro-rock" music resounded with a rhythmic energy that came directly from Africa. When Osibisa were unleashed on the British public, they took audiences by surprise. As one critic put it, Osibisa "grabbed them by the scruff of the neck and

Ojah playing in London, 1979.

made them dance." If Osibisa grabbed the public by the scruff of
the neck, the real story has still to be told.

West African Pop Roots lays bare the inner driving forces and
influences of popular music in Africa since the turn of this century—the great names, their frustrations and struggles, setbacks
and successes; their love of music and of each other; their common
bonds; and their belief in the power of body rhythm.

Here are the personal stories of the artists, as they have never
been told before, based on their life experiences and the living

memories of the older generation. We get behind the screen of the glossy paraphernalia of the superstars, to hear personal anecdotes about the way they live, their families and friends, life on the road, and palm-wine days.

Cross-overs back to Africa are charted from the roots. These include the flourishing of Afro-pop styles inspired by the blues, jazz, the Latin beat, salsa, soul, funk, reggae, disco, and other black dance-styles shaped in South America, the Caribbean, and the United States. But what about minstrelsy, popular already in the early 1900s in West Africa, along with the movies of Al Jolson? It was this in Ghana that led to the concert parties (local comic opera groups), such as the Jaguar Jokers, which combine minstrelsy with folkloric characters such as the traditional Akan spider hero, Ananse.

Who knows about the vaudeville and ragtime hits in West Africa in the 1920s? After that swing became the rage, brought in by the Allied troops stationed there during the Second World War. It was soon taken up by local dance-bands.

Jazz also went to Africa in the 1950s. Louis Armstrong ("Satchmo") visited West Africa in 1956 and 1962. The All-Stars and Satchmo were welcomed at the Accra airport by a massed band of top Ghanaian dance-band musicians.

Later soul met soul in Africa with visits there by James Brown, Millicent Small, Chubby Checker, Wilson Pickett, Ike and Tina Turner, the Staple Singers, Randy Weston, Jimmy Cliff, Bob Marley, Steel Pulse, and many other black artists. From rumba to rap, and ragtime to rock and reggae, the New World music of the black diaspora has found its way back to Africa. *West African Pop Roots* shows the creative impact of these multiple black trans-Atlantic cross-overs. Africa is reaping the harvest of its own seeds.

West African Pop Roots explores other fusions, such as South African kwela, congo jazz, Sierra Leone maringa, Afro-reggae, and Afro-disco. The great names are there—Miriam Makeba, Manu Dibango, Franco, E. T. Mensah, Victor Uwaifo, Ebeneezer Obey, Youssou N'Dour, Fela, Salif Keita, Sunny Ade, and Alpha Blondy—to mention a few.

West African Pop Roots not only presents the outstanding personalities, the developments in cross-overs, and a whole way of life. It is also a cameo of historical episodes in the life of a continent: the colonial intrusions of forts, ports, and the military; insights into what it was like to live in Monrovia, Liberia, in the nineteenth century, when the black American Liberians settled there, bringing along the quadrille and their own cultural resources.

Finally, this book exposes the global reach of the roots of pop, and the search of Western superstars, all returning to Africa. Ginger Baker of Cream and Paul McCartney with Wings went to Nigeria, followed by Mick Fleetwood of Fleetwood Mac and Brian Eno. Since then many other white pop musicians have begun looking to Africa for inspiration—Peter Gabriel, Malcolm McClaren, Sting, Paul Simon, Stewart Copeland, Bob Geldof, David Byrne, and others. These artists are turning more and more to African roots shaped by a dynamic philosophy of cool and hot, the laid-back energy of highlife, the spaciness of Afro-beat, the "criss-cross" power of Afro-rock, and the fever of African dances.

The full circle has turned. As Kofi Ghanaba (Guy Warren), Ghana's famous drummer, notes, "Our artists leave home in search of a new sound, and they end up by going back home." Equalisation is about to occur. This book delves into the past and present of popular African music with its outstanding sounds and personalities, going back to the vortex of it all, the ancient vibrations and wisdom of Africa, and then moving forward to present-day music happenings.

West African Pop Roots

Roots

1   Traditional Cool and Hot Rhythms

African Music in the Space Age

In spite of slavery and colonialism, African dance music has spread to every corner of the world and is flourishing back home. What is so special about it? Where does it get its power and popularity?

First and foremost, music in Africa is for everyone and for every occasion. It is truly folk music, played by and for the people.

Wherever you go in Africa, people play music and dance—from tiny tots to cool and collected elders. There is music for all occasions—a woman pounding yams, a typist putting rhythm into the machine, a carpenter embellishing his hammering, and even a traffic policeman pirouetting on his pedestal. Infants learn rhythm on their mothers' backs, and children have a vast array of musical games and toys.

African music is democratic. Genius and excellence shine from within the whole community, giving inner illumination and providing the opportunity for tuning in to the world of spirit and nature. It is alive from within, not dazzling from without, like some of the works of Western classical composers or modern rock superstars.

This African music for all peoples and all occasions was taken by slaves to the New World, where it burst asunder some of the straitjacketing to which Western creativity had been subjected.

Another feature of African music that has led to its flourishing in modern times is that it is a unifying music. There are no disembodied parts. The head is not separate from the feet. So whether in traditional drumming by moonlight, the guitar-band music of African night-clubs, or the funk and reggae of the discos and sound systems, there is a communion of the beat.

African music brings different aspects of life together since it is performed in association with other art forms, such as dancing, drama, masked parades, and poetry. Ashanti drums may beat out a poem:

> The path has crossed the river,
> The river has crossed the path,
> Which is the elder?
> We made the path and found the river,
> The river is from long ago,
> From the Creator of the Universe.

The tradition of unified art in Africa has continued to the present day. One only has to consider the African concert parties, which fuse music, dance, drama, painting, and comic literature. In the New World black minstrelsy started up and then came vaudeville with its tap-dancing, ragtime music, satire, and comedy acts. Today there are the toasters and disc jockeys, this generation's musicians, poets, comedians, and commentators—all rolled into one.

The Structure of Traditional African Music

African music unifies by binding together the complicated fragments of a song's cross-rhythms and cross-melodies. First and foremost is the beat, the rhythmic totality that is repeated in cycles throughout the music.

The separate strands of music are woven together by call and response, dialogue and overlapping conversation among the various rhythms, voices, instruments, and dancers. Yet each leaves space for the others. Drummers and dancers may respond to each other; the singer and chorus alternate with one another; and gaps are left open for the participants' handclaps. Everyone has a voice in the musical happening.

The Power of the Music

The power of the African arts lies in the fact that they have always been an integral part of life, accompanying all important social functions—weddings, funerals, communal work and play, festivals, religious ceremonies.

African music has a crucial purpose in the transmission of knowledge. There are songs of advice, warning, information, and morality. The Ashanti *okyerema* (court drummer) is the actual symbol of knowledge and wisdom. During court cases he drums out counsel and recommendations. The whole apprentice system is built into African music, where the first lesson in becoming a master musician is patience and discipline, followed by many years spent in learning the skills of the trade and its esoteric wisdom. That is how the master-drummer or court troubadour (or griot or jali as he is called in West Africa) is able to play out the history of his people. He is close to the ancestors and the deeper undercurrents of society.

This concern for origins or roots is evident in the "Awakening" played by the drummers at the start of the Ashanti Adae Festival. Before anything else can begin, the drummers play homage to the ancestors for providing the materials out of which their drums are made, like cedar wood and elephant skin, as well as to the ancestor of all drummers.

Besides containing the cool and collected wisdom of the ancestors and society as a whole, the local music of Africa sparks off hot, disoriented states, where the grip of the dance beat becomes that of possession by the spiritual archetypes of a particular beat. So strong is this African idea of dance as body-prayer that it has

Traditional dancers.

influenced African Separatist churches, the soul and spirituals of America, and the Pocomania, Rastafarianism, and Santería of the Caribbean and the Candomblé of Brazil.

Not only does African music spread wisdom and knowledge, but it is also used to send messages. Messages played on tonal drums imitate Africa's tonal languages. When the first Europeans visited Kumasi, the capital of the Ashanti Empire, they were told that the drums were discussing the current situation of the Napoleonic Wars. The news of a big British defeat in the Ashanti Wars was known in Sierra Leone by the local people before the British because of this "bush telegraph."

African music is not just a tool for social control. It is also an instrument of satire and protest. In the olden days a chief could be literally drummed out of town by the young warrior associations and the secret masked societies. There were even musical duels. Musicians were (and still are) court jesters and social critics.

African musical traditions accommodate change as each generation brings its own ideas and styles, modifying older ones. Even the traditional or "cultural" music that abounds in Africa today is not a fossilised remnant, but the product of thousands of years of experimenting and honing down.

The Balance of Sound and Silence

What of the music itself, which generates its own power from a dynamic balancing of material and nonmaterial, sound and silence, the heat of the rhythms and the cool of the beat? This sound energy of hot rhythms is produced by the clash and interplay of the cross-rhythms, which in turn create space and time.

Rhythms are linked at critical junctions or intersections. The whole network of rhythmic sounds and spaces is locked together like the steel and air of scaffolding. Thus the space and silences between the sounds are as important as the sounds themselves—whether they are the void between the threads of cross-rhythms, the gaps that pairs of rhythms leave for one another in dialogue, or the awareness of the binary impulses of each individual rhythm—the silent upstroke and played downstroke of the drummers, dancers, and clappers. This is why Africans in the New World

Traditional drummer.

were able to turn European rhythm inside out, creating syncopated space for jazz and reggae.

The criss-crossing rhythms of various lengths finally link up as a complete time-cycle. The beat pulsates within the time-cycle, creating an inside rhythm that extends, shortens, and bends the time spans of the individual rhythms—an aural equivalent to the optical illusion of shortening, lengthening, and bending lines. The hot rhythms of Africa make space and bend time, releasing an almost infinite permutation of spaces and times.

With such a complicated pattern of interwoven sounds and spaces, how is it possible to play African music at all? The trick is to be able to flip at will from focusing on sound to focusing on silence, from figure to background. A similar skill is that of the wood carver, who chips away matter to produce space and inner form, for the shape of the carving exists at the boundary of wood and space. In the same way the African musician gives music an inner stability or shape by cutting holes in sound and being able to hear the silence. Only then can the beat really be appreciated and utilised as an anchoring point within the sea of rhythms. The beat is not only the totality of the sounds but also of all the silent gaps and spaces. This is the "hidden rhythm," a stillness within the turmoil of sounds, like the quiet in the eye of a storm.

It's not only what is played that matters, but also what is not sounded—understatement rather than overstatement. This laid-back and cooled-down approach can be achieved only after first mastering all the individual rhythms. Only after many years is it possible to become a master musician, one who can balance sound and silence. The master musician knows when to come in to strengthen a flagging rhythm, or create a silence, or jump into the silence and improvise. In other words, the master is poised between cool silence and hot sounds, the hidden rhythm and the overt beat.

Ibrahim Abdulai, a Ghanaian drummer, expounds some African musical wisdom:

> We say that music is sweet when it is cool, or "baalim"—not "cool" in the way that water or the weather is cool, but rather it means "slow" or "gentle." The young men play "yirin" or "by heart." They don't cool their bodies and take their time. If you do something that is not necessary, if you are rude or rough, if you miss your road and go to the wrong place, that is yirin, it has no meaning. The young people dance faster and they usually play faster too. When they are playing, before an old man will play this or that, the young man is already on top of it. Sometimes when you know something too much, you can do it in a rough way and add something unnecessary inside. If you beat a drum very hard the sound will reduce. And if your wrist is too fast, your drum will not sound. "My wrist is fast," that is not drumming. As you are beating, it is your heart that is talking, and what your heart is going to say, your hand will collect it and play. Unless you cool your heart, your drumming will not stand.
>
> (From John Chernoff, *African Rhythms and African Sensibility* [Chicago: Chicago University Press, 1979], p. 106)

The African master musician is in tune not only with the music, but also with society at large. He leads through balance and cooperation. He can heat people up into states of possession or

Mustapha Tetteh-Addy, one of Ghana's top master-drummers.

cool them down by focusing on inner silence. Music is a micro-cosm of the whole society.

African music is composed of many rhythms (polyrhythms). Africans are traditionally polytheistic (have many gods and god-desses), polygamous (have several spouses), polyglot (speak more than one language), and may live in compound houses. This plu-ralism and psychic space give the traditional system of ritual and protocol much flexibility. There is conformity to the rules, taboos, and regulations and yet spaces or options are left at certain critical positions as symbolic periods of freedom and chaos, upside-down behaviour, and ritual license that punctuate individual and social life.

Poise is therefore a prime virtue needed in balancing these cy-cles of freedom and necessity, chaos and order, a virtue that comes only with maturity. There is great respect for age in Africa, whether for the master musician, elder, or ancestor. Mature wisdom is ultimately obtained by an awareness of the silence and stillness enmeshed within the bustle and noise of everyday life. This gives the African sage stability. Whereas a Dagomba man like Ibrahim Abdulai calls it *baalim*, Akans call it *bokoor*, Gas call it *bleoo*, Ewe people call it *dododo*, and Yorubas call it *itutu*. African Americans call it "Daddy Cool."

Music is a microcosm of society, and African music embodies all the unspoken traditional wisdom of that continent. Black music and black art are bringing this ancient African wisdom to the modern world—the art of expressing space and time symbolically, and participating in that expression through the moving body.

African Music in the West

Africa and its diaspora have influenced a profusion of music and dance-styles that are the nearest thing we have in the twentieth century to a global folk music. At the opening of the century it was ragtime and blues; then the swing and Latin-American ballroom dance crazes of the interwar period; followed by black rhythm and blues, soul, disco, reggae, and rap—recently supplemented by the music of Africa itself.

What is it in the African approach to music that has enabled it to cross all frontiers to become, directly or indirectly, a major force in international music? Or to put the question in a different way, why is it that European classical music (unlike its technology) has not become the dominant form of the twentieth century? In fact, the two questions are linked, for the waning of classical music from the turn of the century (with the emergence of the so-called atonalist modern school) corresponds exactly in time with the proliferation of music-styles that contain seminal black influences.

One could say that the latter filled a vacuum left by classical music, but more positive reasons than this can also be found. Probably the most important is the flexibility and adaptability of African music. Indeed, this is exactly how African slaves in the Americas were able to overcome the problem of having to play the music of their masters. They syncopated it by playing around the rigid

European metre and emphasising the gaps or offbeats largely ignored in white tempo, so creating a significant space for themselves to swing in.

Unlike much of European music, with its score-sheets, metronomes, and baton-wielding conductors, African music emphasises the spontaneity of the players. This creative approach even embraces the African audiences who, unlike European ones, always dance and are just as likely to clap during the performance as after it.

So, generally speaking, the black African influence has had a balancing effect on white Western music. It has balanced the cerebral tendency of classical music with footwork and funk, the onbeat with the offbeat, the performers with their audience, and the mechanical with spontaneity and soul.

Finally, black music has a roots appeal in this modern runaway age (Babylon, as the Rastafarians call it), with much of the present-day fascination with African music being a romantic reaction against the excesses of a mechanised society.

Paradoxically, however, and as I will show later, so-called primitive African music is more relevant to the postindustrial consciousness that will be needed in the relativistic twenty-first century than Western classical music, with its stiff, one-dimensional bias.

Foundations of African Music

The agbadza, discussed here as an example, is a variation of the widespread African rhythm termed the "African signature tune" by musicologist A. M. Jones. The agbadza of eastern Ghana and Togo, a beat used in both traditional ensembles and in the modern guitar- and dance-bands, is a recreational dance of the Ewe people that emerged in the 1920s out of a much faster traditional war-dance.

One: The Parts or Subrhythms (The Hot Aspect)

African music is mostly polyrhythmic, composed of multiple rhythms each with its own particular metre. The friction between these criss-crossing polymetric strands of rhythm is what generates its energy or heat. The first stage in learning to play African music is to acquire the discipline of the separate beats. It is a training that, in Africa, starts in infancy on the dancing mother's back, or from the myriad of children's rhythmic games that abound on the continent.

In the agbadza, there are four subrhythms that create its basic phrase and correspond to one complete agbadza bell pattern. This single basic phrase of the agbadza can be imaginatively treated as being divided into twelve equally spaced time intervals—a temporal framework into which all four subrhythms can fit.

1. The feet (i.e., the dance downsteps) are played evenly four times for each basic phrase: on the first, fourth, seventh, and tenth of the imaginary twelve time intervals mentioned above.

2. The kagan drum is played with two sticks. Its rhythm is made up of groups of three notes. The right stick strikes the open drum twice; the left is then played, but with the skin muted by pressure from the right stick. This results in two high notes followed by a low, muted one. This is played four times to correspond to the twelve imaginary time intervals.

3. The kidi is a hand-drum. Its simplest rhythm is made by the right, left, then right hands striking the perimeter of the drum-skin, producing three open notes, then three muted notes, played twice over in the full agbadza phrase to make up the twelve time intervals.

4. The claves or cow-bell (Ewe *gankogui*) pattern is made up of seven pulses. If a double-headed bell is used, the very first pulse is played on the lower-pitched bell. The spacing of the seven pulses on the twelve imaginary time intervals exactly corresponds to the spacing of the seven major notes (do, re mi, fa, etc.) on the twelve intervals of one octave of the melodic scale. The first agbadza bell pulse is therefore equivalent to the note "do"—and so on up to the seventh bell pulse, which is equivalent to the note "ti."

Of interest here is that the octave scale is thought to have been developed by the Greek mathematician and musician Pythagorus, whose name comes from the sacred python and priestesses (pythia) of the Delphic Oracle. This snake cult, of which he was a member, came to pre-Achaean Greece from North Africa.

Pythagorus actually studied in Egypt, from where many of his geometrical theorems came. If his musical theories also came from Egypt, then an intriguing fact is that Africa has provided the same musical octave arrangement of seven notes/pulses on twelve intervals twice over: once in melodic and once in rhythmic form.

Two: Rhythmic Spacing (The Cool Aspect)

Besides polyrhythms, another feature of African music is the silent gaps between the individual pulses of the rhythm (between the striking of the drum and bell, the clapping of the hands, or the downward movement of the feet).

This characteristic was noted by E. M. von Hornbostel, one of the first European musicologists to become interested in African music. He divided each stroke of a drum into two components: an acoustic downbeat (the note itself) and a silent motor upbeat (when the hand is raised to strike). He believed that while Europeans focused on the sounded aspect, Africans put equal emphasis on both the heard and the unheard.

In the case of the agbadza rhythm, this even-handed stress can be illustrated by the way the maracas (Ewe *axatse*) are played. In the simplest rhythm pattern, the instrument is held in the right hand and beaten on the knee in time with the cow-bell. Instead of leaving the upstroke silent (as in the bell), the upbeat of the maraca is accentuated by striking it against the left hand, which is held above the instrument. This creates a slightly different sound from the downstroke, in a rhythm that is the exact opposite of the cow-bell pattern.

This ability to flip at will from the positive to negative aspect of rhythm is vital to the appreciation of African music, so much of which is based on call and response and interpenetrating rhythms.

Imagine the common picture that illustrates the relationship of figure and ground; it looks either like a vase or two heads facing each other, depending on your focus. If you think of it as a specific rhythm then the vase (figure) would be the sounds and the two faces (ground) the silent gaps in between. Whereas the Europeans focus on only one aspect (i.e., the figure), African musicians are experts at "seeing" the rhythmic boundary or contour from both points of view (the hot sounds and the cool space). And it is precisely this skill that was utilised by black slaves in the New World to turn European music inside out, syncopate it, and, in a sense, colonise it.

Quite another expression of spacing in African music concerns its rhythmic tempo. In the case of the twelve imaginary time intervals of the agbadza, the intervals are absolutely evenly spaced, equivalent to the exact ticks of a chronometer. Yet no drum or instrument actually plays out this rigid common denominator (the kagan comes closest in the agbadza). The drummer, in fact, can use different combinations of rhythmic tempo, anticipating or delaying the downstrokes to create all sorts of "auditory illusions." This heightened awareness of time—or what musicologist and jazz player Richard Waterman calls "metronome sense"—is the basis of swing in African music. Black slaves in the New World used this technique to circumvent the rigid onbeat metre of European music. They simply swung in the spaces between the intervals that the whites ignored.

Take a nonmusical example of a silent rhythm—from the African kitchen! In West Africa there is a favourite dish known as *fufu*. *Fufu* is usually prepared by two people. One pounds the cooked starches with a pestle, and the other turns the dough in a wooden mortar. The men or women who turn the dough have the amazing ability to remove their fingers from the descending pestle just in time. Europeans attempting this perilous operation would probably first focus their attention on the downstroke of the wooden pestle—and then place their hands where the pestle is not, a mental procedure that can easily lead to confusion and crushed fingers. Africans adeptly put their hands directly into the silence between the strokes, a single mental operation that is much safer on the fingers!

Three: The Summation of the Subrhythms (The Balancing Aspect)

The individual rhythmic patterns that constitute a particular style of African music are not fragmentary, but knit together into a total sound or acoustic gestalt—the "Beat."

The "Beat" manifests itself in two ways, the most obvious being that the music moves in cycles. The shortest cycle revolves around one key instrument (the bell in the case of the agbadza). The "Beat" is also found in the sound pulses of any two subrhythms; these sound waves cancel and reinforce each other to create an interference pattern or standing wave.

Precisely the same thing happens with multiple rhythms, although in a more complicated way, for the interference between the subrhythms creates a third or inherent rhythm that no one actually plays and yet has a rhythmic life of its own. The sum is greater than the parts and this inherent rhythm helps hold the beat together. African musicians call it an "inside rhythm."

All the individual cross-rhythms, as well as their resultant inside rhythms, move in cycles of time. The most important thing to note is that the rhythmic phrases do not all start at the same time, but are staggered or out of phase with each other, in the fashion of a musical round or fugue. Thus in the agbadza "Beat" the feet, bell, and maracas open on the first of the twelve intervals, the kagan on the fifth, the kidi on the eighth; master drums such as sogo and the long atsivemu-drum begin on yet other intervals. (One can therefore understand why African musicians call most European music "one-way," as players all take off together with the fall of the conductor's baton.) Of equal importance are the differing endings; where one finishes another takes its place, constituting a rhythmic dialogue among the instruments.

With so many beginnings and endings, one of the skills of master musicians in Africa is their ability to jump anywhere into the "Beat" and, through various rhythmic tricks always, like the proverbial cat, manage to land on their feet. This aptitude completely by-passes the existential problem of how to initiate a creative act, a hesitancy musically equivalent to "writer's block" that can occur if too much emphasis is put on starting correctly. The African approach evades this block, thus enhancing spontaneity and the free flow of creative energy.

Another feature of African music is the silent side of rhythm. The complementary aspects of the maracas and bell pattern have already been discussed. Another is the hand-clapping pattern provided by the audience. Although the claps follow the tempo of the four dance steps, they are not continuous like those of the feet, due to a gap in the hand–claps at interval 4. And it is precisely this quiet space that supplies a crucial anchoring or reference point in what would otherwise be a bewildering and sustained round of rhythm. For a fuller explanation (with diagrams) of the agbadza, including some of its major drum patterns, the reader should consult the *M.U.S.E. Letter,* published by Musicians United for Superior Education Incorporated (1990, pp. 57–68), and edited by Charles Keil of the Department of American Studies, SUNY at Buffalo.

African Rhythms and Einstein

Far from being primitive or archaic, the African rhythmical tradition turns out to be a highly sophisticated music that even has a bearing on advanced physics. It might seem odd that an ancient folk-music genre should have any relevance to such a modern topic. But the African "Beat," with its multidimensional rhythms, manipulation of space, and squeezing and stretching of time, throws us into a relativistic realm reminiscent of Albert Einstein's. Similarly the African play on opposites (on- and offbeats) brings to mind Niels Bohr's concept of complementarity—that everything comes in matching pairs, positive and negative, matter and anti-matter.

The creative swing, flexible metre, and audience participation in African music also provide accoustic metaphors for other discoveries in New Physics. Whereas nineteenth-century physicists thought atomic matter was rigid and separated by nothingness, this void is now known to be filled with ever-changing potential states of being (i.e., virtual particles). Therefore, emptiness invites possibilities rather than a negation of them. African music also fits Heisenberg's famous uncertainty principle, which concerns the indeterminate nature of subatomic entities and the difficulty of trying to fix them absolutely, as they do not exist in categories of exact space and metronomic time. Geoffrey Chew, in his bootstrap theory, goes so far as to argue the ultimate impossibility of scientists even trying to isolate themselves completely from their experiments. They participate in the subatomic show whether they like it or not, for here, as in African music, there is no real separation between players and observers.

Finally, African music is a gestalt of opposites that unifies the up- and downbeat, head and feet, audience and performer, in the communion of the "Beat." Likewise, networks of virtual particles and their corresponding antiparticles connect all material things. There is no separation, only universal "togetherness"—an idea supported by physicist David Bohn, who speculates in his implicate order model that all of reality is enfolded, like a hologram, in each of its parts.

This whole question of the relationship between traditional African music and modern science is the topic of a book I have written entitled *Roots, Rhythms and Relativity: African Music in the Space Age* (forthcoming from Off the Record Press, London).

2 First Fusions— Orchestras and Brass-Bands

E. T. Mensah, the King of Highlife, and King Bruce

Traditional African music is flexible and ever-changing. There have been cross-overs and feedback, Western influences on African music and African influences on Western music.

Modernised traditional music and dance-styles that developed along the West African coast in the nineteenth century demonstrate the subtlety of the interaction between black and white music—styles such as gome (or goombay), ashiko (or asiko), timo, and osibisaaba: rhythms that later were incorporated into highlife and juju music.

Even though no European instruments were used in these first fusions, the songs were sung in hymn-type harmonies. European carpentry techniques were used for the construction of new brands of African drums, such as the square tambourines and the giant gome-drum. Another type of drum that was much simpler to make than the local hand-carved drums was the barrel-drum, made by coopers with planks and iron hoops.

While some African musicians started to incorporate new ideas into their music, others began playing in brass-bands, regimental bands, and dance orchestras.

In the poorer areas of port towns, local musicians learned to play sailors' instruments and created a blend that became known as palm-wine music, ragtime, or "native blues." This developed into guitar-band music.

Brass-bands go all the way back to military brass and fife bands associated with the coastal forts. European, West Indian, and African musicians were employed at these forts. They played military marches, polkas, waltzes, and fusions of their own.

Konkomba Music

About a hundred years ago, a type of African brass-band music called adaha became very popular with the many brass-bands in the Fanti areas of Ghana. Within a short time the whole of the south of Ghana was swinging to this music, and every town of note wanted to have its own brass-band.

When local musicians couldn't afford to buy expensive imported instruments, they made do with drums, voices, and plenty of fancy dress. This poor man's brass-band music, which included drill-like dances, became known as konkomba or konkoma music.

Beni and Dance Orchestras

A similar thing happened in East Africa when, around the turn of the century, military brass-band music was taken up by local people. They combined African and European drums, bugles, and brass instruments with military parade-type dances and called it "beni." This beni ngoma, or beni dance craze, was spread around the rural hinterland of East Africa by the askaris, local African troops during the First World War period. It became progressively Africanised. For instance, the trumpet was replaced by the gourd

Ghanaian regimental band, around World War I.

kazoo. This led to a whole number of even more Africanised dance-styles, like the mgonda, kalela, and chikosa.

Another popular type of music around the turn of the century was performed by the African dance orchestras, complete with brass, woodwind, and stringed instruments. The black and mulatto elites in the towns especially liked this music. There were orchestras such as the Lagos City Orchestra in Nigeria, the Excelsior Orchestra in Accra, the Don't Worry Entertainers of South Africa and the Dapa Dan Jazz Band of Sierra Leone.

These large, prestigious orchestras played waltzes, foxtrots, quicksteps, ragtimes, and other ballroom dance numbers for their top-hatted audiences. Then, they began to orchestrate the local melodies and street music. That's how highlife got its name.

These stylish orchestras went on playing up until the Second World War, and then died out. During the war, tens of thousands of Allied troops were stationed in Africa, and African soldiers fought in Burma and elsewhere. All this affected the popular music scene in Africa. Jazz and swing became all the rage.

So the huge orchestras gave way to the smaller jazz combos of

*Surviving members of the Excelsior Orchestra (formed in Accra
in 1914), 1959.*

the postwar period. The man who pioneered this breakthrough
was E. T. Mensah.

E. T. Mensah

E. T. Mensah, or E. T. as he is known, was born in Accra in 1919.
It was his band, the Tempos, that pioneered urban highlife played
by dance-bands. E. T. started his musical career when, as a small
boy, he joined the Accra Orchestra as a flute player. The Accra
Orchestra was formed by Teacher Lamptey around 1930, based on
a schoolboy band.

Teacher Lamptey, the headmaster of a James Town elementary
school, had been a member of one of the first dance orchestras in
Ghana, the Jazz Kings, formed in the early 1920s. But it was his
Accra Orchestra that became the best-known prewar orchestra,
and many of Ghana's top musicians played in it, including E. T.,
Joe Kelly, and Tommy Gripman.

*The Accra Orchestra was formed in 1930 out of this school brass-band.
The founder, Teacher Lamptey, is seated and wearing a police-type hat.*

E. T. and his older brother Yebuah went on to form their own
Accra Rhythmic Orchestra, which won the Lambeth Walk Dance
Competition in 1939 at the King George Memorial Hall (present-
day Parliament House).

Yebuah Mensah comments on the origin of the term "highlife":

> During the early twenties, during my childhood, the term
> "highlife" was created by people who gathered around the danc-
> ing clubs such as the Rodger Club (built in 1904) to watch and
> listen to the couples enjoying themselves. Highlife started as a
> catch-name for the indigenous songs played at these clubs by
> such early bands as the Jazz Kings, the Cape Coast Sugar Babies,
> the Sekondi Nanshamang, and later the Accra Orchestra. The
> people outside called it "highlife" as they did not reach the class
> of the couples going inside, who not only had to pay a, then,
> relatively high entrance fee of 7s. 6d., but also had to wear full
> evening dress including top-hats.

E. T. Mensah was self-taught at first:

> He taught himself music, starting with the flute. During World
> War Two, saxophonist Sgt. Leopard of the British Army in West

Right to left: *E. T. Mensah and
J. Mallet, members of the Accra
Rhythmic Orchestra, 1937.*

Africa, looking for musicians, took him under his tutelage.
From him, E. T. learnt how to play the alto saxophone. He took
to playing the trumpet and later led the Accra Tempos Band.
E. T. claims that it was watching and listening to Eddie Calvert
play Cherry Pink and Apple Blossom that encouraged him to
play the trumpet the way he does now. Many musicians in
Ghana have passed through his hands; many more extending
outside Ghana have modelled their style on his. His music was
recorded by Decca (West Africa) and admirers gave him the title
"King of Highlife."

(record notes, *Mensah's African Rhythms*)

The high-class dance orchestras were eclipsed during the Second World War, when American and British troops were stationed
in Ghana. They brought in jazz and swing. Night-clubs and dives
were opened with names like Kalamazoo, Weekend-in-Havanna,
and the New York Bar. They also set up dance combos and played
with local musicians.

Jazz and Swing

The first combo was the Black and White Spots, set up by
Sergeant Leopard. E. T. left his brother's orchestra and joined up

with Leopard's jazz combo as sax player in 1940. Sergeant Leopard, a Scot, had been a professional saxophonist in England. According to E. T. it was Leopard himself who taught them jazz techniques:

> It was Sergeant Leopard who taught us the correct methods of intonation, vibrato, tongueing, and breath control, which contributed to place us above the average standard in the town.

Just after the war, E. T. joined the Tempos, set up by Ghanaian pianist Adolf Doku and English engineer Arthur Harriman. At first the band included some white soldiers but after the war, when the Europeans left, the band became completely African and E. T. became its leader. It was a seven-piece band with E. T. doubling on trumpet and sax, Joe Kelly on tenor sax, and Guy Warren on drums.

Guy Warren made an important contribution as he had been playing Afro-Cuban music and calypsos in England. So the Tem-

E. T. Mensah (seated, centre) and his Tempos dance-band,
early 1950s.

pos not only played with a jazz touch, but incorporated calypsos into their repertoire and added the bongos and maracas to the lineup.

It was the Tempos' style of highlife that became all the rage; by the early 1950s the band started touring West Africa and recording for Decca. E. T., who had been a pharmacist, was able to go fully professional.

It was during the 1950s that E. T. was acclaimed the king of highlife throughout West Africa, for although the palm-wine variety of highlife was popular in the rural areas of West Africa, ballroom music and colonial-type orchestras still dominated the urban dance scene.

In Nigeria, highlife music like konkomba, juju, and palm-wine was left to the rural and low-class urban night-spots. High-class clubs featured dance-bands like Bobby Benson's, Sammy Akpabot's, and the Empire Hotel Band, which played only swing and ballroom music. But E. T.'s style of highlife soon began to influence them and create a whole new generation of Nigerian

Bobby Benson's band.

dance-band musicians like Victor Olaiya, Eddie Okunta, Arinze Rex Lawson, Charles Iwegbue, Victor Chukwu, Chief Billy Friday, Enyang Henshaw, King Kennytone, and Roy Chicago.

The Tempos influenced not only these mature Nigerian dance-band musicians, but also the young Victor Uwaifo. As Dan Acquaye, one of E. T.'s musicians, recalls from one of the many of the Tempos' tours of Nigeria:

> In Benin City, Victor Uwaifo, then a schoolboy, would rush down to our hotel after school to watch my cousin Dizzy Acquaye on the guitar. He was determined to play the guitar and used to help Dizzy clean his instrument.

Victor Uwaifo corroborates this story:

> I used to see E. T. Mensah and his Tempos play whenever they were in Benin and I went to see their guitarist, Dizzy Acquaye, to put me through a few chords. I had a guitar book but I didn't understand the chord drawings. Dizzy helped me.

Many musicians passed through the tutelege of the Tempos—Joe Kelly, Tommy Gripman, Saka Acquaye, Spike Anyankor, Ray Ellis, and the first female vocalist Juliana Okine (all from Ghana); and Zeal Onyia and Babyface Paul Osamade from Nigeria.

E. T. on Tour

During the 1950s, the Tempos toured West African countries, where there were no highlife dance-bands. In Sierra Leone there were local palm-wine music and meringue (or maringa), but this was never played by the dance-bands there. So E. T.'s music was an instant success. They played at a party for the prime minister, Doctor Margai, and toured the country. By the early 1960s, dance-bands like the Ticklers were in full swing, playing both highlifes and meringues.

In Liberia, too, local music was not being played by the dance-bands. They were playing the quadrille, a refined Creole music that the American Liberian freed slaves brought over from the southern states of America. In fact, the Tempos were so popular in Liberia that President Tubman invited them to his inauguration. He sent them the following telegram:

The Tempos dance-band, mid-1950s.

I am very pleased to note that you and your band have safely arrived in Accra. We enjoyed the melody, rhythm and tempo of your band and this telegram constitutes an invitation to you and your band to return for the inauguration.

In the French-speaking countries of Guinea and the Côte d'Ivoire, E. T. did not come across an African dance-band or orchestra, let alone one playing indigenous music. In the night-clubs of Conakry and Abidjan he heard white groups playing French music. The Tempos had to show the people there how to dance highlife.

E. T. Mensah's Tempos spread highlife far and wide, until E. T. retired in the 1970s.

When I wrote *E. T. Mensah, the King of Highlife* (published by Off the Record Press, 116 Whitfield Street, London WIP 5RW, in 1986) I was living at Temple House, James Town, in downtown Accra (1974–1979). On many occasions E. T. visited me. He told me he remembered coming to the place as a boy with Teacher Lamptey's Accra Orchestra, which played for Ghanaian "big people" with top hats and tails at balls held in the old tennis courts at the back of the house (now a factory). Oddly enough percussionist Kofi Ayivor also lived there in the 1960s. When I left, Kris

Temple House, James Town, Accra.

Bediako, the leader of A Band Named Bediako and the Third Eye group, moved into my flat.

The house was built around 1900 by a black lawyer named Thomas Hutton-Mills who sponsored the balls. His daughter Violet was a brilliant classical pianist who reluctantly had to give up a professional musical career to become her father's secretary. She died in 1971 and it was her son and daughter-in-law, Tom and Balbil Whittacker, who told me the house's history. They were my landlords. Because of their musical heritage, they never minded my band rehearsing in the house.

King Bruce and the Black Beats

An award was given to Ghanaian musician King Bruce by the Entertainment Critics and Reviewers Association of Ghana (ECRAG) on April 30, 1988, for his "immense contribution to the development of Ghanaian art and culture in the field of highlife music." This musician's career in dance-band music spans nearly forty years.

My first contact with King Bruce was in the mid-1970s, when I hired equipment from him for my own band. For a while we were both on the executive board of the Musicians' Union of Ghana (MUSIGA). In August 1987 King gave a number of interesting presentations at the conference of the International Association for the Study of Popular Music (IASPM) held in Accra (of which I was on the local organising committee) with its theme of "Africa in the World of Popular Music." Since then I've recorded four songs for him—"Esheo Heko" (There Comes a Time), "Onyiemo Feo Mi Feo" (Walk Beautiful), "Ekole" (Perhaps), and "Tsutsu Tsosemo" (Old Time Training)—that King has released locally on cassette.

King Bruce, a Ga, was born in James Town, Accra, in 1922. His musical experiences started early and were varied. His mother belonged to a traditional women's singing group called Etsi Penfo; his eldest brother Kpakpo Thompson taught him piano; another brother, Eddie Bruce, played palm-wine guitar-styles like "fireman" and "dagomba wire" in a group of seamen called Canteen. At the same time, and much against his parents' wishes, King was a keen follower of the Accra street music, such as the alaha, kolomashie, tsibode, koyin, and other popular dance-styles played by the local Ga drumming groups.

At the prestigious Achimota College, King continued to be inspired by music, particularly by some of the teachers who taught there. These included Phillip Gbeho, who composed Ghana's national anthem, and Doctor Ephraim Amu, who, King explains, "was my house-master as well as my music teacher and taught us his Twi and Ewe songs. He had come to Achimota after he lost his appointment as a teacher at the Akropong Training College because of his strong African tendencies. He didn't believe in the idea of going to classes or church in Western-style suits, but always wore traditional kente cloth or batakari. He had these strong feelings about African culture as far back as the 1930s and was welcomed at Achimota, as the founders of the school—Guggisburg, Fraser, and Aggrey—were strongly interested in promoting African ways."

It was at the end of his schooldays at Achimota that King developed a taste for swing and dance-band music, for these "were

the war years and we had British and American army units stationed here. They had bands for their entertainment and so ballroom music progressed very much. The airport was virtually
taken over by the Americans and one wing of Achimota College
itself was taken over by the British resident minister, who was
taking care of the British war effort here. So this was the time of
musicians like Glenn Miller, Benny Goodman, and Artie Shaw; so
by the time I left Achimota I had a definite liking for jazz and
swing."

King did not actually start playing in a dance-band, however,
until he had spent a couple of years in England studying to be a
civil servant with the P&T (Posts and Telegraphs) and learning to
play the trumpet. On returning to Accra in 1950, he hung around
for a while with top musicians like Adolf Doku, E. T. Mensah,
Kofi Ghanaba (Guy Warren), Joe Kelly, and Papa Hughes. He occasionally played clips (claves) for Ghana's leading highlife dance-
band, the Tempos. When King felt he was ready to go on stage
with his trumpet, he joined Teacher Lamptey's Accra Orchestra.

King stayed with this group until 1952, when he and tenor

King Bruce's Black Beats, 1952. King Bruce (far left)
is playing trumpet.

saxist Saka Acquaye formed the Black Beats band. This name, according to King, "just came out spontaneously. One evening when we were coming home from rehearsals Saka asked me what name we were going to use. Without hesitation I said Black Beats. The reason was that Doctor Amu at Achimota had impressed on us the necessity for doing things African. At the same time as a group we were very much enamoured with jazz, swing, and music with a beat. So we were all interested in playing good dance-band music, but keen on giving everything a recognisable African beat."

Unlike the other Ghanaian dance-bands, the Black Beats vocalists (the Black Birds, Lewis Wadawa, and Frank Barnes) dominated the instrumental lineup—and in this they were influenced by the swing and "jump" music of Afro-American Louis Jordan. It was with this format that the Black Beats began to release a string of highlife hits for HMV, Senophone, and Decca composed by King, like "Teeman Sane" (A Confidential Matter), "Laimomo" (Old Lover), "Nkuse Mbaa Dong" (I'll Never Return), "Nomo Noko" (A Thing of Joy), "Srotoi Ye Mli" (Distinctions), and "Agoogyi" (Money—this song being composed by Oscarmore Ofori).

In 1961 disaster struck the band. Alto saxist Jerry Hansen and nine musicians left the semiprofessional Black Beats to form the fully professional Ramblers dance-band. Nevertheless, within a few months King had reorganised his band and with this second-generation Black Beats began releasing more hits for Decca, like "Se Nea Woti Ara" (I Love You Just as You Are), "Kwemo Ni Okagbi" (Take Care You Don't Dry Up), "Odo Fofor" (New Love), and "Nkase Din" (I Am Quietly Poised).

During the whole period when King was running the Black Beats he was slowly working his way up the civil service ladder, but getting a lot of criticism from his superiors for playing on stage. As King comments, "At first the opposition from my employers came in hints. Then in 1967 the opposition came in black and white as a result of a letter I received from the government. It was from the head of the Administrative Civil Service and they told me that I had now got to the stage where I was due for promotion from assistant to full principal secretary and that the only thing that stood in my way was my dance-band playing. So I had to decide whether to continue playing or accept promotion. So I replied that I got commitments to play up to Easter 1968, but that from April and thereafter I would comply with the undertaking and wouldn't play in public anymore."

I asked King how he felt about this. He replied, "I was very much annoyed because I had always believed that it was the actual playing in a band that sharpens your faculties and brings new ideas. When you sit down doing nothing you don't create new music. So the ban on my playing hurt me very much as I had to sacrifice a lot to play music and had always wanted to pursue it and make something out of it."

To keep his band running King handed the Black Beats' leadership to Sammy Odoh. Instead of playing King started managing the band—plus others that became based at his house in James Town. During the 1970s he was running eight "BB" bands: the Black Beats, Barbecues, Barons, Bonafides, Barristers, Boulders, "B" Soyaaya, and Blessed Apostles.

Besides being a senior civil servant, composer, band leader, manager, and teacher of the hundred or so musicians who have passed through his groups, King Bruce has also found time to help organise all three of Ghana's music unions: the 1950s' Gold Coast Association of Musicians, the short-lived (1960–1966) Ghana Musicians Union, and the present-day MUSIGA.

In 1977 King Bruce retired from the civil service. He still actively pursues his musical career. He runs two "BB" bands (the Black Beats and Barristers), has begun to rerecord some of his old hits, is active in MUSIGA, and was involved in the recent changes in the copyright law that now make infringement a criminal offence. In the latest phase of his musical career, he became for a while the manager of the sixteen-track Elephant Walk recording studio in Kaneshie, Accra.

3 Palm-Wine and Guitars

"Sam" (Kwame Asare), Kwaa Mensah, and E. K. Nyame

In spite of their prestigious beginnings, the large dance-bands and brass-bands have all but died out, and almost everywhere in Africa it is the up-dated palm-wine music that dominates the local music scene. This is in spite of the fact that palm-wine music emerged from low-class seaport dives and palm-wine bars. In fact the guitar became so closely associated with this African beer, brewed naturally from the palm-tree, that anyone playing the guitar was considered to be a drunken rascal.

Where sea shanties met African music, palm-wine music was born. The lineup was a combination of local African instruments and those of the sailors—the guitar, concertina, accordion, harmonica, and banjo. Compared to orchestral instruments, these instruments were cheap and portable.

But it was the guitar that became the main melody instrument. It was probably introduced to Africa by Portuguese sailors, completing yet another circuit in the complex to and fro of contemporary African music. The Spanish guitar has its roots in Muslim North Africa, from where it was taken to Spain and Portugal in medieval times.

The first Africans to make the modern guitar their own were the Kru (or Kroo) fishermen who lived in villages along the coast of Liberia. When the Europeans came, the Kroos became famous as seamen on the old sailing and steamships. They also became famous for their guitar-playing, and their African styles like dagomba, fireman, and mainline accompanied them wherever they went. Dagomba was a name they gave to one of their new styles, originating from a Kru expression; fireman probably got its name from the coal-burning steamships; mainline is the first and fundamental African finger-picking style.

These styles, and others that grew out of them, spread through West and Central Africa.

Palm-wine music was introduced to Sierra Leone in the 1920s by Kroos living in Freetown's Kroo-town quarter, where it was known as ragtime. Kroos, such as Foster and the seaman Eku, played their guitars in the red light district of Freetown, accompanied by the giant bass "hand-piano," called the congoma. Other groups featured the guitar and African percussion with the musical saw. Groups like Peter na Leopard and Waking Profit acquired most of their money from wake-keepings. Most popular of all was Ebeneezer Calendar, who raised the status of palm-wine music, and whose guitar-band used the sousaphone to provide the bass line. His meringues, calypsos, and highlifes were popular until the 1960s.

It was Ghanaian palm-wine music, which started at the same time as that of Sierra Leone, that made the first major shift from the coast to the interior and hinterland. This happened when the Akan went guitar mad and added Ashanti blues to the palm-wine repertoire. This is basically their own local music in which the traditional lute (seprewah) is replaced by the guitar.

By the 1930s and 1940s there were dozens of guitar-bands from various Akan areas—Kwerku Bibi, Kwese Manu, Kwese Peperah, Mireku, Yaw Ofori, and Appiah Adjekum. This list is endless, but the first of all was Kwame Asare, or "Sam" as he is fondly remembered in Ghana.

In Ghana, during the early 1950s, palm-wine music became linked with acting. Before this, the local concert parties and comic trios had been accompanied by ballroom music. It was E. K. Nyame from Ghana who made the vital connection between high-life and concert parties. His music became an inspiration throughout Africa during the 1950s. By the end of the 1950s, guitar-bands started going electric.

The Birth of Juju

Palm-wine music appeared in western Nigeria in the 1930s, where it became known as juju music. This was, in fact, a combination of traditional Yoruba music with modernised African styles, like gome or gombe (found all over West Africa), ashiko (an early name for highlife), and konkomba (which spread out from Ghana). Juju music also incorporated contemporary Yoruba street music like denge, played on guitar and samba-drum, and agidigbo, played on hand-piano and drums.

The actual name "juju" was coined by mandolin player Tunde King in the late 1930s. Other formative juju musicians were Ojoge Daniels, who played ukelele and banjo, guitarist Ayinde Bakare, and agidigbo player Adeolu Akinsanya, who later formed the Rio Lindo Orchestra. Then, in the 1950s, Ayinde Bakare and I. K. Dairo turned juju electric.

In central and eastern Nigeria palm-wine music, known there as native blues, first surfaced in the 1930s with Igbo guitarists like Israel Nwaba and G. T. Owuka. In the early 1950s E. K. Nyame's music became immensely popular in eastern Nigeria and guitar-bands there were influenced by his Akan Trio—like those of Aderi Olariechi from Owerri, January from Port Harcourt, and Okonkwo Adigwe from Asaba.

Similar to the palm-wine music of West Africa was dansi music from East Africa, the coastal music of freed slaves. They used sailors' instruments to play local and imported melodies. Unlike its West African counterpart, however, dansi incorporated orchestral instruments and so suffered the same fate as the West African dance orchestras—it died out!

The palm-wine music finger style of guitar-playing became popular in East Africa in the 1950s. It was introduced from Zaire where, in the 1940s, people had gone crazy over the West African finger-picking style of guitar-playing. In 1952 Jean Mwenda Bosco began to release rumbas and local luba music played on Spanish guitar. This style is quite different from the distinctive congo-jazz style of electric guitar-playing that grew out of it in the 1960s. Another early finger-style top guitarist from Zaire was Losta Abelo, whose music, like that of Bosco, spread into East Africa during the 1950s. It influenced musicians there like John Mwale, Paul Muchupa, and Fundi Koude. Later everything went electric.

That nonelectric guitar music remains popular in East Africa is evident in the success of Daniel Kachamba of Kenya, who sings songs while playing guitar, harmonica, bass-drum, and rattle at the same time.

"Sam," the First Palm-Wine Guitarist

The man who spread the palm-wine style far afield was Ghanaian guitarist Kwame Asare (or "Sam," as he is usually known). He popularized the various African seamen's styles like dagomba, fireman, and mainline and the more indigenous and rural native blues (this is a minor chord music played in 6/8 time rather than 4/4 and is usually sung in the vernacular).

Sam composed the famous highlife standard "Yaa Amponsah," a song about a beautiful and alluring dancer, a song that laid down the basis for hundreds of others. In many ways "Yaa Amponsah" is to highlife what the twelve-bar blues is to jazz.

Sam and his trio went to England in the mid-1920s, where they recorded and released scores of palm-wine highlifes on the Zonophone label (EZ series).

Sam's nephew Kwaa Mensah is another famous Ghanaian palm-wine guitarist. Although Sam died in the 1950s, Kwaa continued playing his uncle's style of music. Kwaa comments on his Uncle Sam's early life:

> Sam was born in 1903 in Cape Coast. His father played the concertina and used to take Sam, when he was very small, on his shoulder to play clips. His father played adaha, the music of the flute, fife, and brass bands. And also opim and ohuga (native

*Kwame Asare ("Sam") (right) and his trio recording for Zonophone
in Britain, 1928.*

blues). Opim was a special rhythm for the concertina. Another
rhythm they played was ashiko, a highlife played with concertina
or accordian, clips, and carpenter's saw, where the saw is bent
and an iron is used to rattle its face. Sam later learned to play
guitar, against the wishes of his father, who thought only ruf-
fians played guitar. So Sam ran away to Kumasi, where he met
Kwah Kantah from El Mina and H. E. Biney from Cape Coast.
Kwah Kantah played wooden box and Biney and Sam played
guitars. In 1928 they went to London to make recordings.

Kwaa Mensah was born in Lagos and brought up in Cape
Coast. He describes how he was taught guitar by Sam.

My uncle Sam taught me to play guitar in 1937 and anywhere he
goes, I go with him. We were entertaining the soldiers during
the war at Cape Coast, Kumasi, and Accra. We made music and

Kwaa Mensah, 1977.

mime for the soldiers and army officers. I was the singer and
clips player and Sam was playing guitar, singing, and changing
costumes. He used to dress up as a Sierra Leonese woman and
sometimes as an Ashanti woman.

Kwaa continues his story:

> Before the war I was in an adaha band called the Antwem band. I
> didn't use guitar in this band. I played pati (a small side-drum)
> and fifes. In 1939 the Silver Stars konkomba group was formed
> and I left the Antwem band. The konkomba band has jazz-
> drums, pati-drums, bass alto, tenor tambourines, and thirty
> singers. I was the first to bring guitar to them. We played adaha;
> adesim, which is a fast highlife; Ashanti (native) blues; rumbas;
> foxtrots; bumps-a-daisy; sambas; la congas; Spanish music; and
> dagomba highlifes. I went on to form my own Akote Special
> Konkomba group and left when the war finished. When the war
> finished, konkomba finished. By this time I was a master
> guitarist and formed the Navy Blues, which used giant bass
> hand-piano, pati, tambourines, cigarette tin, and clips. The

Navy Blues band collapsed when I went to Kumasi in 1951, and when I came back I formed Kwaa Mensah's Band, which had the same instruments. My first recordings were with His Masters Voice (HMV, now part of EMI) and we were paid £5 for each side (i.e., £10 a record). Altogether I made nearly two hundred records for them.

Although Kwaa was born in 1920, he continued an active musical career right up until his death in February 1991. During the last few years of his life he taught his traditional style of guitar-playing to many students, first at Cape Coast University and then at the University of Ghana's School of Performing Arts.

E. K. Nyame's Music and Drama

E. K. Nyame was born in 1927 in Ghana. He revolutionised West African music in the 1950s, as he not only updated the highlife music of the palm-wine groups, but also combined it with the acting of the local concert groups.

Like highlife music, the Ghanaian concert parties or comic opera groups started around the turn of the century as stylish affairs in the towns and rapidly spread into the rural hinterland, where they were indigenised. When highlife bands left the towns with their orchestras, the music was known as palm-wine and native blues music and was played by guitar-bands. When concert parties like the Axim Trio and Two Bobs moved into the villages, they incorporated Ananse, the traditional spider-hero, in their acts. Their Joker or "Bob" took on all the mischievous aspects of Ananse.

The music of the early concert parties, however, remained basically Western ballroom music—foxtrots, quicksteps, and ragtimes, played on harmonium and jazz-drums.

E. K. Nyame completed the Africanisation of the concert party by using highlife guitar-bands for the music. He also started using the local language in the plays instead of English. His combination of highlife and concert acting was an instant success. From 1951, when he formed the Akan Trio, practically all the guitar-bands in Ghana linked up with acting groups. In the 1950s E. K.'s band was the supreme guitar-band. He became Nkrumah's favourite musician and accompanied him on many state visits. Many of E. K.'s songs and plays supported Nkrumah and the independence movement. During the 1950s E. K. recorded over four hundred records for Decca, Queenaphone, and HMV and he became popular throughout black Africa.

I was fortunate to know him, and often visited him at his house in James Town, Accra, where he gave me some tips on guitar-playing and let me interview him. E. K. joined his first group, Appiah Adjekum's band, in 1948, when he was just a clerk:

> It was an amateur group and if anyone wanted to make some outdooring (christening) or function we would go there. I played the rhythm guitar and Adjekum played the Hawaiian guitar. There were three oblong tambourines covered in velum. The bass one was sat on (a gome-drum). We also had a four-corner (concertina) and castanets or claves. Adjekum's wife played the guitar.

E. K. explained why he left this band:

> I had the idea of modernising the music to raise the standard. At first we used tambourines, guitar, and clips, but we made a

E. K. Nyame's Akan Trio, around 1950. (E. K. is holding a clarinet.)

change in 1951 and replaced the tambourines with bongos, jazz-drums, and fiddle bass.

What of the Akan Trio's early days?

We staged in English but there were parts of it when a character came in and spoke our dialect (Twi). But we minded the colonial ideology and British mind, so whatever we did in those days was in English. But by 1957 we were using Twi. We were the first concert to use guitar-band, and the first to use Spanish bongos. We played highlifes, ragtimes, and calypsos on rare occasions. I played the Gentleman and Bob. We introduced the show with an opening chorus, a quickstep sung in English.

E. K. described how he got ideas for his stories:

When we created a very good highlife number, it's out of this we built our concert story. Because the whole nation wants to see us performing what we have done on the recording side. One play was called "When you push plantain you have to push banana" [i.e., you have to treat everyone equally]. It was about a man who married two wives but loved one more than the other, and the son of the one he rejected became a chief somewhere else. Later on the father became poor and wretched. And it was the child he neglected that came to his aid and who came and brought the father up again.

E. K. died in 1977. His body was laid out on a golden bed and he was given a state funeral attended by ten thousand people. As E. K. had no wife when he died, the top falsetto singer and lady impersonator in his concert party, Kobina Okai (Okine), dressed in funeral clothes and played the part of E. K.'s distraught and wailing wife at the wake. In fact, I was among the hundreds who offered condolences to him/her—and Okai most certainly wasn't acting the part. He *was* the part.

Okai was born in Ghana's Central Region; when he was 13 years old he joined the See There konkomba group. In those days, however, music was considered a useless profession and so some members of Kobina Okai's family sent him to Accra to study tailoring with Appiah Adjekum. Fortunately for Kobina (and for

Ghana), Adjekum was in the process of forming a guitar-band. Kobina Okai and E. K. promptly joined; they later formed the Akan Trio.

The Akan Trio, as already mentioned, was a firm supporter of Kwame Nkrumah and his Convention People's Party (CPP). They welcomed him out of jail, where he had been imprisoned by the British, with the song "Onim Deefo Kukudurufu Kwame Nkrumah" (Honourable Man and Hero). When he became prime minister, the Akan Trio accompanied him to many state functions. It is because of this that the Ghanaian magazine *Positive Joy* (vol. 31, 1985) stated after Okai's death that "some freedom fighters fight their wars with guns and academic degrees, Kobina Okai fought and helped build Ghana with his voice."

4   *The Man Who Made a "Traditional" Music Called Kpanlogo*

On Africa the sharp distinctions and boundaries between folk and classical music, traditional and modern that Westerners have created do not apply. For African traditional music was and is constantly being created and re-created, both affecting the growth of popular music-styles and in turn being affected by them. This chapter, by focusing on one particular Ghanaian dance craze of the 1960s, the kpanlogo, will highlight this complex and dynamic situation in the African music scene.

The Dynamics of African Folk Music

Just as Europe has its anonymous folk music (the famous and prolific "anon"), so too in Ghana and other African countries there is a vast tradition of ethnic music so old that its creators have been forgotten and their legacy has become part of the national heritage. This music, referred to in Ghana as "cultural" music, is often the basis for other types of new or neotraditional music. For instance, the agbadza dance, which first appeared in Ghana's Volta Region between the two World Wars, developed out of the traditional war-dance of the Ewe people, called the atsiagbevor. Even more recent are the Ewe bor-bor-bor music and the Ga kpanlogo, which grew out of dance-band highlife and local drumming. Many believe that the music of Ghana and West Africa developed in exactly the same way as did black American music—moving from the raw roots sound of the countryside to the more Westernised city version. In Africa it's the reverse, with black and white fusion music first starting up in the coastal towns and later growing roots while spreading into the rural hinterland. Thus, the claim that anything in Africa that sounds cultural must be ancient and anonymous is an oversimplification that separates the actual, individual creators from their works. In South Africa, where the bulk of the traditional African music, both old and new, is classed as cultural or ethnic, and thus beyond copyright, a very clear case of exploitation has occurred. The South African establishment has in a sense "nationalised" black African cultural music for itself and is able to use it on records or in exotic "tribal" performances while not paying a penny in royalties to anyone.

Taken to its logical conclusion, this "nationalisation" approach to cultural music could even lead to the absurd situation of African musicians shunning their own traditions altogether if they had to pay royalties to the state. It would force them to go abroad to develop someone else's musical traditions. Fortunately this sort of alienation has not occurred in West Africa, where innovative local musicians are free to adapt their own ethnic music.

Otoo Lincoln and the Origins of Kpanlogo

When I met the inventor of kpanlogo, the Accra-born Otoo Lincoln, and his manager, Godwin Abbey, the first thing I asked was what the actual meaning of the word "kpanlogo" was.

Otoo Lincoln: It was from a folk story my grandfather told me and the name "Kpanlogo" is the imaginary name of a girl. You see, there were three girl triplets called Kpanlogo, Mma Mma, and Alogodzan. Their father, who was the chief of the town, said that the man who would guess the three girls' names could take all three and marry them—difficult, as they were always kept in the house and didn't come out. So one man went to the house dressed as a madman and met Mma Mma in the yard and she shouted to her two sisters to come and see someone dancing. As they called each other, the man learned the three names. To remember them he kept on singing to himself, "Kpanlogo, Alogodzan, Kpanlogo Mma Mma." He was always singing this song, until the meeting the chief had called for the public to come and guess the girls' names. But if you come and can't show the correct name they kill you. Some people came and they were not fit so the chief cleared them out. But when the man came the chief gave him his daughters.

Q: Your grandfather told you this?

Otoo Lincoln: He told me in 1956, when I was 15 and living at Korle Wokon, in Accra. It was what we call an adisa, or Ananse story, and when he told me it he didn't know I would make it into music.

It was when I used to tell the story to my brothers, sisters, and friends at our family house in Bukom, central Accra, and I used to dance and sing, "Kpanlogo, Alogodzan, Kpanlogo Mma Mma." Some friends started to drum as they liked my kpanlogo dance, which is my own version of highlife. The drummers were Okulay Foes and Ayitey Sugar. It was around 1962.

Q: Then what is the origin of the kpanlogo beat?

Otoo Lincoln: In our house our fathers were playing oge [introduced by Liberian Kru seamen and popular in Accra during the 1950s]. It's like a slow kpanlogo played on one drum, clips, and a saw and nail to scrape it. Kpanlogo is really a mixture of different dances like highlife and oge, there's even a rock and roll in it, as I used to dance rock and roll around 1960 with Frank Lane at the Black Eagles Club.

Q: Can you name a few of the early kpanlogos that came out of your Kpanlogo Special Band?

Otoo Lincoln: One, of course, was the original "Kpanlogo Alogodzan" and another was the "ABC Kpanlogo," which I made when I acted like a teacher teaching children. And we had another popular song called "Ayine Momobiye," which means "Ayine hold pickin' as I am going to dance the kpanlogo."

Q: I believe there was some opposition to kpanlogo at first?

Otoo Lincoln (far left) and his kpanlogo group, mid-1960s.

Otoo Lincoln: The Arts Council called me and I wouldn't go and one of the directors there started to spoil the name of kpanlogo. He called me and said my dance was no good as one of the beats in the dance makes the body move in an indecent way. I told him maybe someone is making the dance like that, but not me. So I had to make demonstration at the Arts Council and they said it was okay. That was in 1964.

Q: But the real outdooring was in 1965?

Otoo Lincoln: Yes, when Mr. G. W. Amarteyefio called me to make dance for the big men (including President Nkrumah) at the stadium in Black Star Square. There were fifty kpanlogo groups that performed, all who copied my Bukom-based band. For instance, Okulay Foes, Koto Lincoln, and Frank Lane formed their group from mine.

Q: Did you go professional?

Otoo Lincoln: The Ga Manche made a group called Obuade with Tetteh-Addy and his three brothers, Mustapha, Obo, and Emmanuel, and called me in to show them kpanlogo in 1967. I stayed with them two years and made shows at places like Bukom Night-Club, the Ambassador, and Continental Hotel. Now I concentrate on my carpentry, but whenever there is a funeral or outdooring we still play.

Television viewers can see Otoo Lincoln, Frank Lane, and the others on television as the Third Eye production team has included these originators of kpanlogo in a seven-part BBC Channel 4 television series on black music called "Repercussions."

Section Two

Feedback

5 Ragtime to Rumba

Since the end of the nineteenth century, black music has been prominent in the international arena—from ragtime to rumba and jazz, right up to today's black and white fusions. Dance music and drama originally from Africa were adapted to the New World, creating an enormous impact there and feeding back into the mainstream of music in Africa itself. This double transformation, brought about by leaving and returning home, has created a truly international music-style in Africa, and yet one that is doubly African.

This black feedback extends far beyond the musical realm. Freed black slaves from the Americas actually set up towns in Africa, like Freetown in Sierra Leone and Monrovia in Liberia. Brazilian architecture came to Africa from South America, and a host of Afro-American and West Indian writers, artists, and politicians who stimulated African nationalism.

Musical Feedback—Ragtime and Minstrelsy

During the mid-nineteenth century, Caribbean melodies were introduced to Africa by members of West Indian regimental bands stationed in West Africa. This cross-over quickly caught on around the turn of the century, when ragtimes, foxtrots, and quicksteps based on the dance music of North American blacks, began to hit Africa. Ironically they were introduced mainly by whites, who had gone crazy over these new dance tunes and began disseminating them as sheet music and on old wax cylindrical records.

These imported styles were far more popular with African audiences than Western classical music. There is an interesting story of a Belgian colonial officer in the Congo during this time, who received a box containing a selection of cylindrical records. He would play these for the locals from time to time on his wind-up gramophone. The classical pieces left them cold, but they loved the "trick" ones, in other words ragtimes and coon-songs.

When ragtime hit Africa, it was accompanied by black minstrelsy with its tap-dancing and plantation humour. Minstrelsy had become part of the mainstream of European entertainment and was part of the vaudeville tradition. The whole show was taken to Africa—the records of the Afro-American vaudeville team of J. Turner Layton and Willie Johnstone, and films of black and white minstrels, such as Al Jolson. A live tour of West Africa was even undertaken in the early 1920s by the Afro-American husband and wife team Glass and Grant.

By the 1920s, Africans were setting up their own minstrel, ragtime, and concert party groups, which performed plays, comedy sketches, and dances—the Two Bobs and their Carolina Girl from Ghana, and the Dark Town Strutters and Hivers Hivers of South Africa. Another early minstrel team from Ghana were Williams and Marbel, who worked with Glass and Grant before launching off on their own.

Ragtime and minstrelsy became so popular in Africa, that they were incorporated into local musical, dance, and dramatic styles. In Ghana there were the concert parties, with their comedian or "Bob" character. "Bob" is a combination of the black minstrel with Ananse, the traditional spider-hero of the Akan. Even the term "Bob" was an expression that Ghana's original Bob Johnson picked up from visiting black American seamen, who entertained everyone at dockside clubs with comedy sketches and dances accompanied by guitarists and banjo players. Highlife absorbed many elements from ragtime, especially in the coastal towns of Fante, an important location for Ghanaian minstrelsy.

In South Africa, ragtime and honky-tonk piano also became part of the black urban marabi music of the 1920s and 1930s, pounded out on pedal-organs in the shebeens (illegal African bars). At a more refined level, pianist Reuben Caluzza combined ragtime

Williams and Marbel, 1923.

with his own Zulu music for choral groups. He was so successful that he was sent to England to record for HMV (His Master's Voice).

African Dance-Styles Come Back to Africa

The feedback of black music from the Americas blew the creative lid off the music scene during colonial times. It wasn't only North American ragtime and minstrelsy that did this, it was also the African-derived dance-styles from South America and the Caribbean— the rumba, samba, conga, mambo, and meringue, which were already being played by African dance orchestras, having been absorbed into the local music before the Second World War. The samba, for instance, was introduced to Nigeria by the descendants of freed Brazilian slaves and affected juju music with its samba-drum. Meringue became the national music of Sierra Leone, where it is called maringa.

In the 1950s and 1960s, calypsos, boleros, cha-cha-chas, pa-changas, and Afro-Cuban percussion became the craze, with the French-speaking African countries going more for Latin-American music and the English-speaking ones for calypso.

Rumba Crazy

One of the earliest and most pervasive of the Afro-Latin and Afro-Caribbean styles is the rumba, which became an international rage during the 1930s. It spread like wildfire in Africa and was incorporated into the local music there during the 1940s. In East Africa, after the Second World War, African soldiers returning from overseas brought the rumba with them and set up bands such as the Rhino Boys, ex-soldiers of the King's African Rifles. Another group was led by Lucas Tututu, who composed the famous song "Malaika," later recorded by Miriam Makeba.

But the rumba had its biggest impact, and one still felt today, on Zaire and Congo Brazzaville. Even the French and Belgian colonialists used to dance the rumba, and a local African version of it called n'goma became popular in French-speaking Central Africa.

6　Jazz Comes Home to Africa

The ragtime and minstrelsy craze in Africa was followed by Dixieland jazz, which became especially popular in South Africa during the 1920s. Many local Dixie bands were formed there, like the Dark Town Strutters and the Big Four of Johannesburg.

In Ghana, too, Dixieland became part of the repertoire of 1920s bands such as the Jazz Kings of Accra. But it wasn't until the 1950s that the king of Dixieland jazz, Louis Armstrong, played live in Africa.

Louis Armstrong Live in Africa

It all started with Ed Murrow of the Columbia Broadcasting System. He had made a film on Africa in 1955, called *See It Now*. This took him to Accra and to E. T. Mensah's Paramount night-club.

The following year CBS was making a film of Armstrong's European tour. Murrow decided to round off the trip with a visit to Accra by Satchmo (Louis Armstrong) and the All-Stars.

When the musicians and film crew got off the plane, they were welcomed by a massed band of top Ghanaian dance-band musicians and the Nigerian comedian Ajax Bukana, who had played bass for Bobby Benson's band.

That day the All-Stars lunched with the Ghanaian premier, Doctor Kwame Nkrumah, and then performed a free open-air show at the Old Polo Ground to a crowd of over one hundred thousand. In the evening the All-Stars played at the Paramount night-club, side by side with E. T. Mensah. According to the

E. T. Mensah at the Paramount
Club in Accra.

Louis Armstrong and the All-Stars welcomed at the Accra airport by Ghanaian musicians and Nigerian comedian Ajax Bukana.

Ghanaian *Daily Graphic* (May 25, 1956), the show was a great success:

> E. T. seems to have been inspired by the presence of the great Louis. His fingers moved over the valves of his silver trumpet to produce the best manipulation of this instrument by any West African trumpeter. Louis must have been surprised. He was moved. He was pleased. He went up to E. T. and shook hands with him.

E. T. also commented on Louis' playing that night:

> Louis was a great player and put all his energy in, from his head to the tip of his toes. We could see everything quivering, sweating all around, and saliva coming out. I observed that if he wanted to play a note, he must force the note to come, come what may. So we could see him pitching high. He found my range and started above it, so that his trumpet sounded like a clarinet. He was pitching high all the time, his lowest note was my top G. We jammed for about half an hour playing "Saint Louis Blues." Then he left the stage and listened to us playing highlifes.

Left to right: *Louis Armstrong, his wife Lucille, and the premier of Ghana, Kwame Nkrumah.*

The next day the All-Stars visited Achimota College and the University at Legon, where they were entertained by traditional African drumming and dancing. At Achimota Louis saw a woman who resembled his mother, and he became convinced that Ghana was his ancestral home. That evening they played at a charity show at the Opera Cinema, which Nkrumah attended. E. T. observed that

> When the show started there was scarcely any applause. The music was thin for us Africans and we wanted more rhythm. For about the first four numbers, when they finished the audience would just look at them. The people had not known how to give heavy applause at the end of the music as is done abroad. So the musicians were getting no encouragement. It was Trummy Young, the trombonist, who saved the situation. He played reclining on his back using his legs to move the slide and he got a huge applause for this. This raised the morale of the public and the musicians and from then on people became interested. The show didn't close until nearly midnight.

The All-Stars enjoyed Ghana so much that their clarinetist Edmund Hall returned the following year and set up a band at the

Ambassador Hotel in Accra. Louis himself returned for a visit in 1962. By then many of the top dance-bands in Ghana were playing Dixieland numbers, like "Tiger Rag" and "Saint Louis Blues." "All for You," the song that welcomed the All-Stars at the Accra airport, shows the inseparable link between black American and African music. For Ghanaians it was one of their old highlife. songs, but Satchmo remembered it as an old Creole song from the Southern states of America.

Readers interested in more details on the jazz influence on Africa should obtain a copy of my "Jazz Feedback to Africa" in *American Music,* vol. 5, no. 2 (Summer 1987): 176–93.

7 *Soul to Soul*

The Influence of Rock and Roll
on the African Music Scene

In the early 1960s the international pop revolution reached Africa in the form of rock and roll, a commercialised version of rhythm and blues, a music created in the 1940s by American blacks who had migrated to the cities.

Not surprisingly, rock and roll, even though mainly played by white musicians, struck a vibration with African youth, who started to play the music of Elvis Presley, Fats Domino, and Cliff Richard. One of the first African pop-bands was the Heartbeats of Sierra Leone, formed in 1961 by Geraldo Pino. This band was to change the face of the music scene on the West African coast. Many student bands were formed in Sierra Leone, taking their cue from the Heartbeats, including the Echoes, Golden Strings, and Red Stars.

During the mid-1960s there was a fertile pop scene, much of which centred around the Yellow Diamond night-club in Freetown, run by a band called the Leone Stars. Here's how Samuel Oju King, an ex-member of the Echoes, describes it:

> The Leone Stars was formed out of the breakup of two visiting bands, Outer Space from Nigeria and a Ghanaian band based at the Tijuana night-club in Freetown. They all teamed up with a Sierra Leonese conga player, then obtained a loan and renovated a vacant club, formerly known as the Swazark Club. Progressive music like jazz and pop was played at the Yellow Diamond, and on Saturday afternoons they had jam-sessions featuring prominent musicians. For instance, there was a black American musi-

cian called Woodie who was a diplomat. Another was a Ghanaian drummer called Buddy Peep who had been in the United States playing jazz.

The musicians who congregated at this club also instigated a twelve-hour jam-session at the Juba Barracks, just outside Freetown. Fourteen bands played, mainly from Sierra Leone, but there was also one band from Guinea and the Formulas from England.

Rock in Ghana

The first pop group in Ghana was formed by a group of soldiers who were members of an army band called the Red Devils. After training in England, where they were exposed to the music of Cliff Richard and the Shadows, they returned to Ghana and formed the Avengers in 1962. Within a few years there were dozens of student pop-bands playing the music of the Beatles, the Rolling Stones, and Spencer Davis: Ricky Telfer's Batchelors and the Sharks, both from Achimota College, the Road Runners, Blues Syndicate, Circuit Five, and the Phantoms. All vied for first place at the countless school pop chains, competitions organised by impressarios like Raymond Azziz and Faisal Helwani.

Rock in Nigeria

In Nigeria it was the same story, with student bands in Lagos like Yinka Balogun's rock and roll outfit, the Spiders; the Cyclops with their bell-bottomed trousers and Chuck Berry music; and the Clusters, hailed as Africa's Beatles (Joni Haastrup of the Clusters has become one of Nigeria's leading rock musicians). Another was Segun Bucknor's Hot Four, formed with the Nelson Cole brothers. Here is what Segun has to say about Nigerian rock-bands:

> Rock and roll bands were school bands and the first one was the Blue Knights. Then the first serious one we saw was the Cyclops; they were just out of school and were formed in 1964. The beginning of pop and rock and roll was at the United States Information Service, as they had an amplifier and a PA. We used to go there at weekends, but as there were no permanent groups we would just team up and give ourselves a name.

The parents of these kids, of course, hated all this, and something of a generation gap developed between the old and young with pop as one of the issues. Up to the mid-1960s it was mainly the music of white bands that caught on—Elvis, the Beatles, the Who, the Hollies, the Dave Clarke Five, the Small Faces, and the Animals. Then all this was overtaken by black pop music.

First there was Millicent Small from Jamaica, or "Millie" as she is generally known, who made two tours of Ghana and Nigeria in 1965 and 1966, introducing West Indian ska music. Her international hit "My Boy Lollipop" was a big success. Then there was Chubby Checker's "Let's Twist Again." Everyone went twist crazy, especially in East Africa. Chubby Checker toured Africa in 1966 and 1967. The Nigerians were so impressed that they created their own king of twist, King Kennytone of the Top Toppers.

The Beginnings of Soul

But the biggest wave of black pop music to sweep over Africa was undoubtedly soul, which hit Africa well before it hit Europe. In fact it was Liberia, with its American Liberians, which first got soul.

Liberia, however, didn't produce Africa's first band to play the music of James Brown, Wilson Pickett, Otis Redding, and Ray Charles. It was Geraldo Pino's Heartbeats, who left Freetown in 1964 and spent two years in Monrovia. They then spent two years spreading soul music in Ghana. In 1968 Chris Okotie took them to Lagos, where they dominated the Nigerian pop scene for two years. They've now split up. Those who stayed in Lagos with Francis Fuster formed Baranta, while Pino went to Kano, where he formed the New Heartbeats with the Plastic Jims from Ghana.

The Heartbeats created a wake of soul-bands wherever they went in the late 1960s. Ghana's first soul group was the El Pollos, led by Stan Todd and Elvis J. Brown. Others soon followed. King Bruce's old Black Beats dance-band went over to soul in 1969 when the youthful Sammy Odoh (Owusu) and Ray Otis took over. Another band especially created by King Bruce to cater to soul music was the Barbecues, led by Tommy Darling.

In Nigeria, the Heartbeats influenced many of the pop-bands,

Geraldo Pino.

like the Clusters and Hykkers, which went overboard for soul, and Joni Haastrup, who became Nigeria's James Brown. Tony Benson, son of the famous old-time band leader Bobby Benson, set up the Strangers, who played at his father's night-club in Lagos, the Caban Bamboo.

Another soul freak was Segun Bucknor who, in 1968, after a two-year trip to the States, shaved off all his hair, teamed up again with the Nelson Cole brothers, and formed Segun Bucknor and his Soul Assembly. It was this group that released popular records like "Lord Give Me Soul" and "I'll Love You No Matter How."

By 1969 Segun was fusing soul with African music and generally becoming more and more original. He changed the name of the group to Segun Bucknor and the Revolution and released a string of controversial songs like "Son of January 15th," a poetical history of modern Nigeria; "Who Say I Tire," a satire on modern life in Lagos; and "Pocket Your Bigmanism" against the nouveau riche of Nigeria.

Even in French-speaking Zaire, soul music became popular and musicians started to produce their own local versions of it. Most well known is "Sukki Sy Man," an archetypal soul number that became a smash hit in West Africa in the late 1960s.

So, by copying pop music, first white and then black, creative young African musicians turned back to their own sources of energy. For the blacks the influx of soul brought its messages of "doing your own thing" and "black and proud." This trend was accelerated by the impact of the ultracreative and psychedelic rock of Jimi Hendrix, Cream, and Santana.

One of the first African bands to play this freak-out music was the Super Eagles of Gambia (now known as Ifang Bondi and the Afro-Mandingue Sounds), which toured West Africa in the late 1960s. In 1968 they visited Ghana, where underground bands like the Aliens, Barristers, and Blue Magic were formed. The psychedelic Aliens released an extended-play record that combined African music with Jimi Hendrix-type guitar-playing. In Nigeria the Afro-collection was formed in 1971 with some of today's leading musicians in Nigeria, like Tee Mac, Berkley Jones, Laolu Akins, Mike Odumosu, and Joni Haastrup.

The period from 1969 to 1971 was one where musicians got away from simply copying Western pop music. When soul crossed over to Africa, young musicians made a quantum leap out of the copy-cat straitjacket. Here's what Segun Bucknor says about his band Revolution, formed in 1969:

> After the Assembly, I changed the name to Revolution as I was experimenting with pop music but using the real basic African beat, the African jungle-beat which we call the kon-kon, in 6/8 time. We did something like Santana did with Latin music and pop. Before Santana there were Latin-American groups that were making it, but not that big. But since Santana came out with a rock-Latin beat, the older Latin-American musicians are coming up, like Mongo Santamaria who's a bongo player. You know Latin-American music and our music is virtually the same.

Tee Mac, leader of the Afro-collection.

It's all in 6/8 time but when you play Latin-American music you have to double the tempo.

The "Soul to Soul Concert"

It was at this time that Fela in Nigeria began his Afro-beat and Ghana's Osibisa, based in London, burst into the European market with their Afro-rock. Another stimulus to the creative scene, this time in Ghana, was the "Soul to Soul Concert" held in 1971— a massive two-day event at which top black American bands played side by side with Ghanaian groups. Tens of thousands flocked to Accra's Black Star Square. This unique happening was recorded and later released on film and record.

There were American artists like gospel singer Roberta Flack, the ghetto music of the Voices of East Harlem, the Staple Singers, soul singers like Ike and Tina Turner and Wilson Pickett. One of the policemen who was on duty for the show got so excited by Wilson Pickett that he jumped up on stage and started dancing with his hero. (Ghana's police and army took a special delight in soul music and have their own soul-bands, such as the Black Berets of the Recce Regiment.) Ghana's own top soul group, El Pollos, also performed at this memorable show, as did the grandad of Ghanaian palm-wine music, Kwaa Mensah.

New creations were also in the air. Ghana's Kofi Ghanaba (Guy Warren) played way-out drum solos backed by a full choir. Another performance that crackled with energy and new vibrations was the Afro-American jazz group of Les McCann and Eddie Harris. They teamed up with Amoah Azangeo, master of the fra-fra calabash of northern Ghana. Unlike the maracas, which are simply shaken, the fra-fra instrument is thrown around the body in a sort of juggling act, providing the framework for complex rhythms. The scintillations created by this combination of fra-fra and Afro-American music had to be heard to be believed, and fortunately can still be heard on the *Soul to Soul* record album. Following exposure to the international arena, Amoah launched out on an experimental phase. Up until then he had been playing his local music for the Ghana Arts Council, but after his Soul to Soul experience he joined up with the Afro-rock band Basa-Basa.

The music that made the deepest and most long-lasting impression on the Ghanaian music scene during this marathon show was, however, Santana's. Their combination of Latin-American music and rock became a source of inspiration for a generation of young Ghanaian musicians who went on to do the same thing with African music and rock.

So with Fela and Segun Bucknor doing their thing in Lagos, Osibisa doing theirs in London, and the "Soul to Soul Concert" staged in Ghana, a profusion of Afro-fusion bands appeared— BLO, Mono-mono, Ofo, and Ofege from Nigeria; and Boombaya, the Zonglo Biiz, Hedzolleh, Sawaaba Soundz, and the Big Beats of Ghana—bands that dominated the local pop market in the mid-1970s.

FESTAC

The biggest soul to soul experience of the 1970s was undoubtedly FESTAC, the Second World Black and African Festival of Arts and Culture, held in Nigeria in 1977. FESTAC brought together the traditional and contemporary arts of the 800 million blacks living throughout the world.

This spectacular was attended by black delegations from sixty-two countries. Events included a traditional durbar, regattas, and performing arts from the host country, Nigeria. A colloquium on black civilisation was attended by seven hundred scholars. There were fifty plays, 150 music and dance shows, eighty films, two hundred poetry and literature sessions, and forty art exhibitions.

It would be impossible to list all the music and dance events, but here are a few: from African countries there were Miriam Makeba, Osibisa, Bembeya Jazz, Les Amazones, the Golden Sounds, Louis Moholo, and Dudu Pukuwana; from the Caribbean, the Mighty Sparrow and the Cuban National Dance Troupe; from Latin America, Omo Alakuta and her Yoruba/Brazilian priestesses and Gilberto Gil's Afro-Latin music; from North America, Stevie Wonder, Sun Ra, and Donald Byrd and the Blackbyrds; from Australia and New Guinea, aborigine dances.

Section Three

Today's
Sounds and
Personalities

8 Fela and the Afro-Beat Revolution

The most spectacular musical figure to come out of Africa in the 1970s was Fela Anikulapo-Kuti, creator of Afro-beat—a fusion of jazz, soul, and West African highlife music. His new beat is pounding out everywhere in Africa, and is even catching on in the West. His blunt antiestablishment lyrics have made him the Bob Dylan and Mick Jagger of Africa.

Everywhere he goes, people stop what they are doing, shout his name, and give him the Black Power salute. Once, at the Surulere football stadium in Lagos, he received an overwhelming ovation, greater even than the head of state had received. Fela had a larger retinue, with scores of musicians, chorus girls, dancers, bodyguards, and wives accompanying him.

In 1974, at the same stadium, there was another demonstration of his popularity during a Jimmy Cliff show. Toward the end of the reggae star's performance, Fela was spotted by the crowd and a huge roar went up. The crowd carried Fela on their shoulders down to the stage in the middle of the football field, and moved around the field. Jimmy Cliff decided that there was no point in going on with the show after that.

Fela and members of the Africa 70.

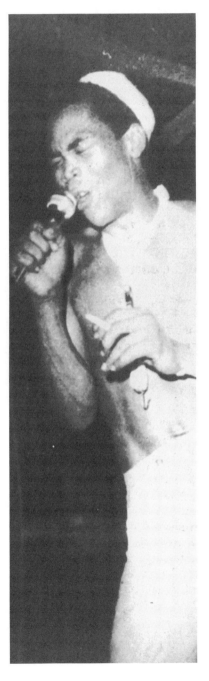

*Fela, injured during a police attack
on his home, was back on stage the
following day.*

The "Kalakuta Republic"

Before it was burned down by the army, Fela's home base was in the ghetto area of Lagos known as Mushin, just across the road from his club, the Africa Shrine. He called his house the "Kalakuta Republic," which in Swahili means "Rascal's Republic"—a name, he explained, that he got from the wall of a Lagos prison cell: "It was when I was in a police cell at the CID headquarters in Lagos, called Alagbon Close. The prisoners called the cell I was in 'The Kalakuta Republic.' So if rascality is going to get us what we want we will use that name, because we are dealing with corrupt people so we have to deal rascally with them."

In every way the Kalakuta was a republic. It had its own rules, court, prison, clinic, and barbed-wire security system. Fela lived inside with his musicians, dancers, twenty-seven wives, his brother, mother, and three children, not to mention a donkey, a baboon, and an Alsatian dog. Fela ruled the place like a traditional chief. Attendants waited on him; he fined and punished wrongdoers and held court every day for visitors.

Fela would often talk to his entourage while sitting on a toilet that adjoined the cushioned "session room" where he held court and entertained visitors. This alcove had no door and, the first time I met him in Lagos in 1974, no curtain either. By 1975, when I went there the second time, he had put a thin curtain between the toilet and the session room so that you could only see his legs and knees; as a result of his growing international popularity, he was advised that some sort of partition was necessary because of the increasing number of foreign visitors who might be shocked. I was surprised myself, but later on discovered that some European kings, like Louis XIV the "Sun King" of France, also sometimes held court for their privileged intimates while sitting on a special throne that doubled as a toilet.

From his Kalakuta Republic Fela and his entourage used to travel the short distance to his Africa Shrine on donkeys. All traffic would stop on the Agege Motor Road until they had passed.

Fela at the Africa Shrine

The shows at the Africa Shrine always start with Fela as chief priest, pouring a libation at a small shrine to Kwame Nkrumah and other leaders of Pan-Africanism. A shrouded figure of death then leaps on stage and the show begins with the Africa 70 band warming up. Fela then comes on stage and has his sax clipped on by an attendant.

While playing, Fela is always flanked by two musicians playing clips and maraccas. The rest of the band is stretched out behind him and includes trumpeters, sax players, guitarists, conga-drummers, and a trap-drummer (originally Tony Allen). Six chorus girls perform. The sexy dancers gyrate on raised platforms. Fela has a foot switch attached to these platforms. If one of the dancers tires, or is not up to standard, Fela switches off her platform light and a fresh dancer takes her place.

"Expensive Shit" and Other Songs

The music of Fela and his Africa 70 is famous throughout Nigeria and Africa.

A very popular number called "Shakara" is about the way Nigerian women demean themselves by copying Europeans:

> I want to tell you about lady-o
> She go say she equal to man,
> She go say she got power like man,
> She go say anything man do she self fit (can) do.
> (But) African women go dance, she go dance the fire dance.
> She know man na (is) master,
> She go cook for him,
> She go do anything he say,
> But lady no be so,
> Lady na (is) master.

Another song that condemns Westernised Nigerian women is "Yellow Fever," about the use of bleaching creams. A song on the same theme about men is "Gentleman." Fela would rather be a natural or original African man than dress up in a European suit. "Confusion" is another of his songs about the problems of modern life:

> Them be three men wey (who) sell for road-side-o,
> Them three speak different languages-o,

Them speak Lagos, Accra and Conakry.
One man comes pay them money-o,
He pay them for pound, dollars and French money,
He remain for them to share-o,
Me, I say no confusion be
        that-o?
(i.e. it will take them hours to work out the change)

"No Bread" is a political song:

For Africa here, him to be home,
Land boku (plenty) from north to south,
Food boku from top to down,
Gold de underground like water,
Diamond de underground like sand,
Oil de flow underground like river,
(but) everything go for overseas
Na from here it de come?

In between songs Fela speaks to his audience about black consciousness, the colonial heritage, government corruption and mis-
management and, of course, the need to legalise NNG, or Natural
Nigerian Grass, for he hates anyone to call it Indian hemp.

He has been charged several times with possession of this leaf
and once the police thought he had swallowed the evidence. They
examined his stool, but could find no trace of the weed. Fela captured the incident in a song called "Expensive Shit."

Trouble at the Kalakuta

Fela is always turning his problems and palavers into music. For
instance, one of his girls had been misbehaving and was put inside
a little prison in the backyard of Kalakuta called the Kala Kosu. It
was a symbolic prison, as the door was only tied with string. The
girl kept up such a racket that she was let out into a circle of Kalakuta people. She shouted at them and they shouted back, calling
and replying, so they soon had a song going.

A more serious incident is described in Fela's song "Kalakuta
Show," about an attack on his house in 1974 by sixty riot police.

Fela, returning from a court appearance in Lagos in 1974, talks to a crowd from the top of a car parked outside his club.

They were looking for a young girl who had been playing truant from home, and who was believed to have become one of Fela's dancers.

By coincidence I was at the Shrine (Empire Hotel) at the time, staying with a group of Ghanaian musicians on a recording trip. None of us had been in Lagos before and our manager warned us about the place the first night we arrived. The very next morning we woke to the smell of tear gas, as we were across the road and downwind of the Kalakuta. We could see the whole thing, including the stiff resistance put up by Fela's people, who were throwing stones and anything they could get their hands on, from the roof of the Kalakuta down onto the police.

There was a show that night, so Fela's stand-in, his lawyer, known as "Feelings," took over the singing. By the next day an injured Fela was back on stage joking about the bandages on his head that made him look like the pope.

The day after that he had more trouble, a court case involving Indian hemp, but he won the case and a crowd of thousands followed him back from the court to Mushin, creating yet another "go slow" (traffic jam) in overcrowded Lagos.

Because of his continual dicing with danger, Fela changed his name from Ransome-Kuti to Anikulapo-Kuti, which means a person who carries death in his pocket. One only has to travel with Fela to know what this means. He loves racing Mercedes Benz cars. Fela will never give way, even with a truck coming the other way. In this test of wills, Fela always comes out on top and the other driver has to give way. This puts all of Fela's people into a good mood.

Fela's most serious confrontation with the establishment was just after the Black Arts Festival, FESTAC (the Second World African and Black Festival of Arts and Culture), held at Lagos and Kaduna. Fela had been needling the authorities for some time before this. He and his cultural organisation, the Young African Pioneers (YAP), had distributed a half-million pamphlets criticising the recently introduced law of on-the-spot whippings for motor offences. They thought it would not be a good idea for the black visitors to FESTAC to see these whippings. He and YAP released another half-million pamphlets condemning the organisers of FESTAC itself. On top of this he released an album called *Zombie,* blasting the military mentality of the establishment. (In fact, because of this record "zombie" has become a term of abuse for the military throughout Africa.)

The final straw for the establishment came when a couple of Fela's people set fire to a motorbike belonging to a soldier from a nearby barracks. The soldiers hit back by raiding the Kalakuta, beating up everyone there and setting fire to the premises, completely gutting it. Fela moved to a new Kalakuta, which is heavily fortified. A later release, *Coffin for Head of State,* refers to this incident. The fold-open cover is a montage of newspaper clippings about the army's burning of Fela's original Kalakuta home.

Fela's Story

Getting Started

What is the story behind this famous musician, who is such a stimulus to the music industry, and such a thorn in the side of the establishment? His parents were famous. His father was a leading Yoruba educationalist and a reverend minister. His mother, Funmilayo Ransome-Kuti, was a leading political figure in Nigeria until her death. Even Fela's grandfather was a well known musician. He wrote Christian Yoruba hymns for the piano, some of which were recorded by EMI in the 1920s. Fela talked about his grandfather:

> He was a preacher and was responsible for bringing Christianity to the Yoruba country here, which I think is very bad, so I have to undo what he has done. His mistakes are colonial and we are now trying to get the colonial thing out.

Fela was brought up in Abeokuta and began his musical career as a highlife musician with the Cool Cats dance-band of Victor Olaiya, based in Lagos. He formed his own highlife group in England called the Highlife Rakers, when he was studying music at Trinity College, London. While in England he was influenced by the jazz of Miles Davis, John Coltrane, and Thad Jones.

When he returned to Nigeria in 1963 he formed his Koola Lobitos, which combined highlife and jazz. During the 1960s his band was based at the Afro-spot (Kakadu Club) in Yaba and competed with other highlife bands of the time like Rex Lawson's, Roy Chicago's, and Eddie Okonta's. The Koola Lobitos got a big boost when they backed Millicent Small and Chubby Checker in their tours of Nigeria in the mid-1960s. Yet Fela's music did not catch on in a big way, so he went to the United States in 1969. There, in Los Angeles, he came into contact with black militants. And, as he explains, what he discovered there completely revolutionised his approach to music:

> You see at the beginning, my musical appreciation was very limited, but later I got opened to many black artists. And I saw that

in Africa we were not open, as at that time they only let us hear what they wanted us to hear. When you played the radio, it was controlled by the government and the white man played us what he wants. So we didn't know anything about black music. In England I was exposed to all these things, but in Africa they cut us off. It was after I was exposed that I started using jazz as a stepping-stone to African music. Later, when I got to America, I was exposed to African history which I was not even exposed to here. It was then that I really began to see that I had not played African music. I had been using jazz to play African music, when really I should be using African music to play jazz. So it was America that brought me back to myself.

When he came back from the United States, Fela changed the name of his band to the Africa 70 and concentrated solely on his Afro-beat. His first two Afro-beat singles, "Jeun Koku" (Chop and Quench) and "Who Are You," were instant hits in Africa. Then the band went to London and recorded their first album at the famous Abbey Road studio. Since then, the Africa 70 has released a string of successful albums for EMI and Decca West Africa.

During this time, the Africa Shrine became a focus for musicians from Africa and abroad. Ginger Baker, the drummer with Cream, came down and did a live recording with Fela; so did Sandra Daniels, an Afro-American vocalist from Los Angeles, who recorded "Upside Down" with the Africa 70. Paul McCartney and Wings also hung around the Shrine for a time.

The Black President

By 1977 Fela thought it time to make a film of his life. He teamed up with Ghanaian producer Faisal Helwani, Ghanaian poet and film director Alex Oduro, and the Ghana Film crew. The film was called *The Black President* and was shot in Accra, Lagos, and Abeokuta. (I played the part of a colonial education officer, Inspector Reynolds.)

I was to have spent four or five days in Nigeria filming my part, but several things went wrong. First, the Ministry of Education prevented the shooting of a part of the film at Abeokuta

One of Fela's many wives.

*John Collins (*right*) as a colonial education officer and Fela (*left*) as a schoolboy during the filming of* The Black President.

Left to right: *Fela, John Collins, and J. K. Braimah during the filming of* The Black President, *1977.*

School where Fela's father (played by Feelings Lawyer) attacks Inspector Reynolds (oddly enough, my grandfather was a Reynolds, from Bristol) and chases him out of the school. During my flight, I knock down Fela, playing himself as a schoolboy. The Ministry thought this scene might embarrass the British government. So we had to shoot this sensitive part back in Lagos in the office of Fela's brother and edit it into the shots of Abeokuta School.

After this delay, my passport was seized by the Lagos inspector general of police, who had accused Fela of hiding two West Indians wanted for questioning (and whom I later met in Ghana). He held on to my passport to put pressure on Fela, and it took almost a month to sort this situation out. The man who took my passport to the IGP was beaten by Fela, as was another young man who sat on and squashed the colonial hat I used in the film. In both cases I tried to prevent the beatings but was told that it was an internal Kalakuta matter and none of my affair.

Fela had enormous respect for his mother, Funmilayo Ransome-Kuti, a leading nationalist and feminist in Nigeria. One day, when I was teaching Fela's children some science at her house in Abeokuta, Fela burst into the room and told me to stop, accusing me of teaching his children colonial mentality. His mother blasted him for this and told Fela she wanted her grandchildren educated even if he didn't and told him to leave the room; he left. Even though Fela had invited and paid me to do the film, for some reason he sometimes confused me with the part I was acting and actually seemed to think I was a colonialist. Mrs. Funmilayo Ransome-Kuti looked kindly on my acting and teaching efforts, however, and when I left Abeokuta she gave me a huge bag of soaps and other commodities that she knew were in desperately short supply in Ghana at that time.

Unfortunately, after the filming was completed the soundtrack was destroyed when the Kalakuta was burned by the army—an awful event that I, Victor Azziz, and the Ghana Film crew narrowly escaped, having left for Ghana a few days before. An attempt was made later in Ghana to redub the sound of the film, but it was unsuccessful as most of the film had been ad-libbed and no one could remember their exact lines. At the Ghana Film dubbing studio, I again met Mrs. Ransome-Kuti. Looking terrible and frail, she was quite unable to recognise me; during the attack on the Kalakuta she had been thrown out of a second-story window by a soldier. Shortly after leaving Ghana for Nigeria she died. Fela expresses his outrage at the way his mother died in his song "Coffin for Head of State."

Since that attack Fela has moved both his Kalakuta Republic and Africa Shrine and is still pumping out his music, now with his son, Femi, up on stage, playing sax. The Africa 70 has made several international tours, particularly to Italy and Germany, and their music is definitely catching on in the West. These European tours were great successes. The band played to audiences of around ten thousand in Brussels, Vienna, and Strasbourg, and a packed fifteen thousand at the famous Hippodrome in Paris.

I saw Fela play at the Amsterdam Woods in the summer of 1981, on one of his European tours. On that trip he brought with him several hundred copies of his latest album *ITT* (International Thief Thief), the lyrics of which condemn the machinations of the American multinational company of that name.

Fela had just made the controversial decision to marry twenty-seven wives. He had gone with his band as well as his numerous dancers and girlfriends to Ghana, where the customs officials at the airport objected to the number of women traveling with him. Fela married them on the spot and brought them into the country as his customary wives.

At the press conference after the show the questions were all about Fela's attitude toward women. Many of the reporters could not understand how he could claim to be a progressive and yet dominate a large harem of wives. One Dutch woman accused him of having no respect for women; Fela replied that women had their own specific duties to perform and that he would never enter a woman's kitchen as it is her domain. He went on to say that in Africa categories like male and female, old and new, day and night are never mixed up as "Nature is clear with no confusions." He added that unisex and uniformity may be fine for Europe but would never work in Africa. Fela uses sexual polarity and tension to create energy for his music.

I visited Fela, J. K. Braimah, and the band, now called the Egypt 80, at their hotel and met a very vexed Fela. He had just discovered that his British tour had been cancelled due to visa problems and put it down to the world of the American CIA and ITT. He talked about the psychological warfare these organisations use against so-called Third World countries in terms of language. He could not see why the terms "third," "undeveloped," or, even worse, "nonaligned" should be used. Nonaligned, for instance, means not straight, crooked, or bent—all of which imply inferiority.

His annoyance with all these derogatory terms found expression in an album the Africa 70 released in 1982, called *Original Sufferhead* (Arista label SPART 1171). Here are a few lines from the title track:

> Those who dey for London live like lords,
> Those who dey for New York live like Kings,
> We wey de (live) for Africa live like servants,

United Nations dem come get name for us, dem call us
    undeveloped nations,
We must be undeveloped to stay ten-ten in one room,
Dem dey call us third world,
We must be craze for head to sleep in dustbin,
Dem dey call us non-aligned nations.
We must be craze for head to sleep under bridge-o.

In 1984 Fela was arrested in Lagos for contravening the Nigerian currency laws; he was sentenced to five years in prison but served only nineteen months, during which time his son Femi managed his band (he has his own band now, called Positive Force). Since his release in 1986 and undeterred by his prison sentence, Fela has continued to play and release records. And with his Egypt 80 band he has traveled extensively in Europe and America, where his confrontation with the law has made him more famous than ever.

Anyone interested in more information on Fela should obtain Carlos Moore's book on this controversial musician, *A Bitch of a Life,* published by Allison and Busby in 1982.

9 The Juju Boom

Of it's slow, spacey music you like, then modern Nigerian juju music is for you. Juju is a more relaxed guitar-band dance music than highlife. It comes from western Nigeria, where it grew out of a fusion of local Yoruba music and highlife, like gombe, konkomba, and ashiko—a fusion that emerged in the 1930s and 1940s with juju pioneers like mandolin player Tunde King, banjoist Ojoge Daniels, and guitarist Ayinde Bakare.

In the 1950s the most popular exponents of Yoruba guitar-band music were the Blue Spots, whose leader, I. K. Dairo, electrified juju music and recorded literally hundreds of records. He was awarded the MBE for his success in the music field.

In spite of Dairo's success, up to the mid-1960s juju music was a poor relation to highlife, as it was street music played in palm-wine bars, at weddings, and at traditional functions. The top-notch night-clubs were in the grip of highlife fever, and most recordings were made of highlife.

Everything changed with the Nigerian civil war, including the sound and popularity of juju music. Many of the top highlife bands in Lagos had been run by easterners and therefore broke up. Only a few dance-bands were left in the Lagos area, like Bobby Benson's, Victor Olaiya's, and Roy Chicago's. Even Roy Chicago's band collapsed when his musicians were drafted into the army as musicians. From this point on, juju music had the field to itself in Lagos and western Nigeria. Whereas highlife continues to be popular in the east of the country, it has never recovered popularity in the west—there it's juju all the way.

I. K. Dairo's Blue Spots juju band.

Since then, and right up to the present, the juju field has been dominated by two outstanding musicians who brought about the main changes in juju music—Ebeneezer Obey, who slowed down the music of I. K. Dairo to a rock-steady beat; and the younger Sunny Ade, who retained the slow tempo but added some ultra-modern effects and a steel guitar.

Ebeneezer Obey

I visited Ebeneezer at his home off Palm Avenue in the Mushin area of Lagos. He told me that the first bands he ever joined, in the 1950s, were the Royal Mambo Orchestra and the Guinea Mambo Orchestra. He moved on to Fatal Rolling Dollars Band and the Federal Rhythm Brothers, before forming his own band in 1964, the International Brothers. He created the band after he had been offered a recording contract by Decca West Africa (Afrodisia). Their first release was the single "Ewa Wowum Ojumi Ri" (People

Ebeneezer Obey.

Come and See What I See), after which they released a series of albums for Decca.

In 1970 he changed the name of the band to Chief Commander Ebeneezer Obey and the Inter-reformers Band and continued to release on the Afrodisia label. One very popular song was dedicated to the "Late General Murtala Muhammed" and another expounded the government policy of "Operation Feed the Nation." Many of his songs have a strong moral behind them, like one about a man, his son, and their donkey. When the father rode the donkey, people called him selfish. When they both rode it they were accused of being cruel to animals. When neither rode but walked behind, they were thought mad. Obey's songs are so popular that on a new album his advance orders alone are over one hundred thousand copies.

The Inter-reformers today are an eighteen-piece band based at Obey's night-club in Lagos, the Miliki Spot. The group's instruments include electric guitars, wooden tambourines, the squeeze- or talking-drum, the shekeres (maracas), agogo (clips), and goumbeh- or gombe-drums. His own pair of gombe-drums are traditional hand-carved drums that have a modern drum-head with screws, rather than wooden drum-pegs.

Compared to the earlier type of 1950s juju music, which I. K. Dairo used to play, Obey's style is much slower and more spacey. In fact the juju music of the 1950s was more similar in tempo to the fast and bubbly highlife music of West Africa than to the ultra-relaxed juju music of today. It is so relaxed, and the live shows are so long, that the bandsmen often sit down behind their amplifiers when playing in public. Not only do the musicians weave a web of cool rhythms, but they also embroider and cross the main melody with snatches of other tunes.

Obey's band is typical of many of the hundreds of juju bands. In all of them the bass-guitar is used like a bass-drum; traditional percussion is used a lot and horns are never used. Like many other bands much of the music of the Inter-reformers is praise music, praising God as in Yoruba hymns, or praising big men and patrons. Sometimes huge sums of money are showered over Ebeneezer and his bandsmen by flattered patrons, who will try to stick hundreds of naira on the musicians' moist brows.

Sunny Ade

Equally popular is Obey's young rival, Sunny Ade, who has brought juju music right up to date. His band, the African Beats, not only uses the guitars and traditional percussion of orthodox juju, but also the vibraphone, moog synthesiser, and steel guitar played by Denola Adepoju.

Sunny's "syncro system," as he calls his sound, is even more distinct from the older generation of juju bands because of a strong dash of pop and Afro-beat. Unlike the older version of juju, which is usually in praise of prominent men, Sunny's lyrics are more about the problems of modern life.

Sunny, whose real name is Sunday Adeniyi, was born in the Ondo State in 1946. He picked up his musical inclinations from his father, who was an organist, and his mother, who was in the church choir. He completed his secondary education in Oshogbo and became leader of the school band there. Then he worked for a time with one of the popular traveling comic theatres, that of Moses Olaiya based at Ibadan. From there he moved to Lagos and joined Victor Olaiya's highlife band, based at the Papingo Club. In 1966 he formed his own band, called the Green Spots, based at the Kue Club in Lagos.

The band's first success came in 1967 with their football song,

"Challenge Cup." Since then Sunny has released over a dozen albums, including Nigeria's first double album. He records and releases everything on his own label, Sunny Alade Records, as he does not trust the big companies. He and his band have made many tours of North America and Europe. In Spain Sunny was acclaimed the "Golden Mercury of Africa."

On stage Sunny has almost telepathic rapport with his eighteen musicians and is constantly introducing new instruments to the band. He denies that his juju music is going synthetic. He thinks of it as traditional Yoruba music refined but not changed by modern instruments. For instance, the local gonje-fiddle has been replaced by the guitar, and the bamboo flute by the clarinet. He's a real believer in musical progress, but progress based on all the traditional cross-rhythms of Africa, not only in the drumming but even in the electric guitars. Each guitar plays its own distinct melodic and rhythmic phrase; all instruments interlace with each other in a subtle way.

Sunny's ideal in life is to have as beneficial an effect as possible on the largest number of people. He is deeply spiritual and has been a devout Christian since age 7. He neither smokes nor drinks. He believes that everyone has a special destiny, and that in his case juju music is his shrine. He even calls his Ariya (Enjoyment) Club a "church from where my message will reach the masses."

His music, like all juju music, has a strong religious and moral bias, and there is a definite overlap of juju music with the Yoruba hymn music of the aladura or "praying" churches, which is often played by electronic guitar-bands. Many of Sunny's lyrics are pessimistic predictions of doom, but again this is in the tradition of the revivalist African churches. Sunny hotly denies that his songs are antiestablishment. They are simply about the happenings in society, including its ills.

Sunny regularly sells two hundred thousand copies of his albums in Nigeria alone; Island Records (who produced the late Bob Marley) signed him up and in 1983 organised American and European tours for his African Beats.

Here are two comments on the packed two-and-a-half hour show held at the London Lyceum in January 1983. *New Musical Express* described the music as "the most exhilarant yet subtle mu-

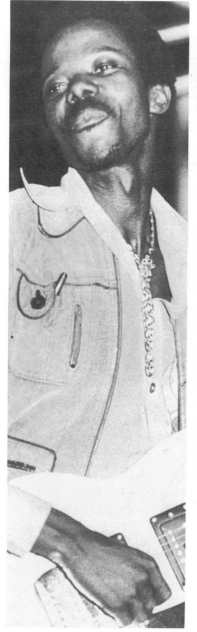

Sunny Ade at the Lyceum.

Sunny Ade.

sic heard in London for ages. Interlocking layers of rhythmic patterns create a seamless loop which at one and the same time combine an unforced airy simplicity with a hugely complex range of inflexions and texture."

The *Guardian* newspaper noted that

> Sunny Ade proved why they call him the 'Chairman.' He functions less as a star performer than as a conductor orchestrating a series of musical dialogues. The show offered a marked contrast with western song structure and our notions of musical climax. Although the set was divided into songs of varying mood and tempo one had the impression it was all part of the same fabric. Each number ended abruptly—in mid sentence as it were—yet without any feeling of discontinuity. They could have all started at any point and played for ever. Their skills and joyful dedication had the effect of making the panorama of English rock music look jaded and trite.

In April 1983, on the televised German programme "Rock Palace" (seen by 200 million viewers), the interviewer asked Sunny how he organises and controls his complex, yet laid-back musical structure. Sunny pointed out that he does not control it—rather he orchestrates the parts. Each musician has a special part to play in the total musical scaffolding. The African Beats' subtle and spacey music always spirals around the main beat, creating ambiguous rhythms difficult to pin down—so different from Western linear music. Even when interviewed, Sunny will never give the opinionated statements expected of a superstar. A master of understatement, he will rather throw the questions back at the interviewer or talk in parables. As in his music, everything is really a question of balancing opposite points of view.

Sunny's growing popularity in the West with his combination of juju and pop has encouraged his main rival, Ebeneezer Obey, to change his tune a bit. And after a short period of retirement and renovation Obey has recently come out with a juju/rock fusion that is also becoming popular with European rock fans, records of which are being released by the new wave record distributor in London, Rough Trade. He has also done some recording for Virgin Records (with Ghana's Joe Mensah as producer) and has toured the United States with his band.

New Trends in Juju

Ebeneezer Obey and Sunny Ade are the two giants of juju, but there are many juju-bands (around three hundred in the Lagos area alone). Their music now ranges from the more traditional types to modern varieties. Many of the old-timers are still playing: I. K. Dairo, Tunde Nightingale, and Daniel Akinolu (who has been the leader of the Inner Circle Orchestra since the death of Ayinde Bakare).

Playing in the style pioneered by Ebeneezer Obey are Sir Skiddo and his Mountain Millionaires, a twelve-man band based at Abeokuta. Oladunni Oduguwa or Mummy Juju and her Decency and Unity Orchestra also play in his style, as does Ayinde Barrister, who has been in Nigeria's Top Twenty for some time. Then there is Sir Shina's band from which Segun Adewele broke away to create a more innovative form of juju.

These days, many juju musicians are innovators, creating their own systems by incorporating new ideas—and generally taking the lead from Sunny Ade's success. For instance, Prince Adekunle and his Western State Brothers are influenced by pop and Afro-beat, as is Pick Peters. Then there is Thony Alex, who has created a blend he calls the "sedico system." Prince Dele Abiodun is another band leader who has combined Afro-beat and juju music, which he releases on the Olumo label. Up to 1970 he was a high-life musician, but then formed the Top Hitters juju-band and created his "adawa system." Bob Aladeniyi, originally second in command of Sunny Ade's African Beats, split away in 1975 to form his Jungle Rock Stars, which actually recruited Fela's Afro-beat musicians, Edo and Tutu Shorunma. Segun Adewele did some Yopop (Yoruba pop) releases in the mid-1980s for Sterns African Records of London, like the album *Ojo Je.*

Juju music quickly absorbs new melodic ideas because musicians use snatches of tunes from anywhere and anyone, incorporating them into a network of criss-crossing melodies. The usual criteria for copyright law break down with juju music. For instance, one juju song copies a phrase from "Somewhere over the Rainbow," but this is only one of four melodies playing simultaneously and it is used to embellish the main theme, a local melody.

Quite a different current within today's juju music is the influence of Muslim Yoruba music-styles like apala and sakara, which are less Westernised than juju and use only traditional instruments such as the hand-piano, the talking-drum, the one-stringed violin, and the sakara, a small tambourine made of clay or bamboo. One juju musician likes this sound so much that he has specialised in fusing juju and apala. Idowu Animashaun, a man of huge proportions, formed his Lisabi Brothers in 1966, which is still going strong.

Apala emerged in the middle 1940s as a mixture of traditional Yoruba music and Muslim music from the north. At first it was called "area" in Lagos and "oshugbo" in Ibadan. The name "apala" was coined in 1947 by the late Haruna Ishola when he formed his Apala Band. He released scores of singles and albums and dominated the apala scene.

If anyone imagines that the more traditional music of apala and sakara attracts old-fashioned people, one only has to turn to Haruna Ishola. In 1979 he opened the first twenty-four-track studio in Africa, at his home town of Ijebu-Igbo near Ibadan. Phonodisc makes three out of every ten records pressed in Nigeria, so the indigenous sounds of apala and juju are getting first-rate treatment. Sunny Ade records there.

The newest craze in the juju scene is the entry of "fuji" music—a juju sound minus the electric guitars and with heavy Islamic influence, created by musicians like Ayinde Barrister, Ayinde Kollington, and Wahabi Ejire.

So juju, fuji, and apala really embrace two worlds, looking forward to technology and backward to roots.

10   *Osibisa's Criss-Cross Rhythms*

*R*ock music, from Elvis to the Beatles, became popular with the youth of Africa during the 1960s, and the rock craze was followed by the progressive rock of Santana, Cream, Jimi Hendrix, and Sly and the Family Stone.

At first, young African musicians simply copied rock and pop music, but later, especially with the influx of progressive rock, they began to experiment and fuse their local music with rock. This is no surprise because, after all, rock and roll is based on black American rhythm and blues, the city version of the even earlier blues, hollas, and work-songs of the Southern plantations, music with roots in Africa.

Osibisa is first and foremost of the Afro-rock bands. They became internationally famous in the early 1970s for their criss-cross rhythms, which became a craze with blacks and whites alike and anticipated the disco-mania of the mid-1970s. This band, based in London, originally came from Ghana. They ended up making a million pounds for British taxes, for which they were awarded the MBE.

Osibisa's Beginnings

How could these extraordinary developments ever have got off the ground in the musical and social climate of the late 1960s? At the end of the 1950s, Teddy Osei and Mac Tontoh were playing in two of Ghana's most popular highlife bands. Teddy had formed the Comets in 1958, which rocketed to fame in West Africa after their "Pete Pete" became a local hit. Mac had joined the Uhurus, in the early days known as the Broadway Band, established in 1958 at Takoradi by Sam Obote, a Nigerian.

But Teddy became fed up with the local scene not really going anywhere. As far as trends in the Western music industry were concerned, the "roots" were virtually nonexistent. Why couldn't the whole range of black-derived Western pop music be broken down into the original African formula and not the other way round? The kind of musical versatility expected of the African musician in the entertainment business should surely make it possible to create a cultural confluence between the old folk tunes (with their own style of rhythm, melody, and timbre qualities, the rich pulsating rhythms, the instrumental variety, the creative energy of Africa) and the various facets of popular music as an overlayer (gospel, blues, jazz, bossanova, soul, funk, and so on). For as Teddy pointed out, "Soul and reggae derive from Africa, so why don't people recognise the original first?"

It was this rather stagnant state of affairs that made Teddy decide to go to London in 1962. In Ghana, after leaving technical building college he was a building inspector, but music was his first love. Born in Kumasi, as a young boy he had already learned to play Ashanti percussion instruments used for various ceremonies, such as the Ashanti atumpan-drums. At school, he played drums for the brass-band. Later he picked up the sax by chance and then the flute. After playing in big name bands like the Star Gazers, with drummer and percussionist Sol Amarfio, he led his own band, the Comets, in which his brother Mac also played. The Comets scored many singles hits throughout West Africa in the late 1950s, the last one "Pete Pete" being simultaneously number 1 in Ghana, Nigeria, and Sierra Leone.

In London, he found that it was not easy to start playing music: "I washed plates in hotels for six months and bought my own saxophone. But no musician was interested in me, so I had to convince them of my worth. Later I got some Africans together and we started playing for Africans during the summer."

The Nkrumah government gave him a scholarship to study music at a London school, training that he later found useful when it came to arranging for his own group. After playing in a few night-clubs, he formed Cat's Paws, which veered toward soul music, as a means of getting work. After a residency in Zurich's Beat Club and a three-month exposure at a 1969 festival in Tunis, Cat's Paws returned to London. "We got so much inspiration that we discovered we had to put more into African music." Teddy brought Mac Tontoh and Sol Amarfio over to London. After Teddy left Ghana in 1962, Mac had spent one year with a military dance-band, playing at top state functions, and then joined the Uhurus, the first big band of its kind in Africa. In addition to the styles they were playing in 1967, their music also ranged from Glenn Miller to Charlie Parker. Sol, born in Accra, was playing maraccas, bongos, and congas with local bands at age 12. When he was 16, he joined the Rhythm Aces, then the Star Gazers. In 1968 he started playing the full conventional drum kit.

After an offer to record a sound-track to a film set in Africa, Teddy started to work on the Osibisa sound, along with four West Africans and two West Indians—later to be joined by a third West Indian. The group included his brother, Mac Tontoh, who had learned to play the Lobi xylophone from Lobi musicians who had settled in his village. In addition, he plays assorted traditional percussion, including drums and Ewe instruments, such as the gangogui (double bell of welded iron) and the axatse (beaded calabash rattle). Other instruments he plays are trumpet and flugel horn. Lofty Lasisi Amao, a Nigerian, playing tenor sax, baritone sax, and congas, had also come to London with Mac and Sol. They were joined by Spartacus R from Grenada, on bass guitar and assorted percussion; Wendell Richardson from Antigua, on lead guitar and vocals; and Robert Bailey from Trinidad, on organ, piano, and timbales. Needless to say, it comes as first nature to all members of the group to play percussion and sing, drawing on African traditions.

Osibisa Takes Off

The name of the group was changed to Osibisa, which means "criss-cross rhythms that explode with happiness." Richard Williams recalled his first meeting with Osibisa:

At that time, Osibisa had nothing—except their instruments, their talent, and their twofold love: for their music and for each other. They were totally unknown, just starting out in one of the world's most competitive arenas.

They played for me that afternoon, and that tiny, cramped room filled up with the sound of joy. To say that I was transfixed would be a massive understatement, and I left the place, a couple of hours later, reeling with the delight of stumbling across something very important indeed.

Soon after that meeting, they were unleashed on the British public, and the effect was astonishing. They took audiences who'd grown used to sitting on the floor and marvelling at superfast lead guitarists, grabbed them by the scruff of the neck and made them dance. They'd come out of the blue: four West Africans and three West Indians, most of whom had been close to starvation for a year or more. They were hungry, and that hunger was plain in their music. It showed itself in an energy and urgency long lost and forgotten by most European musicians, and suddenly audiences everywhere were responding.

(*Woyaya* sleeve notes)

In 1970 Osibisa took off, after releasing their first single, "Music for Gong-Gong," and began to get popular at clubs like Ronnie Scott's, the Roundhouse, and the Country Club—all in London. A number of musicians have passed through the group since

Osibisa with Remi Kabaka at the Royal Albert Hall.

its early days. Originally on bass there was Spartacus R from Grenada, followed by Fred Coker and then Mike Odumosu (both from Nigeria). Del Richardson from Trinidad was their lead guitarist for a long time. Then on congas were Lofty Lasisi Amao from Nigeria and Kofi Ayivor from Ghana. On keyboard were Robert Bailey from Trinidad and Kiki Gyan from Ghana.

From 1971, first on the MCA and then the Bronze label, they released a string of albums and singles—albums like *Osibisa, Heads, Happy Children, Welcome,* and *Black Magic Night;* and singles that got into the British Top Ten, like "Sunshine Day," "Dance the Body Music," and the "Coffee Song."

In the mid-1970s in England, with the decline of rock music and the appearance of disco and new wave, Osibisa's Afro-rock also suffered. So the band packed their bags and spent most of their time outside Britain on international tours of Australia, the East, Europe, and Africa, where they had massive followings.

Of course the one country they kept going back to was Ghana, where they became a constant source of inspiration for the youth. Even in the villages their music was a success, especially their "Music for Gong-Gong," which became a standard among the rural guitar-bands. They also put on big shows in Ghana, like the one they did at the El Wak Stadium in Accra in 1977. They brought over heavy amplification with them.

Ironically they represented, along with other artists, the black and African communities resident in Britain at the Black Arts Festival, FESTAC, held in Nigeria in 1977. They were also invited to the celebrations connected with the independence of Zimbabwe and the inauguration of the Cultural Ministry, and played to a crowd of 25,000 people in the capital. They are getting more and more back to their roots, and in 1980 released, on their own Flying Elephant label, the old South African hit "Pata-Pata."

Fusion

During the summer of 1983 European audiences were given a special treat—a tour by a West African band, the Highlife Stars. This group of musicians combines two streams of highlife music—big-band highlife and guitar-band highlife. The resulting fusion sound is a sensation.

This cross-over came about when members of the internationally known Afro-rock band Osibisa (itself of the big-band format) teamed up with musicians from two of Ghana's top guitar-bands, Kokroko (Mighty) and Ahenfo (Chief). The resulting ten-man supergroup played six gigs, three in Germany and three in Britain, all under the wings of Osibisa's Flying Elephant organisation. The Highlife Stars also recorded an album in London, released on the Flying Elephant label, before the four members of Kokroko and Ahenfo went back home to Ghana.

The European-based members of Highlife Stars will be familiar to many as they form part of Osibisa. They are Mac Tontoh (sax), his son Frank (drums), Potato (congas), and Emmanuel Rentoz (keyboard). Also from Ghana came bass player Martin Owusu (ex–Adam's Apple, now based in Switzerland). Then from Nigeria came trombonist Remi Ola, who used to play with Tony Allen, Fela's former drummer.

Less well known in Europe and brought from Ghana especially for the summer tour were three members of the Kumasi-based band Kokroko: Eric Agyeman (leader and lead guitarist), Thomas Frempong (vocals and percussion), and Tommy King (trumpet). From the Tema-based guitar-band Ahenfo came its leader A. B. Crentsil (vocals and rhythm guitar).

Eric Agyeman began his musical career with the Afro-Boateng band and then for a number of years played with the locally renowned guitar-band the Noble Kings, led by Dr. Gyasi (incidentally, the first Ghanaian guitar-band to feature horns). It was at this time that Eric met up with Thomas Frempong, Dr. Gyasi's drummer, and trumpeter Tommy King.

In 1972 Eric helped form the Sweet Talks, the resident band of a night-club in Tema called the Talk of the Town. Thomas Frempong was with him, as was Tommy King, after doing a stint with the Henrikos Dance Band (run by P. P. Dynamite) and the Complex Sounds, a band financed by the Tema Food Complex.

The Sweet Talks established itself as one of Ghana's leading highlife bands. A B. Crenstil made his popular *Adam and Eve* album with them. Eric's *Hollywood Highlife* album was released after a Sweet Talks tour of the United States. Following the group's collapse in 1979, Eric ran a band called the Super Sweet Talks and released two solo albums, *Safari Highlife* and *Living in the Cold,* before forming Kokroko in 1982.

Crenstil, meanwhile, led a band called the Super Brains and then, before forming Ahenfo, joined up with Smart Nkansah's Sunsum (Spirit) band and released the popular album *Atia* with them. (*Atia* warns of the danger of drinking too much local gin.)

These musicians have made a particularly remarkable break-through with their new musical fusion in the Highlife Stars be-cause the development of the two branches of highlife have been quite distinct. Out of the prewar band orchestras came the Ghanaian highlife dance-bands of the 1950s and 1960s like E. T. Mensah's Tempos, the Black Beats, Ramblers, Uhurus, and Com-ets. And from the acoustic palm-wine groups came the electric guitar-bands that dominate the Ghanaian music scene today.

The gap between these two varieties of highlife was so great that for many years it was impossible to form a single musicians' union, catering to both types of players. In fact, it was only in the early 1980s that the guitar-band musicians joined their dance-band brethren in the united Musicians' Union of Ghana (MUSIGA), with two leading guitar-band musicians heading the union. The president was Koo Nimo, an updated palm-wine guitarist, and the vice-president was Nanu Ampadu, the leader of the famous African Brothers guitar-band.

What was anticipated by this fusion of music organisations in Ghana, finally surfaced musically on stage in 1983 in Europe, with the Highlife Stars. Everybody enjoyed their music; what most people did not realise was that highlife history was being made.

11   *Afro-Rock Catches On*

Osibisa isn't the only group to have influenced the growth of rock in Africa. In Nigeria another stimulus in this direction has come from British drummer Ginger Baker, who played with two of Britain's top rock bands of the 1960s, Cream and Blind Faith.

Ginger Baker's Influence

In 1970 Ginger, by then running a band called Airforce, visited Nigeria. He traveled via Ghana, where he stayed for a time with famous Ghanaian Afro-jazz drummer Guy Warren (Kofi Ghanaba). In Nigeria Ginger was given a big welcome by Afro-beat king Fela, and they jammed together at the Afro-spot. Also playing was one of Nigeria's oldest established pop groups, the Clusters. Ginger was so impressed by their leader, Joni Haastrup, that he took him back to England to play organ for Airforce for eighteen months.

The rest of Clusters—Berkley Jones, Laolu Akins, Mike Odumosu, and Bob Cole—joined up with Tunde Kuboye and Swiss-Nigerian flute player Tee Mac to form the Afro-collection, a band influenced by the progressive rock of Jimi Hendrix, Santana, Sly and the Family Stone, and Blood Sweat and Tears. Tee Mac's Afro-collection was based at the Batakoto Club in Lagos, set up by Ginger Baker and a Nigerian partner.

When Airforce broke up in 1971, Ginger returned to Nigeria across the desert in a Range Rover. At his club he was so taken

Joni Haastrup.

Ginger Baker.

with Afro-collection, that he asked Berkley, Laolu, and Tunde to join a new band called Salt.

The other members of the band were two European musicians, Steve Gregory and Bud Beadle, and two Nigerian vocalists called the Lijadu Sisters. Salt was introduced in Nigeria in 1972 at a huge show at the Kakadu Club in Lagos. Another Afro-rock band was launched then, a six-piece group called Ofo and the Black Company. After this show Salt went to the Olympic Jazz Festival and then on to an American tour.

But Ginger's effect on the Nigerian rock scene didn't stop at moving Nigerian musicians around the world. He also helped set up Africa's first sixteen-track recording studio, the Associated Recording Company (ARC) studio at Ikeja. He put a film together that featured himself, Fela and the Africa 70, the Afro-collection, Segun Bucknor, and artist-musician Twin Seven Seven.

Mono-Mono and BLO

The Ginger Baker–Afro-collection dialogue led to the formation of important rock groups in Nigeria, such as Mono-Mono (which means "lightning") formed in 1971 by Joni Haastrup after his tour with Ginger's Airforce. Mono-Mono's early hit record was a Haastrup composition called "Lidalu." BLO was formed when bassist Mike Odumosu, drummer Laolu Akins, and guitarist Berkley Jones returned from the European-American tour with Salt. The name of the band, BLO, is taken from the initials of the three musicians, and it released a number of successful Afro-rock numbers like "Native Doctor" and "Preacher Man."

The Funkees

Another of the first Nigerian Afro-rock bands, but this time from the east of the country, was the Funkees, formed during the height of the Nigerian civil war in 1969. The band's leader was Jake Solo, who had previously been with the Hykkers, a pop group from Enugu. The Funkees combined pure funk with the local Igbo atilogwu beat, and their first hit single in Nigeria was "Onyemanya," released in 1971, followed by "Akula" and "Dancing Time," both released on the EMI Nigeria label.

Afro-Rock in Ghana

In Ghana, the main stimulus to Afro-rock besides Osibisa was the "Soul to Soul Concert" held in Accra in 1971, which featured the Latin rock of Santana. This gave an incentive to a whole generation of young pop musicians to experiment with rock combined with their own rhythms, just as Carlos Santana had done with Latin-American music and rock.

The Aliens pop-band in Accra went psychedelic, due to the influence of Jimi Hendrix. They released an EP of music that combined Jimi's guitar style with an African backing. They were followed shortly after by a group called Hedzolleh (meaning "freedom"). On stage, they were more African than Osibisa. The group was based at the famous Napoleon Club in Accra.

Another top Ghanaian rock-band in the mid-1970s was Cosmic Boombaya, which was based at Wato's Club overlooking one of Accra's busiest roundabouts. The Q-Masters was based in Ghana but mainly composed of Sierra Leonese musicians. They stayed in Kumasi for several years, where they expounded the

The Grave Diggers (originally the Q-Masters), with leader Papa Maurice Williams (bottom right), percussionist Samuel Oju King (standing, centre), and singer Prince Aji (standing, right).

cross-beat, a combination of rock and the rhythms of the secret Poro society of Sierra Leone.

All over English-speaking Africa, rock became popular. In South Africa it became a craze with the youth in the townships like Soweto. In East Africa, too, there are bands like Matato of Kenya, which plays in the style of BLO, Ofege, and the six-piece rock-band Makonde formed in 1977.

Afro-Rock Goes Abroad

As a consequence of the black and white fusion, many of the African bands that play Afro-rock have ended up in the States and Europe, leading to a great deal of cross-fertilisation in the international rock scene. The members of Afro-collection, who joined Ginger, and Ofo and the Black Company, ended up in the States. The Funkees also went abroad to Britain in 1973. Later Jake Solo played with Osibisa, as did Mike Odumosu of BLO.

The Ghanaian bands Hedzolleh and Boombaya also made the pilgrimage abroad, to the States and Britain, respectively, and both stayed, as did the Sierra Leonese band Super Combo, which was resident in London for a time. Also in London is the Afro/jazz/ rock fusion group from South Africa called Jabula, and Ojah, which was actually formed in London by Ghanaian bassist Nana Tsiboe and English musician Willie Stallibras (originally with the rock group Chilli Willi and the Red Hot Peppers).

Then there have been many individual African musicians working in the American and European rock scenes. One of the first was the Ghanaian conga player Speedy Acquaye, who worked with Georgie Fame and the Blue Flames in the 1960s. Nigerian percussionist Remi Kabaka has worked with Ginger Baker, Steve Winwood, and Mick Jagger. Another Nigerian, Gaspar Lawal, has worked with Ginger's Airforce and with the Rolling Stones. In fact, the idea for the popular Beatles' song "Ob-La-Di Ob-La-Da" was given to them by Jimmy Scott, the Nigerian conga player.

Ojah playing in London, 1979.

Left to right: *Louis Moholo and Speedy Acquaye.*

Eddie Quansah, Ghana's black trumpet, also left home and worked as a session musician in Europe for years. He finally got the money from Island Records to return home and produce a top-selling Afro-rock album called *Che Che Kule.*

Another Ghanaian rock musician, who was actually brought up in Britain, is Kris Bediako. He returned home in the mid-1970s to form his popular "Band called Bediako."

White Rock Goes to Africa

White rock musicians are now going to Africa to play and record. Ginger is one and another is Paul McCartney, whose band Wings recorded *Band on the Run* in Lagos in the mid-1970s. In 1981, Mick Fleetwood of Fleetwood Mac visited Ghana. He came with two American rock musicians, Todd Sharpe and George Hawkins,

Gaspar Lawal (right).

plus twelve tons of equipment and a sixteen-track recording studio with which they recorded their album *The Visitor.* Fleetwood Mac's big hit of the 1960s, "Black Magic Woman," had become fantastically popular in Ghana, especially when Santana did a version of it. This helped blow the creative lid off the local Afro-rock scene.

Afro-Rock Today

Nigeria

Today Afro-rock is still a powerful force in Africa, in spite of the demise of rock in the West. Without doubt the main centre of the African rock industry is Nigeria, with its modern multitrack studios and the release of 20 million records a year. The top Nigerian rock artist at the moment is the young Chris Okotie, who has been a teenage heart-throb since 1980 when he released his first album *I Need Someone.* It sold over one hundred thousand copies in six months and earned Chris a gold disc. He comes from the Bendel State and was a law student at the University of Enugu. He sings rather like an African Bob Dylan, and is influenced by James Brown, Hot Chocolate, and Cat Stevens. On the cover of his second album, *Just for You,* he is dressed as a knight in shining armour, much to the delight of young Nigerian women.

Bongos Ikwue.

Chris Okotie.

Another top rock and pop group is Bongos Ikwue and his Groovies. He started professional singing in 1967 and his first hit came in 1974 with "Sitting on the Beach," sung in the style of Otis Redding. Then he released "Otachik-pokpo" in his own Indoma language, and in 1977 and 1978 was awarded two gold discs for his two albums *Still Searching* and *Something Good*. Bongos sings everything from rock and reggae to funky calypsos and highlife in a distinctively soft, gravelly voice. His harmonies are reminiscent of the Everly Brothers.

Another Nigerian pop star who has more recently risen to fame is Tony Grey and his Black Kings. His *Gospel of Ozzimba* could be termed pop highlife. His album *Please Don't Leave Me,* for instance, is sung in English. He uses a moog-synthesiser, but keeps to West Africa's traditional twelve-beat cycle.

Not all of Nigeria's pop stars are men. Actress/singer Patti Boulaye won the television *New Faces* competition in 1978 and then released her first album, *Patti Boulaye*. This included ballads,

Patti Boulaye.

rock and roll, and soul. Her second album, *Music Machine,* is more disco-oriented and was the soundtrack to a film.

The Lijadu Sisters, Kehinde and Taiwo, are Yoruba identical twins who are related to Fela. They have been singing together since childhood. They have released in Nigeria five albums containing a selection of their own Afro-beats, reggaes, pop songs, disco numbers, and local apala tunes. In 1988, they released another album called *Double Trouble* with the American Shanachie record company and went on a tour of the States with Sunny Ade—where they were described as a West African equivalent of the Pointer Sisters.

Most of Nigeria's first rock artists are still active. Tee Mac is now a music promoter and has his own record label called SKJ Records. Mike Odumosu has set up his own record company in Nigeria, which has released an album called *Sunshine in Africa.* He is currently playing with the Gonzales group in the States. Jake Solo is back in Nigeria and has decided to revive the Hykkers, one of Nigeria's first pop bands. BLO is still around and has done the backing for another female Nigerian rock vocalist, Christine Essien, whose album *Give Me a Chance,* was released on the Decca label in 1981.

Ghana

Despite the serious economic situation, causing many musicians to spend time abroad, Ghana too has many Afro-rock bands

The Lijadu Sisters. (Courtesy Shanachie Records)

today, such as Bob Pinado from Winneba, whose sonobete dance was a hit in Ghana in the late 1960s. After this, like so many others, he had to spend many years abroad and released top tunes, like "The Girl with the Guitar-shaped Body," in Germany. The famous Ghanaian vocalist Pat Thomas has also spent a lot of time in Germany. He was originally with the Sweet Bands run by the Tema Food Complex, which played everything from rock to highlife. He later teamed up with Smart Nkansa's band Sunsum (Soul), whose "Sunsum Beat" is funky rock. Also based in Tema is the young singer Eric Agyeman of the Sweet Talks, who combines highlife and pop. Another of Ghana's leading vocalists, Jeff Tagoe, spends most of his time in Nigeria. When in Ghana he is backed by super pop highlife group Vis-à-Vis.

French-Speaking Africa

Even the French-speaking countries of Africa are now producing their own distinct blend of African rock and pop, with the emphasis on the voice and front-line instruments. Cameroons' Manu Dibango, for instance, is a master of rhythm and blues, rock's progenitor. Some of Pierre Akendengue's (the blind guitarist from Gabon) songs are mainline Afro-French pop, as are many of the songs of Ivorian artists like Pierre Amande, Ernesto Dje Dje, and Aicha Kone.

Rock hasn't affected only the urban music of Africa, but has also penetrated deeply into the traditional guitar-band music. The lineup of a typical guitar-band today is almost identical to that of a rock group: lead, rhythm, and bass guitars; trap-drums; and sometimes an organ. In addition, the guitar-bands use congas and a percussion section, but then many of today's rock bands also include a rhythm section.

A Circuit Completed

Whether it's the juju music of Sunny Ade and Idowu Animashaun, the highlife bands of African Brothers and Eddie Donkor, or the up-dated griot music of the Ambassadors Dance Band of Mali, they are all fusions of African music and rock, or the pop music that has grown out of it.

It's strange to think that rock is now thriving in Africa under so many guises. But it is a circuit completed: African work songs became rhythm and blues; this in turn became white rock and roll; and this in turn ended up back in the African mainstream.

12   *Afro-Disco*

The disco dance craze and the maxi single burst into the mid-1970s at a time when pop fans in the West had stopped dancing and were sitting, listening in stoned-out passivity to the psychedelic music of rock superstars. It was the cross-rhythms of Osibisa that first got them on their feet, until this band's natural rhythms were eclipsed by black American soul and funk, mechanised into disco by German musicians-cum-computer-operators like Kraftwerk. A similar German band, Munich Machine, backed Donna Summers at exactly 154 beats per minute. Boney M also first hit the jackpot in Germany.

This German man-machine fusion swept the world and, for a time, among the youth in Africa, it looked as if disco-mania was going to swamp local music completely. Many bands copied this music. The local live music and open-air clubs dwindled, and everybody started crowding into dark and stuffy discotheques.

Since the initial knock-out shock wave of superproduced disco, African musicians at home and abroad have been on the offensive, creating their own distinct blends of African disco—something that is surely needed, especially as there is a tendency in disco to drift into the watered-down and mediocre Muzak of Euro-pop groups.

Irresistible Disco

It would be impossible to mention all the African disco-bands and artists as so many groups have been influenced by this irresistible dance-music. Osibisa experimented with it before their "Pata-Pata" release of 1980, and several ex-Osibisa members have continued in the disco line—Kiki Gyan, for example, the Ghanaian keyboard player, who has recorded with drummer Glen Warren, and Glen's dad, the famous Guy Warren of Ghana. Likewise congaist Kofi Ayivor is now producing disco music. Then there is the Nigerian bassist Jake Solo, who released a disco record in Europe called *Boogie Legs* and in 1981 in Nigeria released *Shake Your Ya Ya* on the Tabansi label. Jake's first band was the pop group based at Nsukka University called Hykkers, which played Beatles-type music. He then joined up with the Afro-rock groups the Funkees and Osibisa and stayed in England for ten years altogether. Since 1977, with his *Coming Back Home* album, made when he visited

Jake Solo of the Funkees.

FESTAC, he has had the intention of returning home to Enugu to add his professional touch to the music scene there.

Other Nigerian musicians are also producing disco material. Sonny Okosun is creating a kind of disco Ozzidi music. Drummer Remi Kabaka released *Funky Lagos* in 1981. Nigeria's top female pop singer Patti Boulaye made her *Music Machine* album.

A Ghanaian musician who has had some disco works pressed is trumpeter Eddie Quansah. He spent a long time as a session musician in London and then signed a contract with Island Records to make his catchy funky-highlife album *Che Che Kulay*, released simultaneously in Europe and Africa in 1978. Then there is the Ghanaian athlete turned musician, Sidiku Buari, who spent some time in the States and returned home in 1979 after releasing his *Disco Soccer* album.

In 1980 the World Disco Championship, which involved 14,000 contestants, was won by the creative dancing of the thin and lanky South African Godfrey Raseroka.

Akie Deen

An African producer who has created a different mode out of the unstoppable influence of disco music is Akie Deen, a Sierra Leonean based in London, who has moved in a big way into the Afro-Caribbean disco market that has grown up in the last few years. One of the effects of the international disco fever was the updating of calypsos, meringues, sambas, and rumbas by artists like Ed Watson and Mighty Sparrow. Lord Kitchener, whose calypsos were so popular in the 1950s, has also had a new lease on life and his "Sugar Bum Bum" was a major success in the late 1970s and was played at all West Indian parties.

Akie Deen simply moved into this field with his disco versions of Sierra Leonean meringues and Ghanaian highlifes, calling his sound "discolypso" to avoid the prefix "Afro-," which he believes is commercially overplayed.

Akie is a friendly, larger-than-life person who is constantly on the go. He knows practically all the African musicians in the United Kingdom and many come to record as session musicians for his rapidly expanding Afro-disco productions. Ironically, after spending ten years in England and gaining some success there,

Left to right: *Bunny Mack and Akie Deen.*

including several chart hits, his music has now caught on back in Africa. The radio stations are constantly playing his productions, especially the Ivory Coast Radio. In Nigeria one of his records won a gold award in 1981 and he is now busily opening up distribution in East Africa and Zimbabwe.

Akie, who was born in Freetown in 1947, first became interested in music production when he was social secretary of the Sierra Leonese Students' Union in England. It was in 1972 when he had his first opportunity, when he helped organise an eight-week tour of Sierra Leone's top guitar-band, the Afro Nationals. He was also involved with their first releases, the two singles "Dem Kick" and "Wondemuyie."

Even though these records were popular in West Africa, in England there were problems, as he explains:

> It was with great difficulty that I got the first shop in London to take even ten records. Also I had no car and had to put the rec-

ords in a friend's car. We used to attend parties and ask the DJ to play them in order to sell them.

Then in 1973 Akie arranged a tour of the United Kingdom for Ghana's top guitar-band, the African Brothers, and recorded two songs by them, including the popular "Maria" based on a congolese rhythm. At the first pressing only 250 records were made. Akie described how hard it was initially:

> At first I faced great difficulty and I couldn't sell them as the shops wouldn't accept them. That was until I convinced Steve Barnard, a DJ on Radio London's Reggae Time, to play them on the air. Then I got requests for boxes of twenty-five from shops who had only taken a single copy. In one week I got through five hundred.

In 1974 Akie produced two bands. One was Super Combo with whom he made the highlife meringue "Woko." The other group was the Funkees from Nigeria. The first album by this Afro-rock band was called the *Point of No Return,* and was jointly produced by Akie and Dan Jegede.

The following year, members of the Afro Nationals, under the name Sabannah 75, came to London again and, helped by Akie, released three singles, "Susanna," "Konko," and "Carry On." They all became big hits back in Sierra Leone. The band returned yet again in 1977, and Akie released a twelve-inch single version of Rokafil Jazz's "Sweet Mother" with them, under the registered Afro-disco name of Wagadugu.

Miatta Fahnbulleh

In 1977 Akie started working with Liberia's top female vocalist, Miatta Fahnbulleh, who recorded two traditional songs in disco-style with him: "Amo Sakee Sa" and the reggae "Kokolioko." Later she released an album called *The Message of the Revolution,* which contained Pan-African ideas. In spite of her international upbringing (her father was a diplomat in Liberia, Sierra Leone, Kenya, and Britain), her music is rooted in the Liberian culture—a mixture of African, Afro-American, West Indian, and European influences. She describes her music as African music.

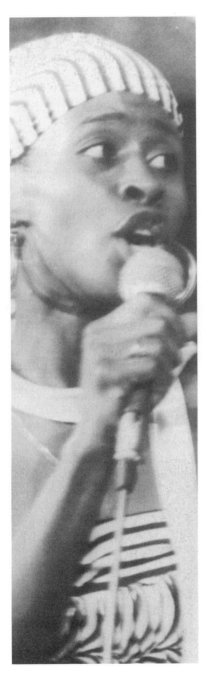

Miatta Fahnbulleh.

It comes from Africa but it embraces the whole world. As far as I see my music, it is to deliver everything that is happening in the so-called commercial music of today, but emphasising the roots as it is.

She is in a good position to add an international touch to the local Liberian folk music, as her traveling continued even after leaving school. For a time she worked for the Voice of Kenya and then went to the States to study journalism. While in New York she sang at the famous Apollo Theatre in Harlem, studied at the American Musical and Dramatic Academy, and worked with the Negro Ensemble Theatre of New York and with Duke Pearson of Blue Note Records.

She returned home in 1973 to appear as a guest artist at President Tolbert's inauguration, and again in 1974 to discover she was a star there. So she toured West Africa with a Sierra Leonean band usually resident in Lagos, called Baranta. After that, she worked with the South African trumpeter Hugh Masekela and with Nigerian artists like Jimi Solanke and Remi Kabaka. In 1977 she represented Liberia at the Black Arts Festival in Lagos.

The same year she went back to England and worked with a number of musicians and producers—Jah Bunny of Matumbi and, of course, Akie Deen of Afro-discs.

More Successes for Akie Deen

After Miatta's disco successes, Akie continued to release his evolving discolypso sound. There was the single "Tumba," and "Carolina" by Addy Foster Jones, who works for Sierra Leone television. Teddy Davies did a version of Lord Kitchener's popular "Just a Little Bit." Akie also produced a single by Nigeria's Jake Solo, licensed by Pye.

But the big breakthrough into the Afro-Caribbean disco market came in 1979, with the release of "Easy Dancing" by Wagadugu, followed by "Discolypso" and "Funny Lady" by Cecil Bunting McCormack (or Bunny Mack) from Sierra Leone.

In January 1980 this was followed by Bunny Mack's first entry into the British pop-charts, "Love Me Love You Forever," which

Remi Kabaka.

Bunny Mack.

got to number 5 in the disco charts and 76 in the singles charts. This was also a hit song in West Africa. In Nigeria it earned a gold disc as it sold over one hundred thousand copies there on the Tab-ansi label.

Akie followed this huge success by even more disco singles like "Weakness for Your Sweetness" by Jimmy Senyah from Barbados, which reached number 25 in the British disco charts and, when released by Scorpion Records in France, got into the French hit parade as well.

Other artists whom Akie is producing include Emmanuel Rentoz, a keyboard player from Ghana, singer Nina da Costa from the West Indies, Yvonne Mobambo from South Africa, Leon Charles from Barbados, and operatic and folk singer Martha Ulaeto from Nigeria.

Akie also organised tours of Nigeria for Bunny Mack to coincide with Mack's release *Supa Frico*. But let's give Akie the last word on his music.

> I've developed a new sound called discolypso, which is a fusion of calypso and African rhythms. This beat, starting off with Bunny Mack's record *Discolypso* progressed to "Let Me Love You Forever" which made an impact on the U.K. market. And I'm going to continue developing that sound until subsequently African music is accepted. It's just a matter of time.

So the story of African disco is a strange one. The roots of disco lie in black American soul and funk. Soul king James Brown admits that he got some of his dance rhythms from East Africa. When it became computerised into disco it swept everything aside. And when introduced to Africa it brought in the idea of dancing in dark, enclosed rooms—quite different from the normal practice of dancing in open-air dance halls and, in the case of traditional music, by moonlight. At first disco had a negative effect on the local African dance scene, but today a new type of Afro-disco musicians and producers has appeared who are now even beginning to affect the Western disco market.

13 Victor Uwaifo, the Guitar Boy

Victor Uwaifo is one of the most dynamic of Africa's modern musicians. He has released over one hundred singles and a dozen albums since he formed his Melody Maestros in 1965. His music has a driving beat based on the local folk music from the Bendel State of Nigeria, merged with a modern touch.

It all started in 1966 when he and his band released three smash hits on the Phonogram label. These singles were "Sirri-Sirri," "Joromi," and "Guitar-boy." "Joromi," based on the story of a legendary hero of Benin City, was so popular that it earned Uwaifo Africa's first Gold Disc Award in 1969. Joromi also became the name for one of the bright African cloth designs.

Since then, Victor has become so famous that the students of Nsukka University knighted him "Sir" Victor Uwaifo, a name that has stayed with him ever since.

The Melody Maestros have made many international tours. They represented Nigeria at the Black Arts Festival held in Dakar in 1966, and played at the Algerian Arts Expo in 1969 and the 1970 World Expo in Japan. They have also toured in the United States, Europe, and Russia.

I first met Victor in 1975 when recording a track on Victor's *Laugh and Cry* album, released by Black Bell.

That Christmas I joined him in Benin City and toured eastern Nigeria with his group. In Benin, I stayed at Victor's hotel on the outskirts of town, called the Joromi Hotel, after his first smash hit. The band was based at a newly opened air-conditioned night-club he owned in the centre of town, known as the Club 400.

Left to right: *Victor Uwaifo and John Collins recording an album, mid-1970s.*

Left to right: *John Collins and Victor Uwaifo rehearsing for a recording session, mid-1970s.*

Victor Uwaifo and midget musician King Pago, mid-1970s.

A typical show would start with the ten-man Melody Maestros warming up with some soul and pop numbers. Then in would
come Victor, wearing some spectacular clothes he designed himself, and he would take over. A one-man show ensued, with Victor
dancing, singing, and playing various instruments, like the flute or
the organ, which he sometimes plays with his chin. But his main
instrument is the guitar and he is a wizard at it. He leaves everyone
spellbound with his amazing "Joromi" solo.

When playing, Victor is backed by two musicians, both midg-
ets, who play clips and maraccas. Sometimes they move backward
and forward across the stage, darting in between Victor's legs.
One of them, King Pago, was with the famous Lagos-based Bobby Benson's Dance Band during the 1950s.

Bicycle Spokes as Frets

Victor was born in 1941 in Benin City, the ancient capital of the Benin Empire. All his family were musical and he became interested in the guitar.

> I used to go around to the palm-wine guitarists downtown. The most famous of these guitarists in Benin was We-We, who had been a soldier during the Second World War. So I made a crude guitar myself, with high-tension wires for strings and bicycle spokes for frets. I begged one of the guitarists to teach me how to tune the guitar and he said he wouldn't, unless I bought him a jug of palm-wine.

Even though his father played accordion, he did not like the idea of Victor playing the guitar, as the instrument was associated with drunkenness.

> I found my home-made guitar very inferior, so I decided to buy one for myself. But it was difficult as I didn't know how to put it to my father. He would never agree. But I earned my one guinea and bought a second-hand guitar. The first time my father saw me playing it he seized it and threatened to destroy it. But my mother saved it.

Victor left Benin and went to secondary school at Saint Gregory's in Lagos. In his spare time he joined the well-established high-life dance-band of Victor Olaiya. In 1962 he won a scholarship to the Yaba College of Technology, where he spent his time on three main interests: studying in the morning, wrestling and athletics in the afternoon, and playing with E. C. Arinze's highlife band at the Kakadu Club in the evenings.

In 1964 he joined the Nigerian Television Service as a graphic artist. It was at this time that he first began to put his own band together.

Colours in Sound

The first sound Victor created was the akwete beat, and his first three hit singles were based on that rhythm. As he explains, it was his knowledge of art that helped him create this, by using colours to represent musical notes.

> It was at art school that I discovered colours in sound, and sound in colours. I was able to transpose them so that do, the strongest note, was black, ray was red, me was blue, fa was green. So, a neutral colour and sound was white, la was yellow, and ti violet. But the whole change came when I transposed the colours of akwete cloth, hand-woven cloth made in eastern Nigeria. It is a very beautiful cloth and you will see that different colours recur, creating a moving rhythm of colour. When I interpreted this, it gave the akwete sound.

By the late 1960s he was fusing this akwete beat with pop influences.

> I developed the "shadow" which was a link between the akwete and the twist. The shadow lasted a year and I made an LP of it, but then soul came, and I started losing fans, so I had to bridge the gap. I had to create a rhythm similar to soul as well as my original sound. This was "mutaba."

Some critics have condemned Victor for his modernising influences, but Victor has an answer.

> They fail to see that the foundation of my music is very cultural, as demonstrated in the beat and the lyrics. The fact that I use modern instruments to produce my sound has not altered the basic character of the music, otherwise we might as well argue that a historian writing ancient history with modern tools, like a Parker pen and paper, is a farce. The tools he uses to write history will not alter the facts and dates of the book. We have experimentation and evolution of ancient African cultures and my music is no exception to this.

Victor has based much of his music on the pure rhythms of Benin, like ekassa.

> It was a royal dance performed during the coronation of a new king. Some people thought it an abomination to hear "ekassa" while the king was still alive, but I didn't mind them as the first tune was a brilliant hit and others followed.

Sasakossa was another of Victor's styles based on tradition:

> There was a time when the Benin Kingdom was overpowered. It was when the king of England sent explorers to Africa to trade with the king of Benin. But the king had an important festival and said he would not grant the British an audience. But they were stubborn to come and were intercepted and killed. A few managed to escape to England where they were reinforced and came back for revenge. It was then that Benin was almost completely destroyed and the *oba* (king) went into hiding. The king had an orderly called Sasakossa, who used to sing in a popular way to warn him that there was danger and it was not safe to come out of hiding. So that's where I got the rhythm for sasakossa.

Never one to stay still for long, Victor has recently begun to experiment with combinations of reggae and the forceful beat of Benin. Victor has a genius for linking up old and new, blended with a touch of his own unique and individual brilliance. In the 1980s Victor established his own television studio, one of the first privately owned studios in Nigeria. He produces his own half-hour shows for Nigerian television.

14 The Drums of Kofi Ayivor

For the last twenty-five years Kofi Ayivor's drumming has been heard all over the world, even in the Arctic circle. Kofi has backed many top musicians and groups such as E. T. Mensah, Miles Davis, Eddy Grant, Alexis Korner, Osibisa, and even a Turkish band. In fact, Kofi is so well traveled that he has fifteen passports. He presently lives in The Netherlands with his Surinamese wife, where he teaches drum and runs his own record company, Ivory Records.

Mastering the Rhythms

But let's go back to the start of Kofi's chequered musical career. One of Kofi's parents was Ghanaian, the other Togolese, and he spent the first ten years of his life at the town of Gusau in Nigeria's Sokoto State. In 1949 his family returned to Deinu in Ghana, on the border with Togo. It was here, in the Ewe region of West Africa, so famous for its knowledge of cross-rhythms, that Kofi first started up on drums. His uncle, who was the master-drummer of Deinu, was his first teacher. It was on this solid foundation that he has been able to master over forty-five drumming styles from all over Africa.

Kofi's father, who was a retailer, hated the idea of his son becoming a drummer, as he wanted him to be a doctor. But Kofi was so eager to play drums that he would walk a twenty-mile round trip to see top Ghanaian bands, like the Black Beats and E. T.

Kofi Ayivor.

Mensah's Tempos, play in the neighbouring town of Lome. And, of course, he would join in.

> Sometimes I would play the maraccas. If the maraccas player was in love with some girl and he was gone, I would take over.

Kofi Joins the Tempos

When he finished school in 1959, Kofi went to Accra and got a job as a lift operator. He decided to try his luck, and went to see E. T. Mensah at his pharmacy on Zion Street.

> Fortunately E. T.'s wife, who is from Calabar, knew my father as she used to buy things from his shop. In fact she started to cry and said my dad was a real human being and a beautiful person— always helping people. So she told E. T. he had to take me. So E. T. had to buy me some heavy clothes, for in those days musicians had to wear trousers, white shirts, and bow-ties.

Kofi became the youngest member of the Tempos. He played bongos for them and was also their *gungadin* (the old West African term for road manager). He toured the whole of West Africa with this band and fondly remembers the help E. T., or the "old man" as he affectionately calls him, gave him at the start of his career.

Rhythm in Demand

When Kofi was offered a job as conga player by Tommy Gripman, he joined the Red Spots dance-band in 1961. He wanted to progress and they gave him room for solos.

This was a busy time for Kofi, as he was so much in demand that he played with other bands as well, including the Gagarin band set up by the Ghana TUC and named after the Russian cosmonaut, Yuri Gagarin. He also teamed up with four Italian musicians belonging to Silvio Cambert's group, which played Latin-American music at cabaret spots in town. They got on so well that, in 1963, the Italians decided to take the band home and on tour, and asked Kofi to choose three more Ghanaian musicians to accompany them. The eight-piece band stayed three months in Italy. Then they drove a Fiat to Yugoslavia, Greece, Turkey, and all the way to Baghdad. In fact they got lost for a time in the desert on Christmas Day but luck was on their side.

> By the grace of God we met one of these camel drivers. They can just look at the sun and tell us exactly which direction to go. So we got to Baghdad and played at the Ali-Baba Club. We were a big success, as Cuban music was popular there.

Trouble eventually arose between the Italian and Ghanaian band members over the problem of playing Turkish music. The Italians had been having trouble with the highlifes, but the Turkish music completely floored them.

> The Turkish music was in 6/8, 9/8, and 12/8 time. The Italians couldn't play it as their syncopations were never there. Then Princess Amina, a Turkish dancer, came to join us and after twelve days the Italians couldn't play for her. We, the Ghanaians, were playing it within three minutes. This led to friction and the band scattered.

Kofi stayed with Princess Amina for four years and toured the Far East, Europe, and West Africa with her, finally parting company in Sweden.

In Sweden he taught music and rhythm at the National Ballet School, and also put together a band, called Modern Sounds, with some West Indian friends. They toured all over Scandinavia. This band used steel drums, congas, trap-drums, piano, and guitars, and played every kind of music, including classical pieces by Bach, Beethoven, and Strauss. Kofi also composed several songs for them, based on the traditional Ewe agbadza beat. These were played on Swedish television, and one song, "Otinku," was recorded by EMI in 1969.

Between gigs and teaching, the ever-dynamic Kofi also played with the Swedish Symphony Orchestra as percussionist. He worked with jazz musicians who visited the country, like Duke Ellington, Jack McDuff, Miles Davis, Alexis Korner, and Sarah Vaughan.

In 1973, after a jam-session in Oslo, he was invited to join the Afro-rock band Osibisa whose leaders, Teddy, Mac, and Sol, he knew well from Ghana.

> When I joined Osibisa it was the same old traveling business. The first record I made with them was *Superfly TNT,* which was the soundtrack of a film about a black American guy going to East Africa. After that we got signed on to Warner Brothers and did *Happy Child* and *Osibirock* for them. Then the band signed up with Bronze in 1975 and we made *Welcome Home.*

Three of Osibisa's successful songs were written by Kofi: "Happy Children," "Somaja," and "Kilele."

In 1977 Osibisa played at FESTAC in Nigeria, did a big show in Ghana, and then went on the road yet again, this time to the West Indies. But, as Kofi explains, he was getting tired of all this traveling.

> I met a lovely woman and decided to be a family man and give up the traveling and living out of a suitcase. So I left Osibisa.

One of the first things he did after leaving them was to release a disco album on the Bronze label with Kiki Gyan, who left Os-

Kofi Ayivor with his family.

ibisa at the same time. Then he went into producing records himself. He started by producing a record with the reggae band called
Tradition and then started to help High Tension, a funk-band
made up of young West Indians living in London whom Kofi
knew.

> For when they were young kids they used to come around to see
> me and sing and I taught them to play drums. Then I got a deal
> for them on Island Records, as Chris Blackwell is a good friend
> of mine. I co-produced them with Alex Sadkin, Bob Marley's
> engineer. Then they hit the charts. The song "Hi Tension" made
> it to number 13 in the British charts, and the follow-up, "British
> Hustle," made it to number 8.

In 1980 Kofi decided to take a short break from family life and
went on a tour of the States and the Caribbean with Jimmy Cliff,
and recorded a few tracks with him.

His last project in England, before going off to The Netherlands, was his very first solo album *Kofi,* on the CBS label. This
was partly recorded at Eddy Grant's Coach House Studios, partly

at Island Studios, and partly at Phonodisc near Ibadan in Nigeria. This album boasts many top West Indian and West African musicians. Ed Bentley (Ghana), Louis Becket (Antigua), and Kiki Gyan (Ghana) on keyboard, Eddy Grant (Guyana) on traps and guitar, Jimmy Hynes (Barbados) on bass, Jake Solo (Nigeria) on guitar, Papa Mensah (Ghana) on drums, Mike Odumosu (Nigeria) and Tokurboh Shortade (Nigeria) on bass, Keith Mackintosh (West Indies) on moog, Ray Allen (Ghana) and Lloys Clark (Jamaica) on sax, Hershall (West Indies) on trumpet, Amoa (Nigeria) on talking-drums, and Uwandile (Zimbabwe) and Dora Ifudu (Nigeria) on vocals. He hopes ultimately to get back home and set up his recording company there.

15 The Afro-Reggae of Sonny Okosun and Alpha Blondy

Sonny Okosun

One of the most successful African sounds is that of Sonny Okosun from Nigeria. Sonny has pounded out a series of distinctive styles, a blend of the local roots music of the Bendel State and Western rock and reggae.

His first sound, which came off the production line in the early 1970s, was the ozzidi beat, in which he combined the highlife music of his hometown of Benin City with a touch of Santana-like guitar. Then, from 1977, he began releasing his Afro-reggae hits and then his own special type of disco music. His music is now heard all over Africa, the Caribbean, and the black communities of Europe and the States. In fact his songs of peace are in such demand that he was the first Nigerian musician to play in newly independent Zimbabwe. He is constantly on tour, both at home and abroad.

He works for London-based EMI and is so ambitious that he wants to become one of their directors. Final touches to Sonny's releases are done at the London studio, but the basic tracks are laid

down at the EMI studio in Lagos. His engineer there is the dedicated and tireless Emmanuel Odemusi, one of the best sound engineers of West Africa.

Salary: One Shirt

But let's start in the eastern Nigerian town of Enugu, where
Sonny was brought up and where he was in contact with artists
right from the beginning. Both his mother and grandmother were
expert singers, dancers, and traditional story-tellers. His first intention was to become a Hollywood actor. When he was a teen-
ager he became a pop fanatic.

> I was inspired by Elvis Presley and watched his film *Loving You*.
> And also Cliff Richard's *Expresso Bongo*. I wanted to be a great
> man like them when I saw how many fans they had. Sometimes I
> used to sleep at the Rio Cinema in Enugu after watching all the
> films.

But when Sonny left school, it was toward acting that he first
turned.

> When I grew up I joined a drama group as I was so interested in
> acting. It was called the Eastern Nigerian Theatre and was led by
> John Okwerri, who started the Mbari Centre in the East. The
> Mbari Centre was an organisation originally started by a white
> man to force us to know our roots. It had big offices at Ibadan
> and Enugu and Nigerian writers like Wole Soyinka and J. P.
> Clarke were seriously involved.

At the centre actors, playwrights, and musicians could meet. It
was there that Sonny first took an interest in playing guitar. His
first guitar was actually bought for him by Miriam Okagbue, now
head of the Imo State Broadcasting and Television station.

At first Sonny began playing just for fun. In 1966, he formed
his first group called the Postmen.

> It was the first pop group in the eastern region and we played the
> music of Elvis, Cliff, and the Beatles. We never earned anything.
> The television people used only to pay us with a shirt each, after
> three months' of weekly performances.

Sonny Okosun. (Courtesy Shanachie Records)

When the Nigerian civil war broke out Sonny moved to Lagos, where he started to work as a graphic designer for television. He wanted to "get as close to acting and music as possible."

In 1969 he teamed up, as second guitarist, with the Melody Maestros, led by the master of the Benin sound, Sir Victor Uwaifo. Sonny learned a great deal during the two years he was a member of this band and toured Europe and Japan with them.

Ozzidi

By 1972 Sonny decided it was time to form his own group, which he first called Paperback Limited. Shortly afterwards he changed the name to Ozzidi, the name of a traditional Ijaw god. Here is Sonny's explanation of how the sound was created:

> I originally wanted to be a playwright and tell the world about Shango, Chaka Zulu, and the deep, deep history of Africa. That's why I named my band Ozzidi. I studied Victor Uwaifo's style of composition so, when I left, I thought if I am to be recognised, I must have my own rhythm. So I combined the African rhythm with the Beatles' style of playing, as I wanted a rhythm that anyone in the world could listen to. I am very proud that they can appreciate my records in America, Britain, and even South Africa.

Sonny's first recording success with his Ozzidi music was the single "Help," which sold over one hundred thousand copies in Nigeria, followed by three albums—*Ozzidi, Living Music,* and *Ozzidi for Sale*—which all sold one hundred thousand. This music was heard up and down the West African coast, and Sonny made many tours with his band and dancers.

Sonny Goes Reggae

In 1977 Sonny changed to a reggae sound. It all happened by chance.

> It was almost an accident, as I was recording six tracks for EMI and needed a seventh to fill the record up. That was my reggae song "Help" which ended up being the biggest hit. It is a simple traditional Bini song but written in English. I got the rhythm

Sonny Okosun.

from Ogunde the playwright. I do believe the reggae rhythm came from our side, for when I met Jimmy Cliff in New York, before he came to Nigeria, he actually said he was playing high-life. And in fact if you listen deeply to reggae it has a highlife formation. The only difference is the modified beat.

It was Afro-reggae that really made Sonny a superstar and after the success of "Help," released on an album and as a single, he made an album specifically featuring his new sound. *Papa's Land* sold 150,000 copies in Nigeria. EMI was so pleased that, in 1977, they sent Sonny to their Abbey Road studio in London, made famous by a band that Sonny idolises—the Beatles. There he recorded *Fire in Soweto* and *Holy Wars,* two albums that sold over

150,000 copies in Nigeria alone, and became best-sellers internationally.

Into Disco

Never one to stand still for a moment, Sonny has recently gone over to a third sound, a disco version of his earlier Ozzidi music. I asked him what made him decide to do this:

> American disco music has taken over Africa. During the days of Victor Olaiya, the Uhurus, and Ramblers dance-bands there was jazz music from America. Then there was pop music. It never gave us musicians a chance to move out. And you know with Africans, anything that comes from England is a gas. Then during the time of Victor Uwaifo and Fela there was this soul music.
>
> I always remember that one day Victor Uwaifo printed some handbills saying that no one should listen to soul music. But I think that soul music is like our aladura (praying) songs— it's a spiritual music. But they came down and took the business from us.
>
> Now these days we have funk, but I'm not lying low and I won't let it take gari (processed cassava or manioc) from my hands. So I have decided to create my own type of African disco music. Believe me sincerely, it is catching on like wildfire. This music we hope to export to America and England.

His first disco song was the track "No More Wars," which appears on his *Third World* album and is sung in Yoruba. This was followed by an album catering exclusively to this music called *The Gospel According to Ozzidi,* sung in both Yoruba and English. When I saw Sonny in 1981, in London, he was putting the finishing touches to a followup to these disco hits.

Many of Sonny's songs, especially the later ones, have a strong theme of African liberation and peace. I asked him what he thought the role of a musician in society should be.

> It is a God-given talent, just like a great football player, a boxer like Muhammad Ali, or Bruce Lee. So a musician owes a lot to society, as he sees more. Whatever we see, we store it in our

memories and it explodes in the studio or on stage. We are talking to the world. You see, a musician is a lecturer and he can't do
anything he likes. He has to wear a good dress or trousers. A
musician has to correct society, as he has followers and fans—as I
once discovered when there was a rumour that I had died. When
I got to Enugu, my friends thought I was a ghost, as did a big
crowd of followers.

I sing protest songs and songs of truth. Like my song "We
Don't Want to Fight Wars No More," which was played on radio
and television in Nigeria when the Nigeria and Cameroon con-
flict burst. I don't sing Tom Jones-type songs about love.

Sonny's social awareness is not only expressed in the lyrics of
his songs, for he is actively involved in helping set up a Musicians'
Industrial Board under the Minister of Culture, to defend artists'
rights and replace the fragmented Musicians' Union of Nigeria.

Sonny is involved in setting up yet another union because he
wants Nigeria to catch up with the Côte d'Ivoire.

When I was in Abidjan I was handled by the Ivory Coast Musicians' Union, a very strong union as you get all your royalties
and mechanical rights. It's one of the best music unions in Africa. About 1978 I discussed with my manager about setting up a
Musicians' Industrial Board and we went about getting some
guys together, like Sunny Ade, Ebeneezer Obey, Victor Uwaifo,
and musicians from the east. In the near future the government
will recognise us, but up to now it hasn't, as our board will take
the cake from the Ministry of Youth, Sport, and Culture who
haven't been active and know little about the modern Nigerian
music scene. We want the board to be represented by a single
Minister of Culture. But when the Industrial Board is recognised it will be stronger than the old musicians' unions.

Alpha Blondy

Sonny Okosun, who sometimes calls his fusion of African highlife and juju music with West Indian calypso and reggae "Afro-
carnival," has worked with reggae star Eddy Grant. A younger
African exponent of reggae who has worked with the Wailers

*Alpha Blondy. (Courtesy
Shanachie Records)*

comes from the Côte d'Ivoire. Alpha Blondy, whose name means "first bandit," was born in 1953 in the town of Dimbokro as Seydou Kone.

As a schoolboy in Abidjan he played for his school's Afro-rock band, the Atomic Vibrations, which was influenced by the music of Jimi Hendrix, Pink Floyd, Wilson Pickett, and Otis Redding. From the Côte d'Ivoire, he went to Liberia, then to New York, where he studied at Columbia University to become an English teacher. He then went to Jamaica, where he remained for a while before returning home to Africa in 1980.

While abroad, he had become affected by the music of Bob Marley and the Wailers and embraced Rastafarianism, wanting to combine Rasta ideas, derived from the Bible, with those of Islam. Because of his strong new beliefs and his decision to become a musician rather than a teacher, however, his parents put him under psychiatric care for two years after his return to Africa.

By 1982, when he made his first hit single, "Brigadier Sabari/Operation Coupe de Poine," about the current police cleanup of Abidjan's gangsters, there was no question about his future in music. Beginning in 1983, Alpha Blondy released a string of reggae albums sung in English, French, and Dioula (a Mandingo language): *Jah Glory, Cocody Rock, Apartheid Is Nazism, Jerusalem* (recorded with the Wailers), and, more recently, *Revolution,* which features Cameroonian saxist Manu Dibango and Côte d'Ivoire's top female vocalist, Aicha Kone.

In 1986, he and his thirteen-piece Solar System band, which includes musicians from the Côte d'Ivoire, Ghana, Togo, and the Cameroons, toured Ghana in a series of "Reggae Festival 88" shows in which they appeared dressed in the colours of the Ghanaian (and Marcus Garvey/Rastafarian) flag. As a result of his Mandingo lyrics, a host of Ghanaian reggae artists have subsequently started to sing in local languages as well as English.

In 1987, the American record company Shanachie released two of his albums and Alpha Blondy went on a forty-city tour in the United States, where Alpha and Ziggy Marley were seen as the true heirs of Bob Marley. In the same year, Alpha Blondy received the Senghor Award for the best male singer in Francophone Africa. (For more about reggae in Africa, see Chapter 28.)

16   Guitar-Band Explosion

Highlife, Maringa, and Makossa

Everywhere in West Africa people are dancing to highlife music, a close cousin of West Indian calypso. If not highlife, then they're grooving to dance-styles related to or derived from it, like juju music, Afro-beat, and kpanlogo.

The name "highlife" was coined in the 1920s, when local African melodies were first orchestrated by brass-bands and stylish black dance orchestras. Later on it was "jazzed up" by famous Ghanaian trumpeter E. T. Mensah, the "King of Highlife," whose Tempos band spread this music around West Africa in the 1950s. But even though highlife started off in the coastal towns, it soon spread into rural areas, where it was played on traditional percussion instruments and the acoustic guitar, and went under names like native blues, palm-wine music, ashiko music, makossa music (Cameroons), and maringa (Sierra Leone). Today, it is this more indigenous form of guitar-band highlife that has burst into the popular music scene.

Highlife in Ghana

Let us turn first to Ghana, the recognised birthplace of highlife. In Ghana in the 1960s, highlife was flowing in two streams: dance-bands like E. T. Mensah's Tempos, Broadway, Uhurus, and the Ramblers playing highlife with a jazz and calypso touch; and guitar-bands playing an electrified palm-wine music, whose audience was the rural and urban poor.

Since the 1960s, the dance-bands have more or less folded up, as the youth identify them with "colo" or colonial and prefer Western pop music. In fact, some of the dance-bands, like the Black Beats, have turned into pop groups.

This did not happen to the guitar-bands, although they did absorb ideas from pop. In the 1970s there was a general expansion of this music, absorbing new ideas while maintaining and strengthening its traditional roots.

One of the first signs of this development was around 1970, with the amazing success of C. K. Mann and his Carousel Seven. They became all the rage with their "osode" music, the roots of highlife on Cape Coast. Their albums on the Essiebons label, such

C. K. Mann.

as *Party Time* and *Funky Highlife,* were in such demand that the shops ran out.

Even some of the older generation of guitar-band leaders, like E. K. Nyame and Kwaa Mensah, started to rerelease, in stereo form, some of their old hit singles from the 1950s. E. K. Nyame started to release a series of albums under the title *Sankofa* ("go back and retrieve") and continued right up to his death in 1977.

Koo Nimo

A fascinating combination of traditional Ashanti palm-wine music, classical guitar, and jazz has been created in Kumasi by Dan Amponsah, or Koo Nimo as he is known in the music business. I first heard one of his tapes in 1970, recorded privately by a friend of mine. From the sound of the music I expected to meet an ancient grey-haired palm-wine guitarist. When I met him in 1973, he

Koo Nimo.

had the appearance of a youngish, vigorous man, as much at ease playing local Ashanti blues as modern jazz. In 1980 he became the president of the Musicians' Union of Ghana (MUSIGA).

Koo Nimo was born in 1934. His father was a guitarist and trumpeter in the local village brass-band. He was given a thorough classical training by German missionaries at the Presbyterian school in Kumasi. Later, when he took up the guitar seriously, there were two major influences on his style. One was the guitar-band leader Onyina from Kumasi who, in the 1950s, began creating a unique blend of highlife using jazz chord progressions. Then there was the English pathologist, Professor Laing, who became Koo Nimo's musical godfather and arranged for him to study classical guitar. He went to England to study as a laboratory technician, where he was exposed to even more musical styles.

> My Spanish influences are from Carulli, Carcassi, Julian Bream, and John Williams (whom I once met). Kurt Anderson, Duke Ellington's first trumpeter, also became a great friend of mine. I met Count Basie's guitarist, Freddie Green. I met Charlie Byrd who influenced me a lot. And I met the prolific composer Jack Duarte who's got a wonderful record library. For guitar, my influences were Django Rheinhardt, Charlie Christian, Wes Montgomery, and Jim Hall. Professor Laing also exposed me to Dizzy Gillespie, Thelonius Monk, and Miles Davis. I also like the Oriental music I heard in Manchester, especially the thing that was like a calabash (tabla drums). In Manchester I got to know the Indian community as I liked their peppers and used to practise yoga.

This is how Koo Nimo sees the development of his music:

> I'm going to marry traditional highlife guitar with Spanish and Latin-American music and Afro-Spanish style, using traditional rhythms and arpeggio. I always use finger-picking, never the plectrum. Also I want to develop an Afro-jazz and use Wes Montgomery and Charlie Christian—type chords in it. I'm also thinking of bringing in the European flute and the durugya, which is the Akan horn played when an old chief dies. It has very low tones and is very melancholic. My other interest is drum-

Koo Nimo.

ming and I've got a boy I have adopted, called Little Noah. I picked him up when he was 9 and he is revolutionising my band. He plays the talking-drums.

Koo Nimo and his Adadam Agoromma (Roots Ensemble) group—which includes Little Noah (now not so little) on percussion and seprewa (traditional Akan lute), Koo Nimo's life-long guitarist friend Kofi Twumasi, and dancers Abena Manu and Nana Yebuah—toured Britain in 1986. In 1988 they toured the States, giving Americans a taste of what Koo Nimo now calls his "up and up" music, Koo Nimo was acclaimed there as an African Segovia. So none can say Koo Nimo's palm-wine music is old-fashioned and on the way out, for he stands at the cross-roads of old and new, traditional and modern, rural and urban, and keeps his sound fresh through constant modifications.

Readers interested in his songs should obtain a copy of his booklet *Ashanti Ballads,* translated into English by Joe Latham and published by Latham Services, 37 Rowallan Gardens, Glasgow, Scotland, UK.

Ga Street Music

A highlife folk revival has been going on in the south of Ghana in and around Accra, where Ga street music, sea-shanties, highlifes, and kpanlogos are now becoming popular with young and old. Until the 1970s Ga music had hardly ever been recorded, unlike the Ashanti or Akan palm-wine and guitar-band music. But since then, a large number of Ga "cultural groups," as they are called, have emerged, using traditional drums and the acoustic or "box" guitar. Wulomei was the first band to make this Ga cultural music commercially successful, and many others have followed, like Abladei, Dzadzaloi, Adjo, African Personality, Agbafoi, and Suku Troupe. After sixty years, Ga music has finally hit the music scene with a vengeance.

Wulomei

Wulomei is a group formed by drummer Nii Ashitey and impressario Saka Acquaye in 1973. On stage Wulomei, which, in Ga means "fetish priests," dress up in the frilly white caps and white cloth of the traditional Ga medicine priests and priestesses. Nii Ashitey, leader and chief priest of the group, darts in and out of his group, directing them with staccato bursts of rhythm on his long osraman-drum, which he slings over his shoulder. Musicians include the solo guitarist, percussionists, vocalists, and bamboo flute players. Percussion instruments are local congas, bells, maraccas, and the giant gome- or gombe-drum that plays the bass line. This huge drum, played with hands and heel, is played by the biggest member of the band, Nii Adu or "Big Boy" who sits on top of it, shaking like a jelly.

Wulomei is not only popular with Gas, but has crossed all boundaries in Ghana. At dances and shows, one finds young and old, rich and poor, Ga and non-Ga, all enjoying themselves. Nii Ashitey formed his group, he said, "to bring something out for the youth, to progress and forget foreign music and do their own thing."

Big Boy playing the calabash with the Wulomei cultural group.

Ashitey started his musical career in the 1940s when, still a small boy, he joined the Navy Babies, one of Accra's many konkomba groups. Later on he became the conga player for E. T. Mensah's Tempos and then went over to Liberia to join President Tubman's Stars Dance Band. After this he returned home to play for the Ghana Police Band and the Workers' Brigade Band Number Two, before going on to form Wulomei.

He told me that Wulomei incorporates music from many local sources, the most important being kpanlogo, a fusion of local Ga music and highlife. In fact, when kpanlogo drumming and dancing was first created in the early 1960s by the Ga youth, the elders banned it as indecent. A terrific row blew up between the young and old, so President Nkrumah was called in to give the final verdict. Happily he gave it the go-ahead.

Wulomei's first album, released in 1974, was an instant success. *Walatu Walasa* was dedicated to the government's self-reliance policy. Then, in 1975, the group signed a three-year contract with Phonogram and released an album called *Wulomei in Drum Con-*

ference. The same year, they accompanied the Kwaa Mensah palm-wine group and the gonje (one-stringed violin) group of Salisu Mahama of northern Ghana on a six-week tour of the United States. The group split after that and Naa Amanua formed Suku Troupe.

The African Brothers

The Ghanaian highlife scene would be incomplete without the African Brothers, top of the league of the approximately 150 electric guitar-bands of the country. The leader of the group is Nana Ampadu from the hilly Kwahu region of Ghana, who formed his band in the early 1960s. Their first big success was the record "Ebi Tie Ye" (Some Live Well) released in 1967, which they later made into a play. The theme of the song is the growing division of society into rich and poor. In the traditional African fashion this topic is dealt with in parable form. Bigger animals push smaller ones away from the warmth of the camp fire.

Nana Ampadu, leader of the African Brothers guitar-band.

Since that first hit, Ampadu and his group of musicians and actors have been barn-storming Africa and have made several international tours as well. The band not only has a full rhythm section of trap-drums, congas, maraccas, and clips, but guitars are also used to set up cross-rhythms. The group uses four guitars that set up a scintillating network of sound, boosted by the distinctive touch of Ancient on keyboards.

Ampadu is a lightly built man who oozes energy. But he does not dominate the stage like a European superstar. Rather he holds back and then suddenly breaks in with a little guitar riff or solo, sending the music of the band to a new and higher level of intensity. Then he retires for a while and comes back again, each time magically raising the vibrations of the players and dancers.

His band doesn't only play top-quality highlifes. Ampadu is always creating new dance beats for his numerous fans: the "locomotive," a funky highlife rhythm; Afro-hili, a combination of highlife and Afro-beat; and a beautiful blend of highlife and reggae called Afro-reggae, to mention a few.

Ampadu's one-time partner was Eddie Donkor, another master of the guitar who has gone on to form his own band. But Ampadu never seems to run out of brilliant musicians. His latest is Mumbi, a female vocalist, whose wistful, melancholy voice fits in perfectly with the bubbling rhythms of the African Brothers.

Since the formation of the African Brothers in 1963—the name chosen in appreciation of President Nkrumah's efforts in forming the Organisation of African Unity—Ampadu has released nearly sixty albums and over one hundred singles. In addition to all this recording and touring, Ampadu also manages to find time to be one of the vice-presidents of the Musicians' Union of Ghana.

Sweet Beans and Sweet Talks

Pat Thomas, the famous Ghanaian leader of the Sweet Beans, was born in 1950; as a schoolboy, he lived in Kumasi with his uncle Kwabena Onyina, who introduced progressive jazz chords to guitar highlife bands in the 1950s. After playing with Onyina for a while, Pat switched to the dance-band type of highlife and worked with the Broadway and Uhurus dance-bands. In 1972, he and Ebo

Taylor were invited to form the Blue Monks band by two of Ghana's leading disc jockeys, Mike Eghan and Carl Bannerman. This group lasted until Ghana's Cocoa Marketing Board decided to set up its own band, the Sweet Beans, which Pat led until 1978. Several years later, Pat settled in Germany, where he released a disco highlife called "Pat Thomas 1980"; he now lives in Canada and continues to record.

A. B. Crenstil (also born in 1950) first played with the El Dorados (of the State Aboso Glass Factory) and the Lantics (of the State Hotel Corporation), then moved from Takoradi to the port town of Tema to become the leader of the Sweet Talks. Before it broke up in 1979, the band released a series of popular albums such as *Adam and Eve, Kusum Beat, Spiritual Ghana,* and *Hollywood Highlife Party* (recorded in the United States). Smart Nkansah went on to form the Black Hustlers and then Sunsum. Eric Agyeman began a successful solo career, while A. B. Crentsil formed the Super Brains and then Ahenfo (Kings), which produced *Moses,* an album controversial for its sexual innuendo. His recent recordings, like *Toronto by Night,* were recorded in Canada and his band tours abroad extensively.

Several other Ghanaian guitar-bands also tour regularly outside the country. Nigeria is an important stop for many, including Eddy Maxwell's Odoyewu Internationals, Canados, Super Seven (all based in eastern Nigeria), and Kofi Sammy's band.

(Ghanaian highlife musicians and bands in Europe and America are discussed in Chapter 30.)

The Maringa of Sierra Leone

Maringa is the popular Sierra Leone equivalent to palm-wine highlife and goes back to roots in the gumbay or goombay music introduced to Freetown in the last century by Jamaican Maroon slaves freed by the British.

The most popular maringa musician was Ebeneezer Calender, who with his Rokel River Boys released songs like "Double Decker Bus" and "Jolloff Rice" in the 1950s and 1960s. Born in 1912, Calender started off as a gumbay drummer before switching to guitar. From 1960 to 1984, he was the director of the traditional music section of the Sierra Leone Broadcasting Service.

Another popular palm-wine guitarist who is still going strong is Sooliman Ernest Rogie. Rogie, influenced by Jimmy Rogers and country and western music, with his Morningstars Band released a number of top West African hits in the early 1960s, such as "My Lovely Elizabeth." In 1973 he settled as a teacher in California and was inactive in the palm-wine music scene for a while. Since his comeback in the 1980s with albums like *The Sixties Sounds of S. E. Rogi,* he regularly tours Europe and the States.

It was only in the late 1950s and early 1960s that dance-band highlife became popular in Sierra Leone (introduced by Ghana's Tempos band) and was played by local groups such as the Ticklers. Congo jazz was introduced at about the same time by Rico Jazz from Zaire and played by Sierra Leonean groups such as Akpata Jazz and Geraldo Pino's Heartbeats (more famous for its soul music).

Today most of Sierra Leone's bands continue to play maringa. Patricia Koroma's Afro Nationals (famous for its song "Money Palaver") and Super Combo (now resident in London) play a maringa style affected by the rumba and local Temne and Mende folk music, and Sabaanah 75 plays a funky disco type of music. In addition, a new updated (but still acoustic) version of gumbay called mailo jazz has become popular locally, played by street groups like Doctor Orloh's.

The Makossa of the Cameroons

Just as Ghana and Nigeria have highlife and Sierra Leone has maringa, the Cameroons dances to makossa music—the latest of a series of guitar-band styles played in palm-wine dives and bar-rooms.

In the 1920s maringa was brought to the Cameroons by West African seamen and it was followed in the 1940s by ashiko or asiko, an early type of highlife found all over West Africa. (The most popular ashiko groups in the Cameroons were those of Jean Aladin Bokoko and Onde Medjo.) The top makossa bands of the 1950s and 1960s were Mama Ohandja's and Ebanda Manfred's. Their guitar music affected the local dance-bands of the period, such as the Black and White Jazz Orchestra and Los Negros.

The word "makossa" didn't surface in the international music scene until Manu Dibango released his "Soul Makossa," a disco hit in the United States in 1973. Sax player Manu Dibàngo (born in 1933) played with Kalle's African Jazz in Zaire from 1961 to 1965. He then went to Paris until 1975, when he became director of the Radio Orchestra of the Côte d'Ivoire. In 1979, he recorded with some of the Wailers in Jamaica, and in 1984 celebrated his thirty years in the music field with his "electric-pop" influenced release, "Abele Dance."

Makossa artists Moni Bile and Sam Fan Thomas (of 1984 African Typic Collection fame) are popular in both the Cameroons and Paris, and in Paris some Cameroonian artists—guitarist Toto Guillaume and Alhadji Toure, for instance—are fusing makossa with the zouk music of the French Antilles. This fusion follows in the wake of another Cameroonian band, Voory's Power, which some years ago worked with the Granadian dance-band in Lagos and combined makossa with Afro-beat.

Mention must also be made of Francis Bebey, a Cameroonian poet, guitarist, recording artist, and musicologist, whose important book on traditional music (*African Music: A People's Art*) was first published in 1968. (The English translation was published by Lawrence Hill, New York, 1975.)

Highlife in Nigeria

Nigeria is now the major centre for highlife because it has recording and pressing facilities. In the 1950s it was all highlife dance-band music, introduced to the country by the Ghanaian Tempos band of E. T. Mensah and copied by musicians in Lagos, such as Victor Olaiya, Bobby Benson, and E. C. Arinze. Guitar-band music was around, but submerged in the commercial music scene.

In the mid-1960s, everything changed because of the Nigerian civil war. Many of the dance-bands, led by Nigerians from the east, collapsed, like those of Charles Iwegbue, Enyang Henshaw, Zeal Onyia, E. C. Arinze, and Rex Lawson. The field was left open for the guitar-bands, which surfaced as a dominant force. In the western part of Nigeria, this guitar-band music was juju music; in the mid-west it was Bini high-life; and in the east it was Igbo highlife.

Victor Uwaifo's music (an internationalised version of the

Victor Olaiya's Cool Cats dance-band.

highlife music of the Bendel State) is in fact a sophisticated variation on the local native blues.

There are many other highlife musicians from that area—Col-
lings Oke and the Odoligue Nobles, who worked with the Melody Maestros; band leader Dandy Oboy; and Mudogo Osegie, who
was with Victor Uwaifo from 1966 but left in 1971 to form the
Muskateers. They play a Bini music they call "bushpower." Another leading musician who was initiated by the Melody Maestros
is Sonny Okosun, whose Ozzidi music is a mixture of rock, reggae, and Uwaifo-type highlife rhythms.

Palm-wine music and guitar-bands have always been popular
in the eastern part of Nigeria. The hundreds of records produced
by E. K. Nyame of Ghana were a formative influence on this style.
There were many local groups too, like Okonkwo Adigwe from
Asaba and Aderi Olariechi from Owerri. In the 1950s and early
1960s it was the highlife dance-bands rather than guitar-bands that
stole the limelight.

With the civil war in Nigeria, the dance-bands collapsed. Then
Rex Lawson, leader of the most popular highlife band, the
Riversmen, was killed in an accident. The highlife tradition was
kept alive by the guitar-bands, Rex Lawson's influence always remaining important. In fact, after Lawson's death, the Riversmen

formed the Professional Seagulls, a top guitar-band right up to the present day. The Peacocks, formed in Owerri in 1970 by Raphael Amanabae, who was a member of the Riversmen, were also influenced by Rex Lawson's music. The Philosophers National, formed by the late Celestine Ukwu, is a top guitar-band in Nigeria today. Born in 1942, at the age of twenty Celestine joined his first group, Michael Eleagha's Paradise Rhythm Orchestra based in Enugu. Celestine then formed his own group in Onitsha in 1966, called the Music Royals, later to become the Philosophers.

Paulson Kalu and his Africana is a very popular band from Aba. From Owerri come the Oriental Brothers, who have recently split into two, one wing led by ace guitarist Dan Satch Opara and the other by the vocalist, Warrior. Both, however, are marketed by the same company, Decca West Africa.

The Soundmakers have been the leading guitar-band from the east since 1964. They were formed by Stephen Osita Osadabe. Born in 1936, he joined Stephen Amechi's band in 1959, then went on to form the Central Dance Band before forming the Soundmakers. The popular Ikengas were formed by a breakaway group from this band.

Rokafil Jazz

In the last few years a new sound has been brewing in the east. This is the combination of highlife with the Congo beat of Zaire, such as the ogene sound of Oliver de Coque. The group largely responsible for popularising this new style is Rokafil Jazz, which has had a series of smash hits in Africa and the Caribbean since their *Sweet Mother* album, released in 1977. That year in Africa everyone began playing *Sweet Mother,* and African prints, nightclubs, chop-bars, and mammy wagons began to bear this name.

The reason for this is clear, as Rokafil Jazz combines all the best from several African countries—the highlife style of eastern Nigeria, the fast makossa music of the Cameroons, and a touch of the guitar-style from neighbouring Zaire. In fact, the leader of the band, Nicholas Mbarga, or Prince Niko as he is known as on stage, is half-Nigerian and half-Cameroonian.

The popularity of *Sweet Mother* was enhanced by the fact that the lyrics were in pidgin English and could be understood from country to country. In addition, Prince Niko's modernised high-life bass line gives a reggae feel.

Rokafil Jazz followed their first hit with more highlife albums in that fast, bouncy style—*Dear Father, Free Education in Nigeria,* and *Music Line* are examples. *Music Line* is literally the story of Nicholas and his band. The song starts with a father warning his son against going into the music business as he will never be able to save enough money to get married and settle down. But it ends happily, with the son becoming so successful through music that he can afford several wives and a big car and is extremely rich and powerful.

Prince Niko has become so successful that he has set up his own hotel and club in his hometown of Onitsha, where he also runs a multitrack studio.

Nicholas was interviewed at the BBC's external Broadcasting Centre, Bush House. I was on the same programme, and was astonished to see a diminutive figure breezing in, flanked by a group of manager-bodyguards. Unlike his boisterous, noisy companions, Nicholas turned out to be a quiet, shy person. He has a lot in common with Nana Ampadu, leader of Ghana's African Brothers band. Both are wiry, slightly built men with sensitive, fine features. Both are wizard musicians. There is even a resemblance in the highlife music they play. Although quiet off-stage, in the limelight Nicholas is completely different. On stage Prince Niko looks larger than real life as he wears stacks, or "guarantee shoes" as they are called in West Africa. After an initial warm-up by the band, he comes on stage dressed like a superstar, wearing bright clothes and a silk cape.

By the end of the two-and-a-half-hour show at a gig I saw in London, he had the audience in the palm of his hand. They were dancing in the aisles and in front of the stage and would have gone on all night if the caretaker hadn't come and closed the place. Prince Niko did only the one gig in London before flying off to Paris to do a promotion tour. His music is popular everywhere and he is spreading highlife music far and wide.

17 "F" Promotions
Ghana's Melting Pot

Faisal Helwani and the Napoleon Night-Club

One of the main catalysts in the Ghanaian music scene has been impressario and producer Faisal Helwani. His Napoleon night-club in Accra has been a central melting pot for musical talent from home and abroad, and from there a stream of top bands has moved into the international field.

Faisal was born in Sekondi in 1946. He has been fascinated by music ever since he launched his "F" Promotions in 1964, when he began organising student pop competitions or "pop chains." In 1968 he formed his first group, the El Sombraros, led by Alfred Bannerman and Johnny Acheampong, and started promoting Fela Anikulapo-Kuti in Ghana. Fela's Koola Lobitos and the El Sombraros toured Ghana several times together.

In 1968 Faisal organised his most ambitious promotion to date; a six-week tour of East Africa by the Uhurus dance-band led by Stan Plange, the Rolling Beats dance troupe, and drummer Kofi Ghanaba (Guy Warren). After this success, he opened up his night-club (and Ghana's first discotheque), first called the Pagadeja and from 1973 the Napoleon.

His first resident band there was Hedzolleh (Freedom), which combined rock and African music and won the Ghana Arts Council dance-band award in 1974. Hedzolleh was led by Stanley Todd of the El Pollos rock group and a number of musicians from the Arts Council, like Nii Poumah on flute and Okyerema Asante on percussion. They played Afro-rock more African than Osibisa. Their biggest hit was "Rekpete," an old Liberian sea-shanty and

Afro-fusion band Hedzolleh.

palm-wine song. Okyerema, incidentally, went on to work with Paul Simon and Mick Fleetwood in the United States.

With this band, Faisal was able to spearhead the movement, experimenting with new African sounds and raising its technical level to the sophistication of disco. Hedzolleh was his first attempt along these lines. The South African trumpeter Hugh Masekela was so impressed by Hedzolleh that he worked on an album with the group called *Introducing Hedzolleh with Hugh Masekela*. They were so successful that Hedzolleh ended up touring the United States with Hugh, where they released a beautiful album called *The Boys Doin It*.

An Afro-American drummer friend, Jumma Santos (James Riley), took me for the first time to the Napoleon in 1974. To be honest I was a bit reluctant to go as I didn't like disco music much at all, after playing with "bush" guitar-bands for some years. But Jumma told me they had a band called the Bunzus that played highlifes and so I went.

They were a sensation. Under Faisal's production they had modernised highlife beautifully. The lead guitarist and leader of the group, Cliff Eck, was using a mellow rock tone on his guitar

Okyerema Asante at the Napoleon Club in Accra, early 1970s.

Left to right: *Faisal Helwani, trumpeter Hugh Masekela, and guitarist Stanley Todd, 1973.*

The "Afro" trap-drums at
the Napoleon Club.

rather than the high-pitched and "tinny" sound favoured by many local bands. Eddie Agyepong, on traps, had an interesting collection of Western bass-drum, cymbals, and high-hat with African cow-bells, up-turned calabashes, and local drums.

Faisal was made up like a gilded and sequined cowboy. Sometimes he would rush up on stage, grab some sticks, and start beating the talking-drums frantically, putting everyone on their toes and generally acting as a tonic.

I'll never forget the therapeutic effect the Napoleon and Faisal had on an Afro-American jazz pianist named Patti Brown. She was languishing, bored and sick, at the Legon University campus, but I got her out of bed and down to the club. That very night she did an organ solo that ended up with her on her back, and the organ on top of her. She got so high she completely forgot about her illness.

Basa-Basa, which means "pandemonium," was the sister band of the Bunzus. Members of the group were mostly Ewes who specialised in rock fusions of their local agbadza beat. There were the Nyarko twins, now based in Lagos, on percussion and Abollo the young master-drummer. The leader, Wallace, was the lead guitarist and floated above everyone on stacks. The bassist was beetle-browed Ashela, the hardest-working man in show business. Vocals were supplied by the charismatic Nii Ayitey II, whom Faisal was building up into a star, but who later managed to slip out of his grasp to Germany.

It was the Bunzus who particularly attracted me at first. That night with Jumma, I asked Faisal for a jam-session with them. This jam immediately produced two Afro-beat creations we called "Onukpa Shwarpo" and "Yea Yea Ku Yea," which were released by Decca on the *Al Haji Tanko* album and later under the titles "Makola Special" and "Volta Suite" by Makossa of New York.

I played at the Napoleon for two years and during this time performed just about everywhere. We played at the Castle for the head of state one Sunday, and the following week at a prison! The enterprising Faisal launched a series of shows for prisoners, the first time such a thing had been done in Ghana. We all had to be searched as we entered Ussher Fort in Accra. When we played, the four hundred male prisoners had to dance "bone to bone" not "flesh to bone" (woman to man). One of them got so carried away that he wanted to jam on congas and Faisal agreed. Several years of bottled-up musical frustration burst out of this prisoner, who soloed for over half an hour. Faisal promised him a job when he came out, and later on this actually happened.

Faisal also took us out of the country several times, to Togo, Nigeria, and the Republic of Benin. We played at Cotonou, the capital of Benin, on the very day of the Marxist revolution and we noticed that everyone seemed to be carrying or waving green branches. In Nigeria we played several times at Fela's Africa Shrine and Victor Olaiya's Papingo night-club.

Whenever we played, the Napoleon's mascot came along. The

late Tawia Brown, a midget "pilot boy," who always sported miniature copies of the latest fashion including ultrahigh guarantee
shoes. Although he could neither speak nor hear, when the spirit
took him, he would jump up on stage and do a James Brown turn,
making odd noises into the microphone, but always on time, as he
could "hear" the beat inside. The Napoleon was his home-base,
and was the place in town where all the musicians, hustlers,
pimps, and "good-time girls" hung around until five or six in the
morning. It is a mazelike building, built by an eccentric Ghanaian
doctor. It has a zoo, aquarium, fountains, and many quiet hidden
corners that the musicians sussed out. The noisiest place, of
course, was the main gate, watched over by a succession of door-
men hired for their lack of charm. Security was of prime importance, as the Napoleon, like the Kalakuta in Lagos, was sometimes
the target of sabotage attempts. The vibes in the Napoleon were
similar to those of the Kalakuta Republic and there was much exchange between these two fraternal establishments.

Faisal's Recording Deal with West Africa

By 1977, I had formed my own band. Faisal asked me to contact
some of the guitar-bands, as he knew I was a member of the
guitar-band co-operative, GHACIMS (Ghana Cooperative Indigenous Musicians Society). I contacted two of Ghana's grand old
men of highlife music, Kwaa Mensah, nephew of the country's
first guitarist, and E. K. Nyame, who combined music with acting. I also contacted a cultural group from Labadi called Abladei
with whom I had played on a television programme, and a little
later the Afro-Spanish guitarist from Kumasi called Koo Nimo.
    The day I took E. K. Nyame to the Napoleon, we bumped
into Fela just as we were about to leave. I remembered Fela had
once told me the high regard he had for E. K.'s pioneering work.
When I told Fela he was standing next to E. K., he got really
excited, blessed the old musician, and invited us the next day to a
party at the Napoleon.
    The guitar-bands were to form part of a massive ten-band pro-
motions and recording deal worked out between Faisal and Decca
West Africa in Nigeria. Besides Faisal's original groups and those I

brought in, there were also the Uhurus dance-band, E. T. Mensah's Tempos, Bokoor, the Voices of East Labadi, and another cultural group called Adjo. E. K. actually never signed up, as he was already under contract.

These groups played at the Tip Toe Gardens in Accra, which became the main musical venue for a while. During this time the Napoleon was given over to a series of successful jazz sessions. The bands finally ended up in Lagos at the Decca studios. Particularly successful was an album of 1950s hits by E. T. Mensah called *The King of Highlife*. Faisal became so inundated with musical material that he had to launch his own radio programme, and finally set up his own multitrack studio in the Napoleon itself.

From 1974 on, the Napoleon not only became the main musical centre of Accra, but also became the headquarters for the Musicians' Union of Ghana (MUSIGA), until it moved in 1980 to the Community Centre on the Accra High Street. For many years Faisal financed the union and fought to revitalise this moribund

Edikanfo (Osei Tutu playing trumpet).

organisation. In 1979 he succeeded in creating a radical interim executive, which organised the great march for recognition the same year. Faisal's latest MUSIGA project is to finance a union newspaper.

From 1979, his preoccupation with music politics didn't leave Faisal much time, so his bands were rather neglected for a while, although many of the tapes were processed and pressed. But once the union was firmly established he was able to turn his full attention again to music. This is when he opened up his own studio and launched a new band called Edikanfo, a large dance ensemble that concentrates on local melodies with a funky touch.

Stars Visit the Napoleon

Many stars have visited the Napoleon. Brian Eno flew in from New York and stayed at the Napoleon as Faisal's guest for three weeks. Brian worked with Edikanfo in Faisal's studio and released an album of them on his EG record label.

In 1981, Mick Fleetwood, George Hawkins, and Todd Sharpe came down to Ghana for a six-week safari, complete with recording engineers, bodyguards, and twelve tons of equipment, including a sixteen-track studio. Mick Fleetwood is the English leader and drummer of Los Angeles–based rock group Fleetwood Mac. They were expecting to trek around in the bush, and even brought mosquito nets and portable latrines with them. Instead everything was laid on for them by MUSIGA and Faisal, and they were put up at the Star Hotel in Accra. Instead of chasing the musicians the musicians came to them, and they were able to spend their whole time recording on the equipment they set up at the Ghana Film studios. An album was later released by them called *The Visitor,* which featured the three musicians plus groups from Ghana like the Super Brains, Koo Nimo's, and a children's group. George Harrison of the Beatles played a dedication to John Lennon on one track.

Although the Napoleon Club is now closed Faisal continues his musical activities. In the 1980s he made local releases of the highlife singer Kobina Okai and the blind musician Onipa Nua, as well as running a recording studio in Liberia for a while.

18

Life on the Road

Modern African Minstrels, the Jaguar Jokers

Drama in Africa is associated with music, dance, and works of art. Together they form a holistic art crucial to society, cementing it together, lampooning it, and accommodating social change through a fusion of creative energy and social process. For example, there are the traditional roving minstrels and troubadors of West Africa, who are historians, praise singers, and entertainers. Then there are the masquerades found throughout the continent and even in the New World, such as the masked Jamaican carnival and the mardi gras. The Ashantis of Ghana also have their dramatised Ananse stories—satirical morality tales that have found their way to North America as Nancy stories, and to Surinam, through the diaspora. African theatre was, and is, performed out of doors. A raised platform separating audience and performers was never used, not even in professional theatres such as the traveling apidan troupes of the Yorubas. The stage was used only in European cantatas or Bible plays and for school plays performed during the heyday of the Empire.

A third influence on African drama was black minstrelsy, introduced from America around the turn of the century by visiting

*Baba John Bull (*left).

vaudeville artists, ragtime performers, and silent movies such as those starring Al Jolson.

It was in Ghana where the fusion of traditional and modern acting first crystallised in the 1920s in what was known as the concert party. By the 1950s there were similar traveling theatres all over Africa. Miriam Makeba worked with one for a time in South Africa. Then in Nigeria there was Hubert Ogunde's theatre. He was the father of modern Nigerian theatre. In Ghana there was the Akan Trio of E. K. Nyame, which combined acting with highlife music.

In those times many of the plays had a nationalistic flavour. One of Ogunde's plays, *Strike the Hunger,* was even banned by the British in 1945. Ghanaian concert parties were staging plays like *Nkrumah Is a Mighty Man* and *Nkrumah Will Never Die.*

Today there are thousands of popular theatres around Africa. In Lagos State alone there are over two hundred traveling theatres, such as those of Baba John Bull, Baba Mero, Oje Lapido, Moses

Olaiya, and Kola Ogunmola. All of them stage plays in Yoruba and Hausa to the accompaniment of local music and dance. Today many acting groups bring out their most popular plays in comic magazine form.

In East Africa, too, traveling theatres abound and governments take them very seriously. They are especially encouraged in socialist countries like Tanzania and Mozambique because these plays develop political awareness and educate people.

Concert Parties in Ghana

In Ghana there are about one hundred concert parties/highlife groups at present and they even formed their own co-operative. The Jaguar Jokers, a Ghanaian concert party, was formed by Mr.

Mr. Bampoe, leader of the JJs.

Bampoe in 1954 and has been on the road ever since. This means that the JJs must surely be one of the hardest-working groups in show business. They've been on the road for almost thirty years, and perform fifteen to twenty shows a month, with each show lasting over six hours. In fact, the first time I joined them, as guitarist, for a three-week trek I lost seven pounds in weight.

The group makes twelve treks a year, touring the towns and villages of Ghana, always starting at the end of the month (pay day) when people have money in their pockets. They send their "pioneer man" ahead of them. He books the gigs, puts advertisements in the papers, and hangs posters all over the place.

When the band hits a village, the twenty actors and musicians unload the minibus and set up their equipment (including a portable generator for places without electricity). There are usually no cinemas and clubs in the smaller venues. Usually one of the compound houses in a village or hamlet has a raised stage in its courtyard. If not, the performers have to put up a make-shift stage constructed of wooden boards and concrete blocks.

Baba John Bull standing by his lorry.

Some of the musicians are released from this work as they have to go out to "campaign" with a speaker on the roof of the bus. Paintings of scenes from the night's show are slung on the sides. Whenever I was with them they used to feature me on these campaigns as a crowd puller, playing fast congo jazz guitar with the conga player. Hordes of children would follow us as we drove slowly through the dusty streets. Everyone in sight would stop what they were doing and start to dance. Women with buckets on their heads and children on their backs would start to sway. Old people would get up from their chairs and do a turn to our music. When we returned, everything would be set up for the night's show and large paintings, or "cartoons" as they are called, were put outside the theatre to pull in the crowd.

Once, while passing through Swedru in southern Ghana, I had the good fortune to meet the artist who does these paintings for the JJs and for many of the concert parties. Mark Anthony started out as a bar artist, painting murals of highlife to attract customers. Later he began to do pictures for the spiritual churches and concert parties and now makes his living from this business. He is in such demand, that he has to rattle off a twenty-square-foot painting in just a couple of days.

The JJs' shows start up at about eight in the evening with the band playing the "Inside Rhythm." The first people begin to trickle in. Nobody ever comes in before they hear something going on inside. They just hang around the gate until they hear the first few notes of music. This warming-up music includes a selection of all the current popular music, like highlifes, souls, reggaes, Afro-beats, congo numbers, pachangas, and smoochie numbers. The band stops playing when the place is full. Then the musicians who accompany the actors play a few of the JJs' best-loved compositions. Anytime between ten and eleven, the play itself starts. First there is an opening chorus. Mr. Bampoe, supported by Mr. Hammond and the lady impersonator Mr. Baidoo, sings and dances ragtimes and foxtrots, just like at the Ghanaian concert parties in the 1920s and 1930s. Mr. Baidoo wears drag with an expensive wig and spectacles and sings in a falsetto voice.

There are no women in the JJs. All female parts are performed by men. This is typical of most Ghanaian concert parties, although a few of the concerts employ women, and some are even led by women. But generally the public has looked down on concert people, making it particularly difficult for women to break into this profession.

After the opening chorus, the three principal actors retire to the changing room or ante-room. During this time the audience is entertained by a comic minstrel, or "Bob" as he is referred to in Ghana, usually complete with black and white make-up.

Then, by midnight at the latest, the three-hour play is under way. The JJs have dozens of plays, but normally stick to one play on any single trek. There are involved stories about orphans and wicked step-parents, the problems of having too many wives, money problems, and the clash between new and old. The very first play the JJs ever performed was about a latrine worker who wasn't being paid for his onerous duties of collecting the night-soil

Kwaa Mensah's concert party, 1950s. (Kwaa is holding a guitar.)

from a certain house. So he went on strike and started throwing excrement from a bucket at his debtors (on stage he used mud).

Mr. Bampoe gets incensed when people claim that concert plays are a corrupting influence. In spite of the slap-stick, he believes that they are educative and uplifting. The derogatory attitude toward concert parties is slowly beginning to change. Even the government has noted the social importance of local comic opera, for in 1973 they initiated the First National Festival of Concert Parties.

Mr. Bampoe started acting when he was 11 years old and formed the JJs when he was only 20. Off-stage he is the quietest of individuals, but in the limelight he literally gets possessed by his bouncy and energetic stage character Opia. Opia is usually a servant in the play— a greedy and mischievous imp whom the audience loves to hate, but who always ends up helping the hero and heroine of the plot. The character of Opia is in fact an updated version of Ananse the spider, just as is the Bob character, who is a fusion of an American minstrel with Ananse. The difference between them is that the Bob character wears the make-up of a black and white minstrel, whereas Opia puts on only dark pancake. Mr. Bampoe originally used to make up like a minstrel, but he realised later that he was copying a white copying a black. So he cut out the white around the eyes and lips altogether.

All sorts of other characters crop up in the plays: good-time girls played by the more slender actors, Hausa-corporals, bush farmers and town slicks, lawyers, teachers, masked ghosts, evils and angels. The lanky Mr. Hammond always plays Mr. Johnson. With his deep and sonorous voice he is the sermoniser, who gives the poetic moral at the end of the night's tale.

Throughout the play the actors keep bursting into song. All movements are accompanied by a guitarist, trap-drummer, hand-drummer, and clip player, who play everything from pop and highlifes to Christian hymns and fetish music.

Even though no scenery is used the crowd really gets into the story and joins in by singing, clapping, and commenting loudly. I've often seen people weeping and if they really dig an actor or musician they will dance up to the stage and "spray" or stick money on the performer's forehead. Sometimes it is the other way around as Opia jumps into the crowd, chasing or being chased by someone or something.

The fact that concert parties involve the audience to such a degree and combine music, acting, dance, poetry, and painting, illustrates the African attitude toward art. From the nineteenth century in Europe there was a marked tendency to fragment the arts into separate categories such as entertainment, music, drama, graphic arts, and ballet and make a sharp distinction between audience and performers. The concert parties simply combine these different facets of Western art, creating something more in tune with the traditionally integrated art forms of Africa.

The plays are performed in the local languages and are unscripted. A show can be lengthened or shortened at will, depending on the size and response of the crowd. There is a great deal of improvisation. The actors cat-nap in the ante-room, but have the uncanny ability to wake up at exactly the right moment they are

One of the JJs' cartoons.

needed on stage. Afterwards they go back to the changing room and fall back to sleep again!

The play usually finishes by three o'clock in the morning with the musicians, who started up the evening's show, playing dance tunes again for an hour. The audience really gets their money's worth! Afterwards the performers just crash out on the floor on their mats. They are up by six in the morning to iron and pack, and back on the road for the next day's show.

Sometimes, of course, things do not go so smoothly. Once, for instance, at a mining town, the executive of the JJs had a dispute with the locals over the entrance fee and so refused to play. People were pouring in from the neighbouring villages and getting angry. So we locked ourselves behind the high walls of the theatre to take cover from a hail of stones. Later, when everything had quieted down, we drove off and had two punctures one after the other. Someone had driven nails into our tires and we had to spend the night stranded in the forest.

On another night we caused a disturbance in a Ga village on the Nsawam–Accra road. We were ready to start the show when a commotion started up outside. The chief ordered us to dismantle our trap- and conga-drums as it was during the Homowo or Yam Festival when there is a thirty-day ban on all drumming. Our promoter had slipped up badly and hadn't bothered to check with the chief, as is the normal procedure when playing in a village. The compound was almost full by the time we got this news. We decided to pack up, for how could we play without drums? The audience, especially the young men, were really upset; they wanted us to stay and told us not to listen to the *kyenkyenma* (decrepit) old men, whom they thought too old-fashioned. We sparked off quite a row between the young people and chief, who finally conceded when we agreed to dash him a bottle of gin to pour libations to the gods. It was a striking incident as it was so reminiscent of similar generational problems in England; in both places clashes occur between new and conservative ideas. Mr. Bampoe told me afterward that a similar thing had happened to them in Saltpond. It was in October, during the ban on drumming during the Akwanbo Festival, when a path is cleared for the chief to go to the fetish. That time the JJs couldn't obtain permission to play at all.

One hazard I never expected to meet as a musician was being hit by giant beetles traveling at thirty miles an hour. Abrim Junction, near Oda, is supplied with electricity. Our bright electric lights attracted rhinoceros beetles, or *amankue,* as Twi speakers call them, that lived in the palm-trees overlooking the open-air theatre. They normally do not touch the ground as they are so heavy they need speed to take off, and the only way they can get this is by jumping from trees. That night they were headed for the stage lights. None of us were hit, although the scene was a bit disconcerting as the insects stunned themselves on the concrete. Even when they recovered, they couldn't obtain the momentum they needed to leave the ground again, so people finished them off by kicking them, like footballs, against a wall. In fact, insects were always buzzing around our lights and if the theatre had wall-lights the moths, bugs, and beetles made beautiful radial patterns around them.

These days the JJs are going farther afield to the Côte d'Ivoire and Liberia in order to obtain precious foreign exchange needed for repairs and new equipment. One would think that after almost thirty years, the now immensely popular JJs would also be bringing in money from record royalties. But this is not so, as many years ago Mr. Bampoe decided never to record. The reason for this was that a close friend of his, who was a well-known concert musician, died under suspicious circumstances. It was claimed that he was poisoned by jealous colleagues who played his record and took the gramophone needles to a fetish priest to cast a spell on them. According to eye-witnesses three needles were found in the dead man's throat.

This happened over twenty years ago and all the time I've known Mr. Bampoe I've tried to persuade him to change his mind and start to record, so that he will be able to collect royalties when he has retired from active show business. The problems of transport and the high cost of equipment are so serious in the country that he is now taking this advice. He came to visit me some time ago and has agreed to record on some recording equipment I have (Bokoor Productions). So his music went straight onto a cassette and there was no problem with poisoned needles!

In September 1982 tragedy struck the JJs when their lorry was involved in an accident in the Aburi Hills. Mr. Baidoo was killed, as were guitarist Kwadwo Doku and percussionist Kwadwo Amankwah. Both Mr. Bampoe and Hammond were injured, but they have since put the band together, made a trip to Britain, and are currently engaged in a film project.

Ajax Bukana—Ghana's Nigerian State Comedian

One of the most famous concert-type clowns in Ghana is Nigerian Ajax Bukana. Arriving in 1952, he became a naturalised Ghanaian citizen in 1961. He was very popular with late President Kwame Nkrumah. He still is so popular that in January 1988 the present PNDC government sent him a letter recognising him as a "state comedian" and put him on a monthly salary. I first encountered Ajax at film shows where he would cleverly pick a quiet moment to sneeze extraordinary loudly, whereupon everyone would shout "Jax." In the early 1970s I got to know him better at the Napoleon Club in Accra, where I was playing guitar and harmonica for one of the resident bands, the Bunzu Sounds, and Ajax was doubling as club doorman and comic.

Ajax, a Yoruba, was born James Kehinde (meaning twin) Ajayi in Lagos in 1920. The son of a policeman, Ajax taught at an elementary school until 1950, when he joined the well-known late Bobby Benson's band. I asked him why he decided to become a dance-band musician.

Ajax: I was very interested in jazz and Bobby Benson was playing plenty of jazz, as well as rumbas, highlifes, and quicksteps. So I started with maracas, then from maracas to congas, from congas I started to learn string bass (double bass), and then I qualify.

Q: What about your comedy act? When did you start doing that?

Ajax: Anytime we had a show we would make a concert and Bobby Benson would give me a part. He used to make some funny top hats and tails for us and I painted my face white and had a walking stick. I used to make short comedies just like in Louis Armstrong's shows. I used to dance jazz and do tap-dancing. It was Bobby Benson who gave me the name "Ajax," by turning my father's name Ajayi into Ajax. And he also gave me the name "Bukana." And I registered that new name on my passport when we were coming to Ghana.

Q: How was it you all went to Ghana?

Ajax: E.T. Mensah came to Nigeria in 1950 and his Tempos band played side by side with us, and then in 1952 he invited Bobby Benson to come to Ghana. At that time there was a night-club in Accra called the Weekend-in-Havana, in James Town, and there E. T. used to play. So he invited us to that place for two weeks. Then I said I'm not going back to Nigeria.

Q: Did you then join a band in Ghana?

Ajax: I look [at] all the bandsmen and don't like the way they don't play jazz, they don't respect their leaders, and they don't dress neat. So I said no I won't join any band. Then I try to make one-man show and go to night-clubs to display. Only sometimes, when they have a police or army band, they would ask me to go with them and gave me a chance to play some numbers on the string bass.

Q: You very quickly came to the attention of the then Prime Minister Kwame Nkrumah. How did this happen?

Ajax: I first met him at Kumasi as I was doing show business at the Hotel de Kingsway; afternoon jumps (shows) on Saturdays and Sundays. At that time Kwame Nkrumah was coming to Kumasi to address the CPP [Nkrumah's political party, the Convention People's Party], and we went to the airport to meet him. I dressed myself fine and started to roll myself around and he looked at me and asked, who is that man. They told him I was a Nigerian man. He said, What is he doing here and they said that he's making a show here. Where is he working and they say he doesn't work. Then Nkrumah said, What! you should send him to Accra to come and see me. So he gave me work at the Guinea Press [now the New Times] and I started working there as a paper packer and later as chief canvassor. They even gave me a motor-bike.

Q: I've been told that you were very free with Kwame Nkrumah?

Ajax: Yes, I could go to Flagstaff House or the Castle and sit down with him. Then he would ask me if I wanted to chop and he would tell them to give me plate and I would chop with him. He loved me too much.

Q: I believe you also worked with the Afro-American jazz trumpeter Louis Armstrong. When did you meet him?

Ajax: I first met him when he came to Ghana in 1956, when we all went to the airport. At the airport E. T. Mensah and all Ghanaian

Nigerian comedian Ajax Bukana with Louis Armstrong during the All-Stars' visit to West Africa, 1956.

trumpeters lined up and I was in the crowd. So I stood on top of a car with my painted face and big belly. And when Satchmo was coming down from the plane he saw me and pointed out and said he wanted to see this man, and the police people brought me down to him.

When he came again around 1960 he asked President Kwame Nkrumah that he wanted to take me on African tour for two weeks with his band as a comedian. So from Ghana we went to Lagos and Kano in Nigeria, then we went to Congo. But when we reached Congo there was a war (the civil war) so we slept in a hotel and the second day we left for Lome in Togo. After we finished at Lome, Satchmo gave me money and I came back to Ghana and he flew on straight to Sierra Leone.

Q: You also met the British queen the same year you played with Louis Armstrong.

Ajax: That's right. When the queen came, President Kwame Nkrumah sent a minister to ask me to entertain her at a parade in Black Star Square. Doctor Kwame said I should make the queen laugh. So the queen sat down, the duke [of Edinburgh] sat down, and the whole place was full of big people. I was told that the time they were marching the queen didn't laugh. I was the last man to display and when I came everyone was shouting and as soon as I reached my point to perform I started to roll myself and threw my shoes and hat up. The queen started to laugh and wanted to fall down. Afterwards I was told that the queen asked Doctor Kwame who was that man and she told Doctor Kwame to send me overseas for training.

Q: And were you sent?

Ajax: Yes, the government sent me to Russia for three years—and I still speak Russian alright. I was at the Moscow State Circus School and was trained there in balancing, juggling, and acrobatics. That was 1961 to 1963 and I had my certificate as a professor. I even appeared on television in Russia. I was the first African at that school.

I met the queen again too. It was when I left Russia and went back home through London. Our high commissioner there met me at the airport and took me to the queen's house at Buckingham Palace, as the queen said she wanted to see me. I put on my tail coat and walking stick and she and her children sat down. They played a gramophone record for me and I joked and danced for just thirty minutes. Then I drink tea and the queen gave me shirt, trousers, and coat.

Q: You said that Kwame Nkrumah helped you get a job at Guinea Press. What happened when he was overthrown?

Ajax: When they made coup against Kwame Nkrumah in 1966, it was the CPP people who were working at Guinea Press—so as all of us there were close to Nkrumah they sack all of us. And the police came and arrested me and took me to the CID headquarters. They arrested all of the CPP security people and myself—as some CID people asked me if I was an informant and I said no. Then they looked through a list of all Nkrumah's security people, but my name was not among them and they left me. But I stayed in the cells for three days.

Q: What did you do after this?

Ajax: I worked with a private press man and continued entertaining at night-clubs, like the Star Hotel for instance. I also worked with Faisal Helwani for three years at his Napoleon Club and sometimes would go with his bands; like when he took his bands to play for the prisoners at Nsawam Prison and Ussher Fort.

Q: Faisal was also helping organise the Musicians' Union [MUSIGA] at the time. Was it through him that you became involved in the union's march for official recognition in May 1979?

Ajax: Yes, and I was also a member. I was with them carrying a placard and went with them all the way to the Castle.

Q: What are you up to these days?

Ajax: I made advertising films for Wiseways Launderies and Club Beer and was also filmed for the Ghanaian *Spear* photo-comic magazine. The comic was called "The Case of the Hunchback Craze." I was a judge. Osofo Dadzie and Bob Cole [two other prominent Ghanaian comedians] were also in it. And every Saturday and Sunday I displayed at the Ambassador Hotel.

Q: What are your future plans?

Ajax: I want to go to New York next summer-time for two weeks as a friend of mine is there. I met him when I went to New York in 1977 as guest artist with a band from Kumasi called Doctor Gyasi's. That time I stayed three months and traveled in eleven states.

Then just now the Moscow State Circus school wrote to the PNDC (Provisional National Defence Council) government for me to go to Russia on March the 15th for two weeks of celebration for all the school's old students from all around the world.

19 The African–French Connection

French-Speaking Africa before Congo Music

Before the emergence of congo music in the 1950s, the French-speaking countries had no modern African dance music. There was plenty of traditional music and imported French music, but the two never influenced each other. The French colonial policy was to keep the indigenous and French cultures separate. This is the exact opposite to the British attitude, which encouraged a more flexible approach to the mixing of cultures. This is probably why highlife and juju music appeared so much earlier than congo music, which only exploded onto the African continent in the 1960s.

E. T. Mensah, the famous Ghanaian "King of Highlife," toured French-speaking West Africa in the 1950s, before this explosion, and has some interesting views on the difference between the English- and French-speaking countries of West Africa.

> In the Ivory Coast they were importing European musicians and actors. We saw more of the whites than the blacks, as the whites could afford the night-club life. The white bands were playing boleros, cha-cha-chas, tangos, and French music. When we played highlifes only a few of the Ghanaians there got up and danced. When we were there I never saw an African dance-band.

In Guinea Bissau there was a similar situation, even in the late 1950s. E. T. Mensah and his Tempos visited that country in 1958, just after the Guineans had said no to De Gaulle's referendum and had opted for complete independence from France. The peeved French authorities left abruptly, disrupting everything as they went. French musicians stayed on and E. T. remembers seeing them in Conakry. White trios were made up of a pianist, violinist, and drummer who played French music, sambas, rumbas, and boleros. E. T. comments:

> The French dominated the blacks socially and this affected the music. They had white musicians from Paris, but the African dance music was small. The developments socially and musically in the French territories have occurred since independence and now they want to catch up.

Ignace de Souza, who joined Alfa Jazz, the Republic of Benin's first African dance-band in 1953, says the same thing.

> By then, you know, it was the French who were ruling the country and they didn't encourage any dance-band music, only the military orchestras. E. T. Mensah and others used to play as we had some night-club owners who went to Ghana to bring them.

Congo—The Fusion of French and African Music

It was in the Congo, now called Zaire, that the first successful fusion of French and African music was created. It all started in the early 1950s when Afro-Cuban and Latin-American music, like the rumba, became incredibly popular in the then Belgian Congo, and was incorporated into the local music. It was played on acoustic guitars and drums and sung in French, Swahili, and Lingala. When everything went electric in the 1960s the two big names of congo jazz, as the music was called, were Grand Master Franco, leader of OK Jazz, and Kalle, leader of African Jazz.

The lineup of congo jazz bands is guitars, trap-drums, Afro-Cuban percussion, and a front line of saxophones. The guitarists do not play lead and rhythm, as in the case of Western pop-bands. Rather, four or five guitarists playing alto, tenor, and soprano, weave in and out of each others' melodies and rhythms, creating an intricate pattern of sound. Because of the rumba influence, this music is quite distinct from that of the former British colonies.

The Zairians compose cooler dance rhythms than those of highlife and jive. In congo music there is usually a subtle beginning to the song, which suddenly stops and is followed by an exciting transition leading to the main dance rhythm.

Grand Master Franco

Grand Master Franco, who is now known as Luambo Makiadi, managed to keep his band going right up to the present day, although a number of his musicians have split away to form their own groups. His one-time saxist, Vercky, formed the Orchestra Vévé. Sam Mangwana was with Franco (after ten years with Tabu Ley) from 1972, leaving in 1976 to form his African All Stars.

From the time Franco formed OK Jazz in 1956 until the time he died in a Belgium hospital in 1989 at age 51, he released literally hundreds of singles and over one hundred albums. One favourite hit on the 1973 *Editions Populaire* album in West Africa was "AZDA," an advertisement for a VolksWagon shop in Kinshasha.

(For further information on this remarkable musician, the reader should consult *Luambo Franco* by Graeme Ewens, published by Off the Record Press, London, 1986.)

Kalle's Demise and the Rise of Tabu Ley

Kalle's band really finished when his two top musicians left to start up their own groups. Doctor Nico, who before joining Kalle had been a technical college teacher, formed his Orchestra African Fiesta in 1966; the vocalist Rochereau left Kalle two years later, and with Guvana and Faugus, two wizard guitarists from the Diamond Blue Band, set up the Orchestra African Fiesta National. After several internal changes Rochereau formed the Orchestra Africa in 1972.

It was that year, during the Zairian indigenisation programme, that he changed his name to Tabu Ley. By this time he was the most well known vocalist in Zaire and had sold over 5 million records.

Tabu Ley was born in 1940 about 150 miles from Leopoldville. He learned to sing during hunting forays.

Zaiko Langa Langa and the New Generation

A new brand of Zairian soukous music appeared on the scene in 1970 with the formation of Zaiko Langa Langa; it didn't use the horn section of the older bands like OK Jazz but percussion and guitars (a rock influence) and produced a string of new dance crazes like "Ye Ye National" and "Zekete Zekete" for the students and youth of Kinshasha. Zaiko, in turn, spawned a host of off-shoots, all jostling to be the country's fashion- and trend-setter, such as the Langa Langa Stars, Grand Zaiko Wa Wa, Papa Wemba's Isifi Lokole, and Cavache International (which had a big hit in West Africa in the mid-1970s with their single "Shama Shama").

In the 1980s female artists finally entered the Zairian soukous field. Abeti Mekekine worked with Doctor Nico before his death in 1985 and M'Pongo Love and M'Bilia Bel worked with Tabu Ley.

The Spread of Congo Music

Today there are over five thousand bands in Zaire, and congo music has spilled out all over Africa.

In South Africa the Zairian style of guitar-playing has influenced some of the township bands like the Zulu group Mshikishi Namagugu. Congo jazz is also extremely popular in East Africa, and many of the contemporary sounds there are based on it. Typical are Gabriel Omollo and his Apollo Komesha, the Les Kinois, the Shirati Jazz band, and Super Mazembe from Kenya; and Salim Abdullah's Cuban marimba band Super Makassy, Orchestra Kamanvola, and Orchestra Safari Sounds from Tanzania.

In Ghana one of the first congo-type bands to become resident in 1966 was the Black Santiagos led by Ignace de Souza.

Today, one of the top guitar-bands that operates in Ghana and the Côte d'Ivoire is Francis Kenya's Riches Big Sound, which plays music in the same mould as that of Zaire, but sung in the local Nzima language.

Congo music has also had a big impact on Nigeria, especially in the eastern part of the country, which is closer to Zaire than the

M'Pongo Love.

rest of the country, and to French-speaking neighbours like Cameroons and Gabon. In the last few years there has been a commercially successful synthesis of Nigerian highlife with congo music by bands like Rokafil Jazz and Oliver de Coque's.

Today, in French-speaking Africa there is a musical ferment going on, and although musicians started producing their own dance-band music later than Nigeria, Ghana, Sierra Leone, and Zaire, they are now catching up.

Togo

Some of the top bands in Togo are the old-established Melo Togos and newer groups like Eryko Jazz, Orchestra Abass, and La Voix d'Agou. Bella Bellow was a very famous pop singer from

Super Mazembe.

Togo. From the late 1960s until her untimely death in 1973, she recorded many highlifes, congo numbers, and traditional songs in the Ewe language. Her most famous release was "Rockia," a Ewe pop song, and she was well on the way to becoming West Africa's Miriam Makeba.

Benin

In the neighbouring country of Benin there is the Orchestra Polyrhythmic de Cotonu, playing Zaire-type music and Afro-beats.

Then there is Elrigo and his Los Commandos, Gnonnas Pedro and his Dadjes dance-band, which has released a number of albums under the Lagos-based Take Your Choice label, and Ignace de Souza's Black Santiagos now resident in Lagos.

Côte d'Ivoire (Ivory Coast)

In the Côte d'Ivoire during the 1960s, the top band playing the Zaire sound was the Francois Lougah Orchestra, but today this

Mzee Makassy, leader of Super Makassy.

band also plays Afro-beats. Amedee Pierre and Ernesto Dje Dje are the main exponents of local highlifes sung in the Dida and Bete languages. Pierre fuses Western music with the Gbege folk music of the Bete peoples, and the late Dje Dje (he died in 1983) combined modern and traditional in a beat he called "ziglibithy." Dje Dje's style is the more modern and sounds a bit like the maringa or meringue style played in Sierra Leone by bands such as the Afro Nationals. Even more Westernised is Aka Jermome's music, which he usually sings in French. The top female vocalist in the country is Aicha Kone, who was recorded recently with Alpha Blondy.

The Côte d'Ivoire has also become a Mecca and base for many Francophone African artists like Les Ambassadeurs of Mali, Mone Bile of the Cameroons, and Sam Mangwana after he left Franco's OK Jazz in 1976.

*The Black Santiagos, Ghanaian dance-band run by Ignace de Souza
(standing, with trumpet), mid-1960s.*

Burkina-Faso (Upper Volta)

Moving northward to Upper Volta, the most famous artist is
Ouedraogo, who is backed by a modern instrumental lineup but
sings all his songs in the local Mossi language.

Another top band that has traveled abroad extensively is the
ten-piece Farafina group formed in 1978 by the balafon (wooden
xylophone) player Mahama Konate. This group employs local instruments and plays the music of the Manoufo, Bobo, and Dioula
traditions.

Guinea, Senegal, and Mali

These three French-speaking countries boast a whole range of
bands that combine a modern electric approach with the griot or
jali tradition and the Cuban rumba, such as Les Ambassadeurs
(that featured the singer Salif Keita), and the Rail Band of Mali;
Bembeya Jazz and Les Amazons of Guinea; the Orchestra Baobab,
the Star Band, and Youssou N'Dour's Super Etoile of Senegal; and
Ali Farka Toure of Mali.

Francis Kenya.

Les Amazons, a fourteen-piece dance band formed in the early 1960s, is composed totally of traffic policewomen. The band broke into the Pan-African scene when they made an appearance at the FESTAC 77 black arts festival held in Lagos in 1977. They have made numerous recordings. In 1983 they had a major hit in Paris with an album recorded there, and since then have made numerous tours of Africa and the West. Two members of the group, M'Mah Sylla and Sona Diabete, have also done independent recordings, like their brilliant Triple Earth release *Sahel.*

Ali Farka Toure started out his musical career by playing the local Malian one-string guitar in 1950 and the acoustic Spanish guitar from 1956. He then went on to become the leader of the 107-strong Niafenke District Cultural Troupe and at the same time became interested in soul music and the blues of Memphis

Slim and John Lee Hooker. As a result he now plays Malian music with a strong touch of the blues. This is not so surprising in that there is strong evidence of a savannah West African influence on the origin of the blues. Readers should consult Paul Oliver's *Savannah Syncopators* (Studio Vista, 1970) for more information on this topic.

Gabon and the Cameroons

A Gabon artist who has recently released a string of beautiful albums sung in French is blind guitarist Pierre Akendengue, whose group plays a modernised griot music. Like the traditional griot music of Africa, Akendengue's lyrics have a strong political and social bias.

He was a student at the Sorbonne and became such an outspoken critic of his government that he had to leave Gabon for a time, until called back to represent his country at FESTAC. His lyrics are present-day parables based on mythological figures like Oreyi, a bloodthirsty monster whom Akendengue equates with a modern head of state in the pay of imperialism. He calls a peace meeting of all the animals and then creates confusion among them so that they devour each other. Marange, the traditional diviner, tries to overthrow the dictator Oreyi.

Cameroons is a neighbour of Gabon and these two countries are tucked between the giants Nigeria and Zaire. Cameroons really gets the best of both musical worlds as it is half English- and half French-speaking. The English-speaking part opted to join Nigeria, so the Cameroons has its own version of highlife, makossa music, which is a very fast and bouncy guitar-band style. Congo music is also popular there, and it is through the Cameroons that Zairian music has influenced the guitar-bands of eastern Nigeria. Nicholas Mbarga, the leader of Rokafil Jazz, is half-Nigerian and half-Cameroonian.

The best-known artist from Cameroons is undoubtedly Manu Dibango. He has been an international star ever since his disco hit of the early 1970s, "Soul Makossa," which got into the charts in the United States. Dibango, who plays saxophone, was brought up on makossa music, but today his interests range far and wide. He is adept at congo music and is also a first-rate jazz and rhythm

Jimmy Kutumba, leader of the Ebonies.

and blues player. For many years he was based in Paris, where he played at the famous Olympia and worked with many top musicians. For instance, he teamed up with the Ivorian musician Francois Lougah with whom he released many albums of congo and makossa music. He also worked with the late Bella Bellow of Togo. Since his smash hit, he has released a number of albums combining local African dance music with jazz and rhythm and blues, and he has a big following, both at home and abroad. He is currently based in Abidjan, where he is the head of the music section and the orchestra of the national radio of the Côte d'Ivoire.

So there's plenty happening in French-speaking Africa today. If things go on like this, maybe this special African fusion music they are creating will come to dominate the French pop scene in France itself.

20 Pushed Out by Apartheid

Although thousands of miles separate West Africa from southern Africa musical influences easily span such distances. Since the late 1940s beginning with South African penny-whistle kwela music and the kwelalike "tsaba tsaba" guitar music of George Sibanda from Bulawayo in Zimbabwe musicians and music forms have come to West Africa from regions to the South. Some South African artists have toured West Africa, such as Miriam Makeba, Letta Mbulu, and Hugh Masekela, who worked in Ghana during 1974.

The South African music scene is quite different from that of the rest of Africa. The local black music (township jazz and kwela) was well known internationally long before highlife, congo jazz, and juju music. During the 1950s and 1960s, while the rest of Africa was gaining independence, the apartheid system was set up in South Africa, nipping the development of local music in the bud and pushing its best players into exile abroad.

Before the 1960s there was a rich musical heritage in the South African towns stretching back to the turn of this century, when Afro-American music first hit the country and when Africa's first recording industry was set up. By the 1940s and 1950s African jazz and variety shows were even becoming popular with whites—the music of Miriam Makeba, Dolly Rathebe, Dollar Brand, and the Manhattan Brothers.

Then came apartheid and everything was put under government control, including the radio and recording industry. Apartheid also meant the systematic enforcement of segregation and the creation of black townships like Soweto. All this had a devastating effect on South Africa's jazzmen, who lost the venues they had been playing at since the 1920s. Alto-saxist Kippie Moeketsi, hailed as South Africa's Charlie Parker, gave up playing altogether for many years. Imported rock and roll filled the musical vacuum for the youth of the newly created black townships.

Many of the black music stars left the country. Pianist Dollar Brand (or Abdullah Ibrahim, as he is now known) settled in the United States in 1960 with the help of Duke Ellington. Miriam Makeba and Letta Mbulu also went abroad. They both had to switch from township music, for which they were famous at home, to their own local Zulu and Xhosa folk songs, for which they have become famous internationally. A whole succession of talented South African musicians left; trumpeter Hugh Masekela went to the States and Dudu Pukwana went to England.

How It All Started

Modern South African music began in 1907, when the record market first opened up and ragtime became a big craze in the African quarters of the towns and cities. In the illegal drinking bars, or shebeens, a local version of ragtime—marabi music—was soon being churned out on barrel-organs and rattles. One of the most popular of the bands playing this music was the Japanese Express. Among the wealthier blacks, ragtimes sung by refined choirs at evening soirees became the vogue. The most famous of these was conducted by Reuben Caluzza, who composed ragtimes in Zulu and went on to record 150 songs for HMV by 1930.

Black American minstrelsy was also popular during the 1920s and many black vaudeville groups and concert parties were set up in South Africa. The Dark Town Strutters, Hivers Hivers, and Africans Own Entertainers tap-danced, sang ragtimes and spirituals, and performed comic sketches.

In the 1930s came jazz and swing, and the music of Louis Armstrong and Duke Ellington began to influence local bands. The Jazz Maniacs and the Merry Blackbirds began to create the distinctive South African township jazz. When the kids on the streets began to play local jazz, they created a poor man's version of it on penny whistles and called it kwela. Later, in 1954, a penny-whistle tune, "Tom Harke," by Aaron Lerole, became an international hit.

Popular in the towns from the 1930s on were variety troupes like the Lucky Stars, which staged plays and played every sort of music from traditional African dances to township jazz. The most famous of these troupes were the Manhattan Brothers, who sang Zulu and Xhosa versions of American close harmony music and made so much money for Galo Africa that this record company employed Griffiths Motsieloa, the first black talent scout, in 1938. These black variety shows even became popular with whites. The Pitch Black Follies was set up in 1937; the variety show "Zonk" was popular with black and white troops during the Second World War.

King Kong starred Miriam Makeba and the Manhattan Brothers and opened in Johannesburg in 1959. It was so successful that it was taken to London in 1960. As by then conditions were getting intolerable for musicians back home, half the musicians stayed abroad. This exodus of musical talent has been the picture right up to the present, so let us take a closer look at some of the South African stars who have become musicians in exile.

Miriam Makeba

Miriam Makeba is Africa's number 1 female vocalist. Her story is a classic one of rags to riches. She was brought up in Johannesburg, where her mother was a servant. Miriam loved singing. She joined her school choir and sang at funerals and weddings, both in English and her native Xhosa, a language full of complicated click sounds.

Her first band was the Cuban Brothers. At age 17, she joined the eleven-strong Black Manhattan Brothers, the close harmony group modeled on Afro-American bands like the Mills Brothers. Miriam joined them in the mid-1950s and stayed with them for three years, during which time she traveled all over Zaire, Zimbabwe, Zambia, and South Africa in a dilapidated bus that kept breaking down.

After she left this hard-working group, she got the lead part in

Miriam Makeba.

the Black opera *King Kong,* based on the true story of a boxer who kills his lover. In 1960, after the London tour of this show, she stayed on and went on to New York. There Harry Belafonte helped her get her first recording contract in the States. Here her musical repertoire enlarged to include calypsos and ballads as well as jazz and South African folk songs, and she got her own female harmony group together, the Skylarks or Sunbeams.

Since then she has released many records, like her famous *Pha-tha-Phatha* and *Malaika* and has made many international tours. Miriam never sings in Afrikaans. She is an outspoken opponent of the apartheid system. Some of her songs criticise the repression there, and she says she will only return home when her country is independent. In fact, she visited South Africa in 1990, when

Nelson Mandela was released from prison and political changes still in progress were beginning.

She often visits and tours independent Africa, and sang at FESTAC in Nigeria in 1977 and at the packed El Wak stadium in Accra, Ghana, backed by local musicians such as the Todd brothers. Her voice is as powerful as ever. Her daughter, Bongi Makeba, followed in her mother's footsteps before her death in Guinea.

Dudu Pukwana

Many of South Africa's jazz musicians have worked with Dudu Pukwana. He was born and brought up in Port Elizabeth, and was taught his first instrument, the piano, by his father when he was 10 years old. In the late 1950s he joined his first jazz-band, Tete Mbambisa's Four Yanks, based in Capetown. After this, he formed his own band, the Jazz Giants, which won a jazz award in South Africa in 1963. In that year, he changed over to saxophone and joined the Blue Notes, a jazz-band with some of South Africa's leading musical names—pianist Chris McGregor, drummer Louis Moholo, cornet player Mongeza Feza, bassist Johnny Dyani, and the late Nick Moyake. They played at the Antibes Jazz Festival

Dudu Pukwana (left) and Pinise Saul (right).

Louis Moholo.   *Johnny Dyani.*

in 1964. As the band was multiracial they had to leave South Africa
that year. They first went to France and Switzerland and finally
settled in England, where they received help from English jazz
musician Ronnie Scott. They were based in London as the Brotherhood of Breath until 1973, when Chris McGregor left for the
south of France.

During the late 1960s and early 1970s, Dudu Pukuwana and
Mongeza Feza, until his untimely death in 1975, asked many of the
Blue Notes or Brotherhood of Breath musicians to work with
their own groups Spear and Assegai. Dudu worked with many
other musicians during this time. He made an album with Hugh
Masekela in 1972 called *Home Is Where the Music Is,* and worked
with American-based South African trombonist Jonas Gwangwa,
Miriam Makeba's music arranger.

Some of the many musicians who passed through Spear and
Assegai were Nigerian guitarist Fred Coker, bassist Chad Cheido,

Ghanaian conga player Terrie Quaye, sax players Bizo Mnqikana and Fred Fredericks, conga player Smiley de Jonnes, drummer Julian Bahula, and vocalist Princess Audrey. The name of Dudu's present band is Zila, which means "We are here."

Many South African musicians who have worked with Dudu in the past are now running their own bands. Johnny Dyani is in Denmark with his group Witchdoctor's Son. Louis Moholo is running two bands at the same time, Culture Shock and Spirits Rejoice. Julian Bahula, who went to England in 1973 after running a band in South Africa called Malombo Jazz, is now leading a London-based band known as Jabula.

Waiting for Liberation Day

Due to its rigid apartheid laws, South Africa has lost an enormous amount of musical talent since the 1960s. As a consequence the music scenes of the States and Europe have been enriched, particularly in the field of jazz. Exiled musicians often play in independent black African countries and many attended and played at FESTAC in Nigeria in 1977, including Jonas Gwangwa, Miriam Makeba, Johnny Dyani, Louis Moholo, and Julian Bahula. None of them planned to return home to South Africa until Liberation

Otingo, a South African musical playing in the West.

Day, but with the recent developments in South Africa some have already visited their home country.

Music or Porridge?

After the exodus of musical talent from South Africa during the 1960s a vacuum was left in the local music scene. Watered-down folk and rock were fostered by the government. Local township bands and choirs continued to thrive, however, and literally millions of their records have been produced, usually in backyard studios. This is why all this urban jive is often referred to as "mbaqanga music"—the name derived from the term for quickly made steamed mealie porridge (i.e., cheaply made records).

In the 1970s things began to pick up for the mbaqanga bands. Some of them have become so popular that even South Africa radio plays some of their tunes, although any controversial lyrics are censored.

Some of the top mbaqanga vocalists are Steve Kekana and the late Jacob Mpharanyana, whose records, backed by the Cannibals, often sell fifty thousand or more. Even more spectacular are the Soul Brothers, who have had total record sales approaching the 5-million mark. Female vocalists are also in demand such as Patience Africa, voted top lady vocalist by the South African Broadcasting Corporation in 1977 and 1980. Margaret Singana, SABC's choice in 1978, was the first local artist to receive a platinum disc for sales of one hundred thousand records.

Back to Roots

Some of South Africa's top bands have turned back to their black roots. The Afro-rock band Harari, whose members originally started off in the 1960s playing Beatles-type music, now sing about black awareness. Another Afro-rock band called Era, formed in 1976, had their first album *Manyano* (Unity) banned on South African radio. Also banned was Juluka's single "Africa, The Innocent Weep." Juluka was formed by a white and a black musician, Johnny Clegg and Sipho Mchunu. Clegg has since formed a new group called Savuka.

Many banned songs are played on the Bantustan radio stations, whose signals can be picked up throughout southern Africa. Another wind of change in the music has come about since Zimbabwe's independence and the surfacing of local guitar-band music there (music influenced by South Africa's township beat, but which uses melodies borrowed from the local hand-piano tradition). Two of the most popular of these sorts of band today are the Shona groups, Oliver and his Black Spirits and Thomas Mapfumu and the Blacks Unlimited, who were both detained under the Smith regime. Another musician is Dewera Ngawena, who plays more in the Zulu style.

In spite of all attempts to deport musicians and bottle up black South African musicians, their sounds are coming through loud and clear. European music fans' sudden interest in mbaqanga is evident in Virgin Records' *Rhythms of Resistance,* Rough Trade's *Soweto* compilation album, the Soul Brothers' single released by Earthworks Records, and Paul Simon's famous *Graceland* album.

Readers interested in more details on southern African popular music should consult the following books:

1. *In Township Tonight,* by David Coplan (published by Ravan Press, Johannesburg, 1985)
2. *Music in the Mix,* by Muff Anderson (published by Ravan Press, Johannesburg, 1981)
3. *Roots Rocking in Zimbabwe,* by Fred Zindi (published by Mambo Press, Zimbabwe, 1985)
4. *Makeba—My Story,* by Miriam Makeba with James Hall (published by The New American Library, New York/Canada, 1987)

21 The Liberian Pop Scene

On September 1984 I spent several weeks in Monrovia, the capital of Liberia, as the guest of Ghanaian producer Faisal Helwani, who had just set up the country's first multitrack recording studio. He wanted me to do some interviews and publicity on some of the thirty-six artists he had recorded there in the space of ten months. So I flew from Ghana to Liberia with Faisal and his graphic designer Sammy (Slim) Bentil (whom I had once been in an Achimota school band with). We landed in a typical Liberian rainstorm (everyone carried umbrellas there) and headed for Faisal's eight-track Studio 99 near the sea at Sinkor.

There we met Faisal's twenty-year-old son and recording engineer Sammy and strong-arm assistant Roger Brisson, also known as Al Capone son of a Money Lender. They were in the middle of a recording session with the thirty-two members of the Lott Carey Baptist Mission. The whole place was full of school boys and girls. Their choir, led by Rudolph von Ballmoos, was doing some African hymns.

After they left I had chance to talk to some of the musicians who were hanging around at the time. I met Ciaffa Barclay, who had just done a recording at the Bongos Sound studio backed by two Ghanaian session men Faisal had brought over from Ghana, Aweke Glyman and B. B. Dowuna-Hammond. Ciaffa said that previously he had been working with the Liberian rock group Kapingbi, which had released three albums in Germany in the late 1970s. I even bumped into my old friend from Ghana, Francis

Francis Kenya's tour bus.

Kenya, who was touring Liberia at the time with his Nzima high-life band and was making a master-tape at Studio 99.

A few days later I chatted with the joint leaders of the Monrovian Brothers guitar-band that was run by Donald Cooper (on keyboard) and T. Kpan Limley (on guitar) and who had recorded some reggae-highlifes and funky meringues at the studio, backed by Ghanaian B. B. on bass and Afro-American Salim on horns. Cooper had formerly played with the Afro-rock group Kabassa run by radio disc jockey Dougha Caranda, and then had moved on to Alfred Kollie's Kalafadaya. Limley started his musical career in a schoolboy pop group called the Jesus People and then joined the late Fred Smith's Smiths Dimension, before forming his own group in 1977 called Suhgbaydaytee (Unity) in 1977, which played at the OAU conference in Monrovia in 1979. They told me that Liberian pop and Afro-rock bands go back to 1970s groups like the Dynamics, Shades, and Psychedelic Six (later known as the Afrodelics), and more recently Willie Dee's Oxygen and Ox Walker's Humble Rebels, both of which had recorded at Studio 99.

From my own research in Ghana and Nigeria I knew that some of the earliest highlife guitar techniques and palm-wine styles had come from the coastal Kru people of Liberia who were famous as sailors. I asked Donald Cooper to take me to his seventy-seven-year-old grandfather, David Kwee Bedell, who plays guitar and accordion. Mr. Bedell told me that modern Westernised Liberian music was not only started up by sailors but also by marching brass-bands, mainly in the coastal Maryland County inhabited by the Kru and Grebo peoples. The sort of music these early groups played were local quadrilles, folk songs, calypsos, and foxtrots. Mr. Bedell recalled the names of two Grebo palm-wine guitarists of the 1920s, Alfred Collins and Gyedata Johnson, who were accompanied by musicians playing banjos, accordions, musical saws, clips or claves, and maraccas. In spite of Kru-inspired guitar music catching on and being recorded in Ghana, Nigeria, and Sierra Leone, it was never recorded in Liberia. In Liberia modern music has always tended to be swamped by American music— quadrilles right through to soul and disco music. In fact, Liberia was founded in the mid-nineteenth century as an American colony for liberated slaves (thus the name "Liberia") and so there has always been a strong connection. Ghanaian musician E. T. Mensah said of Liberia in the 1950s that "they had first night-club there, but no bands, only music such as swing and jazz played on hi-fi amplifiers." In fact there were local bands around then like those of the guitarist Tom Brown and Handy Coleman, but they never played at posh night-clubs—the sort of venue that E. T. Mensah's Tempos played at—but rather at low-class palm-wine bars. And they never had chance to record as there were no studios in Liberia until the 1960s.

The first studio in Liberia was a two-track ABC studio set up in Monrovia by a Lebanese man. It began recording some of the guitar-bands, like those of Jones Dopoe, Jerome Payne, John Dweh, and Morris Dorley, and women artists such as the Sherman Sisters, who had a big hit with the "Bassa Love" record, and Yatta Zoe, who has released twenty-four singles and six albums in the Gola and Mandinke languages since 1964 and who represented Liberia at Nigeria's FESTAC in 1977. In the 1970s other women artists came on the Liberian popular music scene, such as Christine

Clinton, who recorded with South African trumpeter Hugh Masekela, and Miatta Fahnbulleh, who worked with Sierra Leonean producer Akie Deen and Daisy Moore.

I interviewed Daisy Moore, who was also recording with Faisal. She told me that she got her musical inclinations from her father, who had been a member of the Greenwood Singers danceband of the 1950s. Daisy, born in 1955, started singing professionally at age 5, began composing music and playing the guitar at age 8, and was on the radio and television by the time she was age 10. Her first album, *Just Daisy,* was recorded in Monrovia's short-lived Studio One that Hugh Masekela has been involved with. Her recording at Studio 99 was a collection of meringues and rumbas with a conga jazz or soukous touch from the lead guitarist and leader of a visiting Guinean band called Africanium, which also recorded at Faisal's studio.

Another woman artist I met at Studio 99 was Fatu Gayflor,

Fatu Gayflor.

who was lead singer and dancer of the Liberian National Cultural Troupe. She has been singing since she was age 8 and has become known as the "Golden Voice of Liberia." Her compositions are based on the traditional music of the Lorma people of north-western Liberia. On Faisal's production she did a particularly beautiful song called "E La Lokpeh," with guitar licks provided by Aweke Glyman.

I also talked to thirty-eight-year-old Gola guitarist Morris Dorley, who had turned up at the studio personally to sign all nine thousand cassette cards for his new release with Faisal. (Faisal was releasing all Liberian productions on cassette [there being no rec-ord-pressing facilities in the country] and got all artists to sign the covers as a way of preventing piracy, which was rampant in Libe-ria.) Dorley told me about his career, which started out when he played the congoma or giant hand-piano when he was 16. An American bought him a guitar and he learned to play palm-wine music. He went on to form his Sunset Boys, which recorded at Mr. Shafi's record shop in 1970 and at the ABC studio in 1970. He sings meringues, rumbas, and dagomba highlifes in a distinctive high-pitched voice.

Faisal has also recorded the Monrovia Brothers, one of the most popular guitar-bands in Liberia since the early 1970s. They play highlifes, pachangas, and traditional songs from Nimba

Morris Dorley.

Robert Toe.

County. The group was formed by Sony Halawanga and palm-wine guitarist Jerome Payne.

Also at the studio was Kruboy Emmanuel Koffa, a vocalist and drummer who has played with the Voices Liberia guitar-band. He is the principal exponent of darjze music, which is associated with football matches and is played on drums, harmonicas, musical saws, and sasa (maraccas). O. J. Brown sings rumbas, soca music, and folk songs. He used to be with the Sierra Leonean Afro-rock group the Godfathers, but is now with the Ducar Inter-Continental Hotel dance-band.

There were some army musicians recording at Studio 99 as well. One was thirty-year-old warrant office Robert Toe, whose father had been in the Liberian army and had played trombone in a military band. Toe had learned guitar from palm-wine musician Jones Dopoe before joining the army band in 1973. Jimmy Diggs was the leader of the Lofa Zoes (Lofa Wizards) band, which was making a cassette of songs in the Gbandii language backed by the brilliant soukous-type guitar-playing of Old Man Pratt from Sierra Leone.

22 Francophone West Africa and the Jali Experience

By Flemming Harrev

Although I have firsthand experience of the music scenes of most of the English-speaking West African countries, my musical work, tours, and research into the French-speaking countries have been much more limited. As this book is primarily a result of direct contact with West African music and its musicians, and is not based on secondary sources or interviews with African musicians in Europe and America, I have asked Danish radio journalist Flemming Harrev to write this chapter. He has traveled widely in French-speaking West Africa and has met and interviewed many of the top musicians there in their home countries. This chapter reflects his own direct encounter with the popular music in West Africa.

(John Collins)

Senegal and Youssou N'Dour

On a night in 1983, it's almost 11 P.M. when I arrive at Dakar's marina. Outside are several hundred bystanders. Sold out? Is it too late?

Youssou N'Dour in Dakar night-club, 1983.

I make my way to the small lattice gate leading into the courtyard behind the wall. People, mostly boys and young men, are drifting around outside. I pay 3,000 francs CFA (U.S. $12) for my ticket, slip through the gate, and pass two guards in uniforms who close quickly behind me. For the people in the street, it crosses my mind, the entrance fee must equal several days' wages. They can't afford a *grande manifestation culturelle et recretive* but have to satisfy themselves by listening across the wall. Nevertheless, they have come to hear their favourite band, Youssou N'Dour et le Super Etoile de Dakar.

In Senegal, Youssou N'Dour is simply *le phénomene*, the undisputed number 1 singer and probably the most popular person in the country. With his exceptionally beautiful voice and electrifying phrasing technique he has sung his way into people's hearts— not just in Senegal, but also in neighbouring Gambia.

Like most places in Africa, live performances in Senegal's clubs and hotels are for the few who can afford to attend. Ordinary people have to be content with music on radio or cassette, occasional concerts at stadiums, or, like this evening, by trying to get a glimpse of their heroes through the gate.

Inside the people display a style that is rather distinguished, elegant, but relaxed; they have come to have fun and have arrived in their finest clothes—the women in elegant French-designed clothes, the men in European suits and ties or several layers of richly decorated traditional *boubous*. The average age seems well above 20.

For the occasion a big enclosure has been made with a dance floor in the middle. Along the sides runs a roofless area where people sit. At the far end, opposite the band, is a low podium with a long table covered with a white cloth. These are seats for the invited government dignitaries and the leading members of the sponsoring club.

Tonight it's the marina club that has organised the event in the harbor area. People fill the seats and the dance floor, and the hostesses—easily identified by their pink robes and skillfully plaited hair—carry soft drinks, beer, and grilled meat to the tables. The service is French-style. Special tickets are bought from a man in a white jacket, which are then given to the hostesses.

The open area in the middle is reserved for dancing. Each time Youssou N'Dour et le Super Etoile de Dakar starts a new number, there's a metallic rattling of the chairs and tables. It's like people are being sucked onto the dance floor. And almost imperceptibly—just before the number ends—everything rattles again as people sit down before the music stops. Nobody applauds; appreciation for the music is expressed by dancing.

Couples and small groups of people come onto the dance floor cheering and singing—the more energetically the better the music is. Many make a serious attempt to do the traditional dances of Senegal, but the highlight of the evening is a group of women who pull out the tama percussionist during intermission to strike up for *le ventilateur*. In a series of astounding outbursts of energy with high and wry leg movements they move into the middle of the floor. Stout middle-aged women kick off their sandals to give solo performances. The tama percussionist adapts the rhythm to the movements of each woman. After a half-minute it's all over. The many layers of the *boubou* are put back in order and the mama smilingly steps back into the circle of clapping women while another takes her place.

In fact, what we are witnessing this night in Dakar in 1983 is a minor social revolution. Until the late 1970s modern music in Sen-

Traditional performance by Farafina ensemble.

egal was still dominated by a local adaptation of the Afro-Cuban rumba, with many numbers even sung in Spanish. Dancing was for couples only—the European way. Like the other countries in French-speaking West and Central Africa, the dance-bands, with congas and a brass section, had been introduced in the 1940s and 1950s and were heavily influenced by Cuban music. Whereas other countries had developed their own independent styles relatively early, each drawing from indigenous musical traditions, nothing much had changed in Senegal.

In the course of only five or six years, a new generation of young musicians led by Youssou N'Dour had changed all that. Instead of Spanish they were now singing in Senegal's own African languages, notably Wolof. Traditional percussion instruments like the tama and sabar-drums had replaced Afro-Cuban instruments.

What was most significant about this change was the short-circuiting of the antagonism between the music of the French-speaking elite of the major cities and the traditional music of the rural population, which the elite regarded as worthless and old-

Youssou N'Dour.
(Courtesy Flemming
Harrev)

fashioned. For the first time, the Senegalese have a modern music
built on their own traditions that includes the whole population.
The same development can be seen all over the continent. What
makes the change and the new generation of musicians in Senegal
so interesting is the dramatic speed with which the change took
place—and that it happened so late—even compared to the rest of
French-speaking West Africa.

Speaking to Youssou N'Dour a couple of days after the performance at the marina club, I learned that his dreams for the future
go far beyond Senegal itself.

> For years Senegalese music has lagged behind and we didn't have
> an independent modern music of our own. But those of us who

were young in the 1970s knew Senegal had its own culture. In the beginning, we struggled to reproduce the Cuban rhythm and only play it half the time. By composing music which rhythmically was totally Senegalese, we eventually made the audience interested in our own folklore. And they liked it. But to begin with, it was difficult because we didn't know exactly how to bring the African elements out.

Earlier on we had never been noticed abroad in the field of music. So now, the next step for us is to make it on the international market. Just like the music of Zaire and other styles have become known. As a Senegalese musician, it's necessary to promote Senegal's own music.

To go far away and succeed—and then return prestigiously home—seems a typical African strategy. But in 1983, to go on international tours was still a dream for Youssou N'Dour et le Super Etoile de Dakar. During the band's first major tour of Europe in 1984, they were hardly noticed by the broader public. No records were available. But persistently, they came back the following years. And the rumours about the astounding dynamism at their live performances started to spread, giving them some of the best reviews achieved by an African band at the time. Eventually a couple of albums were released in France.

It was also at this stage Youssou N'Dour got in touch with the

Youssou N'Dour et le Super Etoile de Dakar, 1985.
(Courtesy Flemming Harrev)

WOMAD festival in Britain and began working with Peter Gabriel. This collaboration in time brought Youssou N'Dour, the only artist from a non-English-speaking country, to the stage with Sting, Tracy Chapman, Peter Gabriel, and Bruce Springsteen in Amnesty International's world tour in 1988 for the promotion of human rights.

The band's international exposure also opened doors to the multinational record companies. To start with, the band had its music released only on cassettes distributed locally in Senegal. Then a couple of albums were released in Paris for the growing market for African music in Europe. Finally in 1989 came the band's first worldwide distributed album, *The Lion,* released by Virgin Records.

French- and English-Speaking West Africa

The story of Youssou N'Dour's gradual steps toward international stardom in many ways resembles that of two other artists from French-speaking West Africa who have also signed up with multinational record companies—the outstanding modern Mandingo singer Salif Keita from Mali and kora-player and singer Mory Kante from Guinea. Still, they represent only a tiny portion of Africa's talented artists.

With the steadily growing interest in the world music of the 1990s, the West African music scene today seems totally dominated by artists from the French-speaking countries, especially the Mandingo-speaking areas of Senegal, Mali, Gambia, and Guinea. This, however, is a very recent development. In comparison to the neighbouring English-speaking countries, especially Ghana and Nigeria, modern music in French-speaking West Africa started much later, during the 1960s.

Following World War II, when the highlife dance-bands perfected their now classical style, the elite of the French-speaking countries were dancing to imported Afro-Cuban music and records from Congo and Zaire. These outside musical influences (which would affect the subsequent development of pop music in French-speaking West Africa) arrived largely in the form of records, but a much older musical connection once existed between

Gambian national troupe, WOMAD, 1986.
(Courtesy Flemming Harrev)

the former English and French colonies. In the 1920s and 1930s
goumbe (goombay or gome) and asiko—from which most of the
early styles of urban music in Sierra Leone, Ghana, and Nigeria
took off—had spread via associations of returned migrant workers, and later youth groups, to all the French colonies. But there it
never succeeded in making a similar impact on the development of
modern music as it had already done in English-speaking West
Africa.

There is no single explanation for this. On the one hand, compared to Ghana and Nigeria, the process of urbanization started
late in the relatively densely populated French colonies. Also a ma-
jority of the population were Muslims, who maintained their own
culture to a much higher degree than the Christianized coastal regions to the south. On the other hand, the policy of colonial administration also played a significant part, distinguishing between
les evoluées, those who accepted wholeheartedly the French way of
life, education, and culture, and *les indigènes,* those who, despite
tight administrative control by the French after the destruction of
the ancient chiefdoms, maintained their highly developed social
hierarchy and traditional musical culture.

Over the past thirty years, modern music in French-speaking West Africa has grown basically out of these two opposites. On the one hand, there were the modern elitist dance-bands, playing saxophones, trumpets, electric guitars, congas, and jazz- or trap-drums. Their music was based on French pop, Afro-Cuban and Congo-Zairian prototypes, and traditional music. The recent intermarriage of the two, coupled with an international sound supplied by synthesizers, is the dominant force in today's mainstream music. An important influence on the modernisation of traditional music still affecting the ideas of many musicians has been the formation of a national ballet and its experiments with rearranging traditional music, dances, tales, and costumes into stage shows for the concert hall.

Guinea and Its National Ballet

The idea, now widespread across Africa, of forming a national troupe goes back to 1948, when Fodeba Keita from Guinea started his legendary Les Ballets Africains in Paris. Following the breakthrough performance at Paris' prestigious Salle Pleyel in 1952, the troupe began a number of extensive tours throughout the world in the 1950s and 1960s. Initially, the members were students, but following the troupe's artistic as well as financial success, Fodeba Keita was able to return to Guinea to search for local talent. He toured the country for almost a year, organising competitions in the villages to find the best musicians, singers, and dancers.

Fodeba Keita's efforts to recreate Les Ballets Africains in many ways served as a laboratory for the nationalistic cultural policy implemented by Guinea following independence and the country's militant break from the French community in 1958. Les Ballets Africains was made the official national ensemble of Guinea and the members became state employees. Every second year, following a range of festivals throughout the country starting at the district level then moving on to the regional level, a national festival of traditional and modern dance, music, and theatre was held in the capital of Conakry. As Sekou Legrow Camara, trumpet player and one of the founding members of Bembeya Jazz, recalls, the support of modern dance-bands grew directly out of a clash with colonial mentality.

It was just before independence, as president Sekou Toure always loved to recall, when he was elected mayor of Conakry for
the first time in 1957. He had arranged for an orchestra from
Dakar to come and play at the celebration of his installment as
mayor. All the modern bands that existed in Guinea at the time
were led by Europeans. The Africans didn't have modern dance-
bands, and all the other bands refused to play in his honour. So,
after independence in 1958, one of his first concerns was to
launch a policy of cultural rehabilitation, and the decision was
made to hand out modern instruments to all young people who
wanted to play. It was after this the modern bands were
organised on the local level, in all parts of the major towns and in
the districts. This decision supplied the basic equipment, then
followed a recording studio, and organisations to coordinate the
activities of the dance-bands and regulate the rights of the
musicians.

Modern instruments were handed out generously, and the
state provided the necessary infrastructure for the distribution of
Guinea's own music. A recording studio was established at the
national radio station La voix de la revolution (the voice of the
revolution) and foreign music was banned. A state-run record
company was started in the late 1960s, distributing out of France.
Twenty years later it had released almost eighty albums and hundreds of single records. Many have since become classics, and as
nothing similar existed in the other French-speaking countries at
the time, Guinean music predictably came to dominate the scene
throughout the 1960s and most of the 1970s. The only other styles
of modern music that enjoyed widespread popularity in French-
speaking West Africa in those years were the highlife bands from
Ghana, Afro-Cuban music, and the rumba bands from Congo and
Zaire.

One of the singers discovered by Fodeba Keita in Guinea was
Kandia Kouyate, nicknamed "Sory," who, in the French fashion of
placing the family name first, became known as Kouyate "Sory"
Kandia. His uniquely powerful male mezzosoprano could, without amplification, fill a concert hall. He is considered one of the
most virtuoso traditional singers of all times. He usually was ac-

companied by traditional instruments like the twenty-one-string harp-lute (kora), the three-stringed bass (bolon), the wooden xylophone (bala) with calabash resonators, and the lute (koni) with three to five strings. Occasionally he also sang with modern bands.

Kouyate "Sory" Kandia, like most of today's modern musicians and singers in French-speaking West Africa, was a jali, that is, he was born into a family of hereditary musicians, singers, dancers, acrobats, and counselors. Traditionally the jali families form a professional class of their own and are a cultural institution unique to West Africa. In precolonial times, they preserved the family's history, praising the righteousness and deeds of heroes in their epics, which were learned by heart and handed down from generation to generation. No major festival or ceremony would be complete without the presence of the jalis. Even today many influential and wealthy persons have a jali staying in the family compound, as in the case of Dembo Konte, who between festivals and concerts in Europe and America, still goes on tour with his group to visit his patrons in Gambia. But even less wealthy families will send for the jalis for a naming ceremony, to celebrate a wedding, or for a religious festival.

Besides the epic praise songs, perhaps the most spectacular feature of the jalis is the twenty-one-string kora. According to oral tradition, it is the newest instrument embraced by the jalis, invented only some three hundred years ago, as Dembo Konte explains:

> The kora came first to Guinea-Bissau, that's the Gabu. Then they got the kora in Casamance in the south of Senegal. And then, after that, they even got the kora in Gambia. It has been passed on from generation to generation. I take to the kora after my great-grandfather. My grandfather taught my father. My father taught me. And I'm going to teach my sons. In fact, I'm teaching my son right now.

Not surprisingly, a large number of sons and daughters of jalis also found their way into the modern dance-bands throughout West Africa. And in Guinea, after independence, they played a major part in creating the repertoire for the thirty regional bands supported by the government and the six national bands: Keletigui et

Dembo Konte (left) playing kora, 1988.

ses Tambourinis, Balla et ses Balladins, Bembeya Jazz, Super Boiro Band, Horoya Band, and the all-women Les Amazones de Guinee. Modeled on the Afro-Cuban instrumental lineup (also found in Congelese and Zairian music), they developed a style largely based on the jali repertoire, including many of the characteristics of traditional instruments and vocal style.

A look at the almost eighty Guinean Sylipone albums also reveals that a large portion of the songs are credited as traditional songs. One special feature of the modern bands that has developed over the years is the solo guitar style, which is based on the melodic figures of the kora. The style is unique to this region of Africa and today is being perfected by Sekou Diabate, Kante Manfila, and Ousmane Kouyate. Yet another important aspect of the cultural policy of Guinea was the emphasis on women's participation. For many years the country played host to the exiled South African artist Miriam Makeba. Since 1965 the female wing of the national police force, *la gendermerie,* has had its own all-women dance band, Les Amazones de Guinee, which has toured all over Africa and, since the 1970s, in Europe.

Besides creating a new repertoire and a new style, the modern dance-bands continued the traditional role of the jalis as praise singers, now in independent Guinea singing in praise of the country, the single party, and President Sekou Toure. In the years leading up to his death in 1984, the government of Sekou Toure developed into an oppressive system that held political rivals and opposition groups in detention camps and had an economy in total disarray. Today, after Guinea's break with the past and introduction of the second republic, the songs in praise of the old regime, full of all the political rhetoric of the time, seem rather out of place and embarrassing.

What began as a progressive nationalistic cultural policy in the 1960s ended as the imposition of restrictions on musicians and the use of bands as tools of propaganda. Guinea's economic decline toward the end of the Sekou Toure regime badly affected the music scene. Officially, the government turned inward in search of traditional sources, but in 1977 recordings came to a complete standstill and none of the groups were seen on tours abroad. Nearly eight years passed before the country's top modern dance-band, Bembeya Jazz National, was able to enter a recording studio again and resume tours of Europe. Also, the activities of the world-famous national ensemble Les Ballets Africains almost ceased completely; the troupe, now under the artistic direction of Italo Zambo, who himself started as a member of the troupe in the 1960s, was revitalised for a world tour in 1990. The legacy of the best aspects of Guinea's former progressive cultural policy is nonetheless still very noticeable, as Italo Zambo notes:

> Les Ballets Africains is not a commercial ensemble. Ever since the troupe was made a national ensemble after independence in 1958, it has always—first and foremost—been a cultural troupe. It's the same ideas, the same line we are pursuing today. This is also why we, in Guinea, are being seen as ambassadors for African culture and art—not just as ambassadors of Guinea, but for the whole of Africa.
>
> Now, with the second republic, we have a new way of looking at things, a new mentality. And we don't want to lag behind the development in the rest of the world. We have seen what has

happened even in the Soviet Union. Disregarding race, young people all over the world have heard about it and welcome the new ideas and change. They want freedom and true democracy, they don't want war, but peace among all peoples. This characterises the development under the second republic as well. Les Ballet Africains can breathe more easily today. And it is in light of this, one should see our return, in full force, to pay our tribute to freedom, brotherhood, friendship, and peace in the world.

The period of secluded development of Guinean national music under Sekou Toure has left Guinea with a formidable legacy and the potential for blending traditional music with a modern sound. The groups Fatal, based in Holland, Bembeya Jazz, and Les Amazones, and artists like Kante Manfila, Djeli Moussa Diawara, Ousmane Kouyate, Tata "Bembo" Koutate, and Sona Diabete (who in recent years has been on tour internationally) have so far shown only a glimpse of a culture that is exceptionally vital—even when compared to the other rich cultures of French-speaking West Africa. Proof of the potential of the Guinean music scene was

Mory Kante (centre) playing kora, 1989.
(Courtesy Flemming Harrev)

given by Mory Kante who, with his blend of the kora, traditional singing, and a modern band with synthesizers, in 1988 topped the European singles charts with his rearranged version of the traditional song "Yeke Yeke." No other African artist has reached this level of popularity and the unique all-out, high-tech international sound of Mory Kante's albums recorded in Paris, rather than a more acoustic sound, seems to be the key to his commercial success. Nonetheless, even Mory Kante, himself from a jali family, primarily sees this music as yet another variation of Mandingo music.

> Mandingo music has many forms. Many. It's the music which has been disseminated by the jalis. It's our way of making music. Sometimes it's educational, sometimes it's encouraging. It depends on what it's trying to achieve. On what I want to tell. They're the great songs which are sung in the evening, like "Tara," "Djand-jon," and "Soundiata." These great songs I will sing for three hours nonstop. Also they are very good for dancing. Then, there are the songs of rejoicing for young people, and it is this form for the young I put out on the records. And, talking about Mandingo rhythms, there's not that great a difference between our rhythms and today's contemporary rhythms, like *le funky,* which our young people play. When you listen to a group of young Mandingos playing, it very quickly becomes "funky" or universal. I can't explain how. It really attracts a universal, contemporary rhythm. It's not because *le funky* is there right now, that I do it. For me it's not a matter of funky, Afro-Cuban music, or anything like that. What I do, is what we have. I elaborate on it, maybe I create something different on top of it. My form of music is very strong now, but in all I do it has a true colour of Mandingo music.

The Scene in Mali

Mali adopted a similar approach to Guinea's nationalistic support of national culture. Following the country's independence in 1960, a national ballet (L'Ensemble Instrumental National du Mali), largely made up of jalis was set up in the capital of Bamako. A number of state-sponsored modern dance-bands were started in all the major regional towns—Kayes, Segou, Sikasso, Mopti, and in Bamako, the capital. Mali Kunkan, a state-run record company, was established by the Ministry of Youth, Sport, Art, and Culture; and a national festival, *Semaine de la jeunesse* (youth week). In Mali, as in Guinea, the newly formed modern dance-bands came from Afro-Cuban music, and like several musicians from Guinea, some Malians went to Cuba to study the real thing in the 1960s. For example, the Maravillas du Mali, a group formed by Malian musicians in Havana, later reorganised at home as National Badema, featuring singer Kasse Mady Diabate. Other renowned bands during these formative years were L'Orchestre national "A" de la Republique du Mali, Le Kene-Star de Sikasso, Super Biton de Segou, and Zani Diabete et le Super Djata Band.

But it was two other bands formed in 1969 and 1970 that really captured the essence of the livelier and rougher Malian Mandingo sound and subsequently paved the way for an international breakthrough, not only in other parts of French-speaking West Africa, but eventually even in Europe, Japan, and America. Le Rail Band de le Buffet Hotel de la Gare de Bamako (or simply the Rail Band) was sponsored by the Ministry of Information and had regular venues at the railway station hotel and refreshment room in Bamako. The other band was Les Ambassadeurs du Motel de Bamako, which in 1978 moved to Abidjan, the capital of the Côte d'Ivoire, and changed its name to L'Ambassadeurs Internationaux. What links the development of the two groups is Salif Keita, Mali's most outstanding singer today. As his family name indicates, he stems from the royal family, the descendants of the legendary Soundiata Keita, who founded the Mali Empire in 1240. His becoming a singer represents a total breach of his status as a member of a royal family. Singing is a profession reserved solely for the lower caste of jalis; a keita never spoke—let alone sang—in public. If he had anything to say, he would say it through a jali. And it was always the jali who sang for the royal family—in praise of the deeds and exploits of ancestors.

Salif Keita started his professional career with the formation of the Rail Band in 1970, which he left four years later to join up with solo guitarist Kante Manfila in Les Ambassadeurs du Motel de

Salif Keita. (Courtesy J. M. Birraux)

Bamako. With the Rail Band, he had played tribute to his ancestor Soundiata in several versions of the traditional song rearranged for a modern dance-band. But it is yet another version of "Soundiata" that in retrospect stands out as the landmark and proof of the maturity of modern Malian music, with its sophisticated blend of the jali heritage and the Afro-Cuban instrumental lineup. When Salif Keita left the Rail Band, the position as solo singer was taken over by bala player Mory Kante who, since childhood, had been trained in a family of jalis in Upper Guinea. His expressive vocal interpretation of "Soundiata"—twenty-eight minutes long and masterfully underlined by the instrumental arrangement—captures the drama of the ancient epic and makes the thirteenth-century cavalry chase across the savanna come to life.

For Mory Kante, the Rail Band, where both he and Salif Keita began their careers, was his first encounter with modern music. In the late 1970s he moved to Abidjan to form a band of his own, featuring the kora as his new solo instrument, a musical formula he has since developed very successfully with a new group based in

Paris. The Rail Band still exists, however, as one of the most prominent bands on the music scene of Bamako, playing at dances every weekend. It was in the 1970s that the modern Mandingo musicians working out of Mali increasingly came to dominate the music scene in French-speaking West Africa, following the economic decline and unstable political climate in Guinea. Although the members of the national dance-bands and traditional troupes in Guinea were state employees, they found it increasingly hard to make ends meet, as there was no way of earning money besides "dance nights," that is, by making records. Also the lack of artistic inspiration and censorship proved a problem. So for innovative musicians like Manfila and Mory, half-cousins from the same Kante family of jalis in Upper Guinea, it meant going to Mali and the Côte d'Ivoire. But as Kante Manfila points out, it takes more than being a jali to become a great musician.

> Just because you're born into a jali family, it doesn't necessarily make you a good musician. Some never compose anything themselves. There's a confusion about playing our traditional music—about if you arrange it your own way or compose something new altogether. It isn't the same thing. I do both, that's my strength. I'm not altogether satisfied with the way I play the guitar and the way I sing, but I'm very satisfied with the way I'm composing.

Kante Manfila, once a member of Les Ballets Africains, later embarked on a career of his own in Abidjan. There, due to his compositional skills and ways of developing a new Mandingo style for the solo guitar, he became the first artist without a proper band of his own to record for a local record company. When he went up to Bamako in 1971, a journey that eventually led him to join Les Ambassadeurs du Motel, he found things to be different.

> When I joined the band, I didn't play our music but French pop hits and Afro-Cuban music. All this changed when Salif Keita took over as lead singer in 1974. From then on the repertoire was based exclusively on our own traditional music. And it's this direction I've pursued ever since.

With Salif Keita as new lead singer Les Ambassadeurs du Motel de Babako, the first dance-band in Mali, was signed up by a French record company distributing out of Paris. In Bamako, they still played dance nights at the motel, but their music was now heard all over French-speaking West Africa. An arrangement with the Malian copyright association was made to secure Kante Manfila's returns as composer. But when the payment finally came through for three albums and a dozen singles, he was paid only FF 400 (U.S. $80). Disappointed and disgusted with the whole situation, he decided to leave Mali and return to the Côte d'Ivoire, where he had better personal contacts. With him also went five members of Les Ambassadeurs, including Salif Keita and rhythm guitarist Ousmane Kouyate, who reorganised the band in Abidjan as L'Ambassadeurs Internationaux. This move marked a decisive

Kante Manfila with L'Ambassadeurs Internationaux, 1983.

Salif Keita with L'Ambas-
sadeurs Internationaux,
singing on Ivory Coast
television, 1983.

turning point in the development of modern Mandingo music, particularly as it coincided with a boom in the local record industry in the Côte d'Ivoire.

Abidjan and the Côte d'Ivoire

Since independence the economic growth of the Côte d'Ivoire has been astonishing. It is, in fact, the most prosperous nation in French-speaking West Africa. In just forty years in the capital, Abidjan, the number of inhabitants exploded from 25,000 to more than 2 million. The city center is located on a peninsula. Seen at sunset from the international deluxe L'Hotel Ivoire on the mainland, the lights of the fancy high-rise towers on Le Plateau glitter on the other side of the lagoon. Abidjan is one of Africa's most beautiful cities and symbolises a fantasy already come true of a modern Africa moving at full speed into the twenty-first century. Big motorways head north or inland, or from Le Plateau across bridges and past the harbor and the old suburb of Trechville, onto the ten-lane motorway that passes Marcory and Koumassi toward the international airport. Public transport is efficient and served by the latest Saviem buses from France. With its apartment flats in Cocody resembling those of southern Europe, Abidjan seems to hold promises of affluence.

All kinds of music can be found in Abidjan. Afro-Cuban records for the older generation, zouk and reggae for the young.

Goumbe, the earliest form of urban music, is still played by groups in the poorer suburbs of Trechville and Adjame. Juju and fuji records are imported directly from Nigeria by Yoruba merchants. And there is music from the whole of French-speaking Africa. The ethnic composition of the Côte d'Ivoire almost invites this variety. To the north, people speak Mandingo. The country plays host to a large number of Mossi people from Burkina Faso, and in the southeast people belong to the Akan-speaking group, the dominant language of neighbouring Ghana, and this is probably why highlife has always found a big audience with the Ivorians as well. In the Côte d'Ivoire, the most successful highlife artist is Eba Aka Jerome, with his group Le Sanwi Star. Over the years many Ghanaian artists have also been attracted to Abidjan, with its many night-clubs and record companies. Perhaps most successful in the 1980s was Asabea Cropper, a former member of the Sweet Talks, Ghana's famous highlife band led by A. B. Crentsil. Asabea explains how she came to the Côte d'Ivoire:

> I used to do a group called the Black Hustlers Band, and after having toured Germany for a couple of months we went back to Ghana. When we got home, someone invited us to the Ivory Coast to perform for two weeks. We did some TV performances and had a lot of contracts. This first was for three months; later it turned out to be a one-year contract.

As in the rest of French-speaking West Africa, Congolese and Zairian music have always been very popular. Since the 1960s many Central African musicians have visited Abidjan, including Franco Luambo Makiadi and OK Jazz, Tabu Ley (seigneur Rochereau) et L'Afrisa International, and L'Empire Bakuba. Some even stayed for longer periods of time, most notably Sam Mangwana who, in the late 1970s, worked out of Abidjan for four years with the outstanding group L'African All Stars, led by guitarists Dizzy Mandjekou and Lokassa ya M'Bongo. The opportunities of playing clubs and the boom in LP production attracted more Central African musicians, including Nyboma Mwandido, who made his classic Zaire album *Double Double* in Abidjan.

Sam Mangwana, however, originally arrived in Abidjan in search of new inspiration. Blending elements of biguine from the

Caribbean with highlife, Sam Mangwana and L'African All Stars renewed Zairian music; playing in a style that strongly emphasises long interwoven guitar passages, they omitted the brass section and sang in pidgin French (*francais petit negre*). Subsequently, songs like "Matinda," "Georgette Eckins," and "Affaire Video," dealing with male-female relationships, captured the imagination of both the rural and urban populations of the Côte d'Ivoire and French-speaking West Africa. This use of pidgin French became yet another of Sam Mangwana's trademarks developed during his stay in Abidjan, as people in West Africa were otherwise excluded by the use of Lingala in the lyrics of Congolese and Zairian music. More than a hundred LPs of Congo and Zaire music were released by local companies in Abidjan in the late 1970s. And when most of the artists, including Sam Mangwana, left for Paris, the formula had already been worked out in Abidjan for the high-tech Congo and Zaire sounds that have been coming out of French-language recording studios since the 1980s.

Peaking in the mid-1980s, the Côte d'Ivoire had more than seventy-five record producers, including five major companies. A pressing plant had also gone into operation in 1975, at a time when the format shifted from the single record to LP, demand exploded, and modern studios were established. So the whole infrastructure necessary for mass distribution of modern music was available in Abidjan, attracting musicians from all over West Africa as well as Cameroons, Congo, and Zaire. Also no other country in French-speaking West Africa has, as vigorously as the Côte d'Ivoire, pursued an effective copyright policy and tried to stamp out piracy.

The record industry boom since the 1970s also meant an upsurge in the development of the country's own musical styles, notably that of the Bete people living in the central part of the Côte d'Ivoire. Traditional music was adapted for the modern dance-band by Amedee Pierre, and later even more successfully by Ernesto Dje Dje into the ziglibithy, the most original purely Ivorian style to date. So from a humble start, copying French pop songs and Afro-Cuban music, the musicians of the Côte d'Ivoire eventually reached back to their own roots, creating something uniquely their own, as Amedee Pierre puts it:

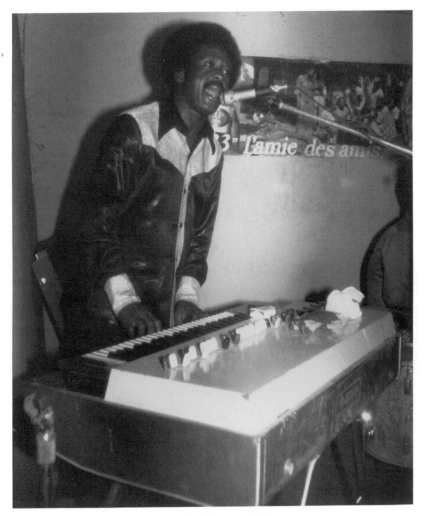

Amedee Pierre, 1983.

When it dawned on me that people actually liked what I was doing, I tried to interest all young people in music. They began with my band and after four or five years—or after eight years as in the case of Ernesto Dje Dje—left my "school." I've participated in creating almost every modern Ivorian style. When one of my students left, he had to create something different in order to develop Ivorian music. However, the "ziglibithy," the rhythm perfected by Ernesto Dje Dje, was his own creation.

Ernesto Dje Dje died under mysterious circumstances in 1983, but his musical legacy is felt very strongly, and today the ziglibithy, with its spectacular dance routines, is still carried on successfully by Sery Simplice, another student of Amedee Pierre, and by Sehia Luckson Padaud. Besides the record industry, the radio, popular press, and especially television have been very important in exposing new local talent to a wider audience. To support the artists, Ivorian television uses its own dance-band that in the 1980s was led by such experienced arrangers as Manu Dibango as well as Bocana Maika, a Malian who studied music in Cuba in the 1960s.

It's a far cry from the situation of the 1960s when the first generation of artists, Amedee Pierre, Mamadou Doumbia, and Anouma Brou Felix, had to build up a reputation from live performances in clubs and when Ernesto Dje Dje worked years to perfect the ziglibithy. Francois Lougah, another early star of the 1970s, actually started out as a James Brown impersonator during the "soul-craze" years, before arriving at his own, up-tempo, highly danceable style. The careers of a younger generation of artists like Justin Stanislas, Beny Bezy, Bailly Spinto, Paul Nemlin, and Jean-Baptiste Zobodi have been helped by the record industry and the media.

These new developments have also helped female artists. In the Côte d'Ivoire, female artists are more visible than in most African countries; Diane Solo, Nyanka Bell, Kassy Perpetue, Reine Pelangie, and Aicha Kone all have secured respectable positions in the public eye because of the level of sophistication of the music scene. Even Bebe Manga from Cameroons, with her international hit album *Ami*, and Zairian singer Tshala Mouna, renowned for her snakelike dance routines, started their international careers in Abidjan. Ghanaian singer/saxist Eugenia Asabea Cropper and her Sawa Band were based in Abidjan for a time. Things are not always easy for women in African show business, however, as Aicha Kone explains:

Traditionally, there are dances for women, which men will never do. There are dances the men would do before they went to war that are only done by men. Traditionally, there has always been a difference in Africa. There is one role for the men and one for women. But when it comes to the modern development, men and women can dance in the same way today. Still, not all families will accept a woman to be an artist and embrace her as a bride. Lack of trust in female artists sometimes creates problems in our personal lives. You are rejected in your marriage. They think an artist cannot be a serious person. That she is never at home, traveling all the time. But we had the first lady Miriam Makeba who put her message out through the songs as a way of communicating. So now women do have a role in modern music alongside the men.

Burkina Faso, Togo, and Benin

Throughout the 1980s in the Côte d'Ivoire, the music of Ghana, Guinea, and Mali dominated the music scene, with the country's own artists less in evidence. The record industry also attracted musicians from neighbouring Burkina Faso. Following in the footsteps of Volta Jazz, Les Imbattables Leopards, Echo del Africa National, and L'Harmonie Voltaique—renowned groups of the 1960s such as those of George Ouedraogo, Traore Saidou Richard, Kabore Oger, as well as Le prince Edouard Ouedraogo et l'orchestre Nakombisse—belonged to a younger generation of musicians who went to Abidjan to make records. Although modern music in Burkina Faso's capital, Ouagadougou, has been played for as long a time as in Abidjan, the conditions for the musicians, as Traore Saidou Richard explains, are quite different and much more limiting:

In Ouagadougou, we have about five open-air bars with modern bands. That's not enough to give a good pay. It's too expensive to order your own instruments from abroad. So, usually the band leader goes and talks to the bar owner. We come, play, and we get the entrance. The bar owner gets the drinks. We have arrangements, so it works. That's business. Then you have the owner of the instruments, a private person or the band leader, who might take 50 percent and give the other 50 percent to the band. Sometimes the owner of the instruments might also pay the musicians on a monthly basis. For individual singers like myself, it's when you play concerts at Maison du People, a hall with 3,000 seats, you can get a really good return. That's privately organised, where you have to pay for the hall and the band yourself.

With no recording studios and few places for live music, the music scene in Burkina Faso has, more than in any other country, really been an extension of what happened in Abidjan, with the music from Congo and Zaire, Guinea and Mali, and the artists from the Côte d'Ivoire ranking among the most popular from other countries. In later years, the best internationally known group from Burkina Faso has been Farafina, a traditional group with djembe-drums and bala, partly made up of former members of the national dance troupe. Managed by a Swiss agency, they have been able to follow up on their first impressive performances at festivals in France and Switzerland, eventually touring most of Western Europe, Japan, and the United States. These tours have opened opportunities for their appearances as guest artists on albums by Jon Hassell and the Rolling Stones.

Apart from Burkina Faso, the interests of the record producers in Abidjan also branched off into Togo and Benin. The Satel pressing plant in Cotonou is of special importance as it also supplied most of the matrices used in Abidjan. Whereas Togo shares the highlife and concert party music with Ghana to the west, Benin is one of the few countries outside Nigeria where juju and fuji find a big audience. Besides artists from the Côte d'Ivoire, music from Congo and Zaire over the years has been most popular in Benin. For, like Central African music, many groups in Togo and Benin also were influenced by the Afro-Cuban dance-bands. Most notably in Benin, there was Gonnas Pedro y sus Panchos de Cotonou, the Black Santiagos led by Ignace de Souza, and the present top dance-band T. P. Orchestre Poly Rythmo de Cotonou, Benin. Based on the Afro-Cuban instrumental lineup, the bands in Benin have developed their own immediately recognisable, energetic, up-tempo style, with sudden guitar and brass riffs between the lead singer and the chorus.

Paradoxical Modernisation— The Africanisation Process

The case of Benin could serve as yet another example of one of the dominant tendencies found in African music when seen over a certain period of time: the more modern music gets, the more African it gets as well. According to musicians all over West Africa, the influence from Afro-Cuban music is almost universally ascribed to the shellac records released by His Master's Voice in the GV series. Daniel Cuxac, the owner of Disco Stock, one of Abidjan's leading record companies, explains it this way:

> In all French-speaking countries there's a certain, important story which needs to be mentioned. The influence of French music and culture itself. Everything that was à la mode in France, say thirty or forty years ago, also became à la mode here in Africa a year or so later. When the French went to the colonies they brought with them the music which was à la mode in Paris. In the late 1940s the *son* dominated Latin music. But people here didn't know what to call it. So they called it "GV"—from the records edited for Africans by a company in Venezuela. In fact, "GV" is short for *Grabado en Venezuela,* pressed in Venezuela. You see, that's why we called it "GV" no. 1-2-3-4-5 and so on. And if you meet people here who are maybe fifty or sixty years old they'll say, "Oh, I remember 'GV'!" In Cuba where it was very strong, a certain part of the music became cha-cha-cha around 1950. And, of course, it also became à la mode in France and eventually even here in Africa. In particular in Dakar, the capital of the French West African colonies, but there was a big influence of cha-cha-cha everywhere in Africa at that time. It was also popular in Belgium—in old Zaire music [from the former Belgian Congo] you'll find cha-cha-cha. They called it differently—rumba and all kinds of things—but it wasn't really rumba, rather it was a very simple cha-cha-cha.

The first records in the GV series were released by La voix de son maître, or HMV, in 1933 and in advertisements at the time presented as "hits from Cuban and South American shores." In French-speaking West Africa the impact of the GV records really caught on after World War II and the influence from these records is still very noticeable today, from Senegal, Guinea, and Mali, right across West Africa, to Congo and Zaire. Everywhere they inspired young people to form groups with an instrumental lineup similar to the Afro-Cuban dance-band. But whereas the original impact from GV music came from the same records, sold all over French-speaking West and Central Africa, local music eventually evolved into a number of quite different styles. Over the years the musicians of each country have moulded and re-Africanised the dance-bands over and over again according to their own musical traditions. When comparing modern Mandingo music, the Sene-galese mbalax of Youssou N'Dour, to the music of the Côte d'Ivoire, Burkina Faso, and Benin—or even to the classic Central African dance-bands of Franco Luambo Makiadi and Tabu Ley—they bear very little resemblance, yet they all started some forty years ago listening to the same GV record.

For instance, in modern Mandingo music a significant devel-opment took place when Salif Keita and Kante Manfila left Bamako and went to Abidjan in 1978 to reorganise their band as L'Ambassadeurs Internationaux. Aided by the big record pro-ducers operating on the local music scene, they released a whole range of now classic modern Mandingo songs—"Jean ou Paul," "Mana Mani," "Primpin'," and "Kanke-len-Tigui"—in addition to the two wholly acoustic LPs *Dans l'autenticité*. But the album that stands out as a masterpiece—in the same class as Mory Kante and Rail Band's interpretation of "Soundiata"—is *Mandjou*, with its thirteen-minute-long epic title song. The title song is notewor-thy not only because of its original musical arrangement—blend-ing Salif Keita's vocal interpretation with horns, Mandingo solo guitar, and a bala replacing the rhythm guitar—but also as an out-standing contemporary praise song. In West Africa *Mandjou* is widely regarded as a tribute to Guinea's former President Sekou Toure, a leader today renounced for his political persecutions. One might therefore think that the song today would be considered

rather controversial. Nevertheless, Salif Keita still sings "Mandjou" at his European concerts as he sees the song in a somewhat
wider context.

> It's a tribute to all the Toures—including Sekou Toure. There are
> many Toure families. I'm not a politician, I'm an artist. It's true I
> sang "Mandjou" for the occasion when Sekou Toure arrived in
> Mali. But it's not a political song. I wrote it because I like the
> man as an African, and because he has honoured me and gave me
> a medal. Voila! We have a proverb which says: In a marriage, you
> always observe other marriages whilst amongst neighbours, you
> always watch other people. Thus as a professional, you always
> look toward some other professional.

The point Salif Keita underlines is that no man is ever perfect
and without faults. "Mandjou" can stand as a tribute to the most
progressive aspect of Sekou Toure's policies, when—after independence—the nationalistic cultural campaign was launched in
order to re-create pride in the culture of Guinea.

Another example of this modernisation/Africanisation process
is the case of Mory Kante, for whom the sophisticated setting of
Abidjan provided the opportunity to set up a band of his own,
blending the kora, bala, and traditional singing with synthesizers
and electric guitars. Incidentally, *N'Diarabi,* one of his best albums, was recorded in Paris and produced by the African-American company Mandingo Productions, operating out of Abidjan.

The travels abroad and the subsequent rerelease of their records in Europe made Salif Keita, Kante Manfila, and Mory Kante
contemplate leaving Abidjan and embarking on a career in Europe. They were well informed about the growing interest in African music in the early 1980s. They also knew that Island Records
had signed up the Nigerian juju star King Sunny Ade and that
Virgin Records was attempting to promote East African bands.
And they had seen how most of the Zairian artists in Abidjan,
including Sam Mangwana and Nyboma Mwandido, had already
left for Paris. The opportunities seemed ripe, and by the
mid-1980s they had all left West Africa in order to try their luck in
Europe and around the world.

Be it the thriving music scene of the Côte d'Ivoire or the rich jali tradition of the Mandingo-speaking areas of West Africa, so far it's been the music from Senegal that has generated the biggest interest in Europe, Japan, and North America. This is almost a paradox since the Senegalese started very late with their first attempts to develop a modern style based on their own folklore. Modern dance-bands have existed in Senegal since the 1950s, but the influence from Afro-Cuban music and French pop songs lasted longer there than anywhere else in French-speaking West Africa. The band that dominated the Senegalese music scene in those early years was the Star Band de Dakar led by Gambian saxophone player Dexter Johnson, renowned for his collaboration with singer Laba Sosseh. In the 1970s Laba Sosseh went to New York and recorded with American salsa musicians, remaining true to his original musical influences. Already in the 1960s he had introduced many Spanish-language songs into the repertoire of the Star Band de Dakar as well as songs in French and English and the first attempt to sing in Wolof with a modern dance-band. The idea of singing in Wolof, the language spoken by half the population of Senegal, was later carried on in the 1970s by Orchestre Baobab Gouye-Gui de Dakar, which also started to introduce Wolof rhythms into their music. The overall influence was still Afro-Cuban, but Baobab evolved toward a highly sophisticated style of their own with sensitive arrangements underlined by the suggestive guitar solos of Barthelemy Attisso and the melancholy voice of Thione Seck. In many ways the classical Baobab recordings resemble the same instrumental sophistication reached by the Ghanaian highlife dance-bands of the 1950s. It was a highly unique and refined music, yet in retrospect also very European in its whole approach. Star Band de Dakar was reorganised several times and it was in one of these later formations that singer Youssou N'Dour made his professional debut in the late 1970s. Still in his teens, Youssou N'Dour, with a background as a singer at street drum parties, perceived himself quite differently than the older generation of musicians. What he wanted to do was to fuse the traditional music of the rural population with the Afro-Cuban elitist dance-bands in the urban centers. As he explains:

Our music is based on percussion. The tama-drum is very important; it's a solo instrument. When it sparkles, it makes people move and the dancers go wild. How really to describe it, I don't know, other than the rhythm of tama evolves into a grandiose improvisation. It starts accompanying the rhythm and then plays a solo which dominates for a while. It is here the Senegalese have an opportunity to display themselves through dance. This has nothing to do with the basic beat found in European music. Then there's also the sabar-drums, usually a set of three drums which have a more accompanying function.

It still took some time for the audience to appreciate the new music and for the musicians to find out exactly how to present the Senegalese elements. But after just five years the music scene in Senegal had surrendered completely to the new style. Dominated by Wolof rhythms and percussion instruments, it was subsequently labeled mbalax (after the traditional wrestling games and the music that went along with it) by Oussin Ndiaye, Youssou N'Dour's uncle and tenor singer in his band.

From an African perspective, there is nothing unusual about

Youssou N'Dour et le Super Etoile de Dakar, 1985.
(Courtesy Flemming Harrev)

the way Senegal arrived at a modern style based on its own traditional music. What makes it so special is that it came so late compared to the rest of French-speaking West Africa and the dramatic speed with which the change took place. For older Afro-Cuban bands like Baobab Gouye-Gui de Dakar, it meant total abandonment by the public at their night-club gigs, resulting in the dissolution of the group in 1984. Youssou N'Dour, on the other hand, moved from Star Band to Etoile de Dakar, where he was featured as co-lead singer alongside Eladj Faye. Dissatisfied with the businessman running the band and the artistic aspirations of the members, he left, and set up his own group in 1982, Le Super Etoile de Dakar.

The rest of the old Etoile de Dakar, reorganised under Eladj Faye as leader, became Etoile 2000. They brought the new and raw Wolof sound to its limits, with full use of all the timbre and echo-effects the local Dakar Studio 2000 could muster. To Super Diamono de Dakar, another group started in the 1970s, the new Senegalese music meant abandoning their earlier experiments with elements of Afro-beat and a more jazzy style. Still featuring *le slow* and the soulful interpretations of singers Omar Pene and Ismael Lo, they presented the audience with a more international sound. As Omar Pene comments:

> We would like to reach the same high international standard, with our music, already achieved by jazz and soul. There's lots of good music in Senegal and this is what we want to play. We have existed for many years now and in the future we would like to play for other people as well—in Europe and America. This is really what we want to do. Our ambition is to reach something *extraordinaire* like other Senegalese bands. There are many going abroad now, including Xalam and Toure Kunda. But there's a difference between the music of those living abroad and us, who still maintain our base in Senegal, despite the hardships of getting equipment, et cetera. We want to do music which is 100 percent Senegalese—or more precisely, Sene-Gambian.

The "Sene-Gambian" reference reflects the enormous popularity enjoyed by the Senegalese bands in neighbouring Gambia, largely due to the very similar ethnic composition of the two countries. In Gambia, Senegalese bands are generally referred to simply as "N'Daka," that is, music from Dakar. Not all music, in fact, comes from Dakar. Both Xalam and Toure Kunda have stayed in France for many years. Toure Kunda—a group from the Mandingo-dominated southern region of Casamance and led by the three Toure brothers—has been one of France's most successful African bands, with an audience made up almost entirely of Europeans. Heavily promoted, their music—with its somewhat blurred ethnic character—has emphasised a more generalised West African feeling, a quality also underlined by the members, both African and European musicians. And like Mory Kante, as well as Johnny Clegg and Savuka from South Africa, Toure Kunda hit records in France have an air and feeling of international pop music.

On a wider international level, the artist who indisputably—more than most—promoted Senegalese music throughout the 1980s is Youssou N'Dour with his group, le Super Etoile de Dakar. Starting out at night-clubs in Dakar and subsequently playing at clubs and stadiums throughout Senegal and Gambia, he has also established his own company to present the band on the thriving local market for prerecorded cassettes. Today his latest cassette released in Senegal corresponds with his albums, distributed worldwide by Virgin Records. But before this happened, almost thirty cassette productions had been released locally, of which only a few so far have found their way on vinyl outside Senegal itself.

While Youssou N'Dour et le Super Etoile de Dakar has spent much time in recent years on international tours, new names have surfaced, which have also been able to benefit from the rising interest—especially in Europe—in Senegalese music. After the collapse of Afro-Cuban music and the dissolution of Orchestre Baobab Gouye-Gui de Dakar, lead singer Thione Seck left and set up his own band, Le Raam Daan. After spending years at home working out how to merge the new percussive style with his rather sentimental voice and releasing several prerecorded cassettes on the local market, he has now made a couple of albums, produced while on tour in Europe. While Thione Seck, Xalam, Super Diamono, Youssou N'Dour, and Ismael Lo (former lead singer with

Super Diamono now pursuing a solo career in France) all sing in Wolof, the greatest new talent in recent years, the singer Baba Maal, comes from the Fulani-speaking region to the far north. Traditionally, the Fulanis are cattle-herding nomads, and it is from this cultural background that Baba Maal draws his inspiration. As he explains:

> I began to sing at the age of 5. In my family, my mother used to sing—not professionally—just like every woman in Africa, at ceremonies in our village, together with other women. But it wasn't the only inspiration I had. When I look at society, at everyday life, my feelings make me sing about it in the Fulani form of singing. Fulanis are nomads. They have many cows and when they walk about in nature, they sing from early morning. The nomads sing in a particular way—slowly and very high— about what they see, in order to express their feelings and to tell other people about their life with the cows.

A university graduate, Baba Maal spent almost ten years in a traditional group before setting up his own modern band, Le

Left to right: *Baba Maal and Masour Seck, 1988.*

Dande Lenol. His powerful, high-pitched voice and some highly original arrangements, reflecting his Fulani background, first caught the imagination of the Senegalese audience. This was also how he was first presented on local cassettes and reached new fans abroad. On subsequent tours of Europe as well as his European albums he began to project a modern sound as well as a purely acoustic one.

Section Four

Music Business

23 The African Recording Industry

Early Days

The African record business goes all the way back to 1907, when records were first sold in South Africa at two shillings each. The main companies were the French-owned Pathe and British-owned Zonophone. By 1914, one hundred thousand records a year were being sold there.

In the 1920s, other foreign companies came onto the scene. His Master's Voice (HMV), for instance, sold over one million records in South Africa in 1927. HMV started recording "native" songs at about the same time as Zonophone and Brunswick.

During the 1930s, black South African close-harmony and ragtime groups modeled on Afro-American groups became popular. Many of them were sent to England to record with EMI (formed by the merger of HMV, Zonophone, and Columbia in 1931).

In the 1940s, the first African record company was set up. Gallo-Africa employed the first African talent scouts and producers like Griffiths Motsieloa. Their initial major success was August Musurugwa's hit song "Skokian," which he sold for a few pounds and which made Gallo-Africa hundreds of thousands of pounds.

In East Africa, records in English and Hindi were first imported in the early 1920s. But by the late 1920s HMV, Odeon, Columbia, Zonophone, and Pathe were recording and releasing local African music sung in Swahili, Luganda, and Somali. For instance, in

1939 HMV/Zonophone sold over two hundred thousand records, of which eighty thousand were in the vernacular languages of East Africa.

West Africa lagged a bit behind. By 1930, however, HMV/Zonophone released 180,000 records there. From 1930 to 1933 the major record companies sold 8 million records in West Africa.

During the Second World War, record production remained low because of the war effort. Afterwards it started up again and during the 1950s records of African and European artists were flooding into Africa. Columbia, for instance, released over two thousand different records of African artists in its East Africa series. In 1954 they even had a major hit with an African song in Britain. They made a quarter-million pounds from South African Aaron Lerole's penny-whistle tune "Tom Harke."

Decca launched its West Africa series in 1947, when almost fifty thousand records were released of top Ghanaian, Nigerian, and Sierra Leonean artists. So successful was this that a permanent studio was built near Accra and portable equipment sent to Lagos twice a year. By the end of the 1950s, Decca West Africa was pressing almost a quarter-million singles a year.

The biggest recording company in Africa operating from France during the 1950s was Pathe-Marconi, which had offices in Nigeria, Kenya, and South Africa.

The first pressing plants actually built in Africa were those of Gallo-Africa, EMI, and Pathe-Marconi in South Africa, all fully operational in the 1950s. In the early 1960s Phonogram (Polygram) and EMI built pressing plants in Nigeria.

The Situation Today

South Africa

Today in South Africa records are still produced largely by the big companies, like home-grown Gallo-Africa and the foreign multinationals Pathe-Marconi and EMI. But many records, especially singles, are being made by the small numerous local companies, such as Imbongi, HVN, Soweto, Shonalanga, and Smanjo Manje. These companies deal exclusively in singles of popular songs—jives, kwela music, traditional songs, and township music—that are usually sung in Zulu, Shona, and Sotho.

The problems facing the South African local music industry are many. But surprisingly, in spite of the undemocratic political system, there are effective copyright laws, a problem that still has not been solved in the rest of black Africa. In 1964 the South African government introduced record royalties, and the record companies agreed to pay them, as there is great competition for popular black artists, who often sell gold discs on the local market.

But there is still opposition to the idea of copyrighting African music from those who argue that African music is communal and modern tunes are reworkings of traditional ones. This seemingly "democratic" idea has become, in the hands of some producers, simply another way of ripping off black artists—particularly so in the case of certain white producers of exotic "African tribal musicals," who do not want to pay royalties for the African dances and compositions they use.

In spite of the copyright laws, the number of black musicians who register and claim royalties are few and far between. Many are illiterate and are pawns in the hands of paternalistic companies who control their savings right up to retirement. These companies prefer to have salaried musicians whom they can move about at will, rather than complete bands. In this way it becomes difficult to pinpoint copyright and the company producers can therefore claim it.

As if these problems were not enough, the apartheid political system has two direct negative effects on the black music business. First, musicians are not allowed to form their own trade union and therefore remain as a pool of unorganised and easily exploitable labour. Second, many of South Africa's top black artists, who sing out against their racist government, have had to flee abroad.

East Africa

The big multinationals in East Africa are Phonogram (Polygram), EMI, Pathe-Marconi, and Decca. The first local East African company, the Jambo label, was begun in Kenya just after the Second World War. Today dozens of small local record companies print singles of popular guitar-band music, hymns, and Afro-

Swahili tarab music—companies like AIT in Kenya and the Seychelles, ACPI in Kenya, Ray's Music Room in the Seychelles, the Green Carpet in Zambia, Discomad in Madagascar, and the Tanzanian Film company, which produces a half-million singles a year in Tanzania.

In East Africa, very few albums are pressed, and the market, mainly in singles, is very small, with a top single selling around fifty thousand copies. According to Hans Kinzl, managing director of Phonogram East Africa, "the market is so small that in one year we only sell as many records in East Africa as we do one good record in Europe or the States." The album market is so tiny that when EMI set up its pressing plant in Nairobi in 1976, it kept going by manufacturing one hundred thousand records a year for the Nigerian market.

Pirating is another problem in the music business, and pirate cassette production has almost become a cottage industry in East Africa. It has cut deeply into the profits of record companies, both foreign and local. It has become so bad that the Kenyan government has tried to outlaw pirating.

Another problem in Kenya was the introduction in 1978 of a 55 percent sales tax on records. Ron Andrews, who runs AIT, reckons it has become cheaper to import records than to manufacture the records locally. Also in 1978 the Nigerian government banned the import of records. EMI therefore lost its Nigerian market and had to close down its Nairobi factory.

Generally speaking the East African record business is far smaller than that of West Africa and is lagging behind.

West Africa

The main international companies catering to the huge local market in Zaire and the French-speaking West African countries are Decca, Phonogram (Polygram), and WEA Fillipachi, a subsidiary of Warner Brothers. Decca's African records and cassettes fill an eighty-page catalogue. WEA Fillipachi has an office in the Côte d'Ivoire and has organised a thirty-two-day African concert tour (Africa Special) of its artists.

French-based companies in West Africa are Pathe-Marconi, now in decline; Safari Ambiance, which releases albums of artists from Zaire, the Cameroons, the Côte d'Ivoire, Upper Volta, and Gabon; and Sono-Disc, which releases records and cassettes of artists from the Côte d'Ivoire, the Cameroons, and Zaire.

The record business of the French-speaking West African countries is generally behind that of the English-speaking ones. Most of the production has been in the hands of the international companies, especially those based in France. For instance, at the 13th International Trade Fair of Record and Musical Productions (MIDEM) held at Cannes in 1979, only three African record producers attended—from Nigeria, Algeria, and South Africa. There were none from the French-speaking African countries. Things are beginning to change. Local recording studios and pressing plants are now being set up in Zaire, the Côte d'Ivoire, and Senegal. In Togo there is the twenty-four-track Studio de la Nouvelle Marche and in the Republic of Benin a twenty-four-track studio is about to be set up by Bernard Dohounzo of SATEL.

In the English-speaking countries of West Africa like Sierra Leone, Liberia, Ghana, and Nigeria, the local record industry is more developed, especially in Ghana and Nigeria, where albums are now more important than singles.

In Ghana by the late 1970s there were four recording studios: the eight-track Ghanaian Ambassador Studio near Kumasi; the Ghana Film studio in Accra, which has just gone over from two track to eight track; a recently opened eight-track studio at Faisal Helwani's Napoleon Club; and the four-track Polygram studio, also in Accra (now closed).

There were also two pressing plants in the country: Ambassador Records, which both pressed records and did recordings, and the Record Manufacturers of Ghana Limited, which is 50 percent owned by Polygram. Between 1969 and 1975 Polygram was producing a half-million singles and a hundred thousand albums a year. But by the mid-1970s the whole of the Ghanaian record business met with many difficulties due to the general economic decline of the country. Record production went down to one-quarter of its former total. This created a bottleneck in the industry that had several serious repercussions. Many of Ghana's top musicians and bands went abroad to record and often never returned home, like Eddie Quansah, Bob Pinado, Boombaya, Pat Thomas, Oscar

Sulley, Kiki Gyan, Kofi Ayivor, Basa-Basa, and Jeff Tagoe. As local music could not be produced the music market was flooded with funk and disco music.

March on the Government

By the late 1970s things got so bad that the Musicians' Union (MUSIGA) organised a march on the seat of government at the Castle in Accra. The government finally woke up to the situation, broke the monopoly of the two pressing companies, and re-distributed record vinyl to independent producers. They reduced the retail price of records dramatically and ordered that 75 percent of all imported vinyl should be used to manufacture local music, rather than imported music under license. The Prices and Incomes

MUSIGA march through Accra, Ghana, 1979.

Ghanaian musicians march to the Castle in Accra for official recognition, 1979.

Board collected over one hundred thousand pounds in unpaid record royalties and passed it on to musicians who were owed money.

Whereas Ghana had been suffering serious economic problems, Nigeria was enjoying an oil boom, which boosted the record industry (records are actually made from oil). The record business was also helped in 1978, when the government banned the import of records. By 1979 Nigeria was pressing all its own records, which that year numbered 12 million albums and reached over 20 million in the 1980s.

Today there are many pressing plants in the country. The largest is the Record Manufacturers of Nigeria Limited at Ikeja, which can press up to twenty thousand albums a day. RMNL is jointly owned by Decca (35%), EMI (25%), Take Your Choice Records (20%), and Northern Nigerian Investment Limited (20%).

Polygram has a large pressing plant in Lagos. It is 60 percent Nigerian-owned and can manufacture 4 million records a year. Apala king Haruna Ishola's record factory was opened in 1979 near Ibadan and is now producing almost a third of Nigerian records. It has a maximum capacity of thirty thousand records a day. There is also a fully automated plant at Onitsha, set up by Prince Tabansi.

Multitrack studios abound in Nigeria. One of the first was the ARC sixteen-track studio, set up in Lagos with the help of English drummer Ginger Baker. Haruna Ishola has a twenty-four track studio near Ibadan that has been used by Sunny Ade, Fela, Tee Mac, and Chris Okotie. Prince Tabansi has a twenty-four-track studio in Onitsha. Decca's sixteen-track studio in Lagos is about to go twenty-four. Artists on the Decca label include Ebeneezer Obey, the Oriental Brothers, the Ikengas, Kabaka International, Christine Essien, and Manu Dibango.

Nigeria's record industry is so far in advance of that of other African countries, that it is the first country in black Africa to have its own pop magazine, *Africa Music,* and its Top Ten of best-selling records.

The Live-Music Scene

Since the mid-1980s, the live-music scene in Nigeria has had a setback, with many of the clubs closing down. For instance, in Lagos the few remaining live night-spots are Fela's Shrine and Sunny Ade's club (when they're in town), Victor Olaiya's Stadium Club, guitarist Tunde Kuboye's Jazz 38 Club, and Art's Place (run by pianist Art Alade). Live music is now mainly focused on marathon all-day open-air concerts such as the Lekki Sunsplash and the Freedom Day concerts held in 1988.

The demise of live-music clubs occurred for several reasons. First, the purchasing power of Nigerian naira (needed to buy imported band equipment) was reduced 50 percent between 1986 and 1989. Second, because of fear of armed robbers, few people go out at night. Third, many of the night-clubs that are operating, like Niteshift, Klass, Lords, Peak, Princess, and Duroof, feature disco music and lip-sync shows by artists such as Lagos's heart-throb Mike Okri.

The Ghanaian live-music scene is also in a similar position because "spinners" (i.e., disc jockeys with mobile sound systems) have moved out of the discos and onto the night-club dance floors with their sophisticated sound equipment, strobes, and laser lights and are having a disastrous effect on the live-music scene, especially in Accra and Tema. The musicians are split on the issue. Some want to send the spinners back to the discos and a petition to that effect went to the Musicians' Union of Ghana. Another group of musicians opposes this sanction, as the Ministry of Information's Copyright Administration has imposed a tax on spinners so that musicians are now receiving money indirectly from them.

Now a compromise is being sought. One of the best suggestions appeared in Ghana's weekly music magazine, the *Hit Parade,* of August 10, 1988: "the Musicians' Union must get the mobile disco operators to agree to involve the live bands in their shows. By allowing the bands to use their heavy sound and lighting equipment the mobile discos would be giving the bands a better chance to promote themselves."

The spinner phenomenon follows in the wake of the disco music craze of the 1970s, which had a negative influence on live music in open-air clubs like the Tip Toe, Silver Cup, Metropole, Lido, and Apollo Theatre, which catered to both home-grown pop-bands and the few remaining highlife dance-bands. In the 1970s many of the Accra youth preferred dancing to records in dark discotheques such as Virgins, Keteke, Blow-up, and Black Caesar. The one exception was the Napoleon Club in Osu, whose proprietor Faisal Helwani ran a disco that included live-music bands that experimented with Afro-pop fusions, like Hedzolleh, Basa-Basa, the Bunzu Sounds, and Edikanfo.

Now, after the disco craze, the latest blow to live music are the ten or more spinners in the Accra-Tema area with names like Willie Chii, Skyhawks, Mobisco, and Studio 44. In the main, the damage they have done is not to the guitar-bands and concert parties, like the African Brothers, Sunsum, A. B. Crentsil, and Jewel Ackah, who have simply moved into the countryside and hardly bother with Accra, but to the imitative "copyright" bands that cover the music of foreign musicians like Bob Marley and Michael Jackson and cannot compete with records played on the spinners' top-quality sound equipment. This competition might force the copyright bands to be less imitative and lend more vitality to live music in the long run. At the same time, a new type of venue for live bands has appeared in Accra—restaurants like Dimples, Afrikiko, Quelquechose, the Sunrise, Jimmy's, and Mandarin. If the bands that play at these places simply continue to churn out imported pop music, the spinners will have no problem pushing them out of their last Accra refuge as well.

24 African Music Unions

There are no musicians' unions in South or East Africa, but in the West African countries of Ghana and Nigeria, there has been a series of unions since the 1950s.

The first was the Association of Gold Coast Musicians, set up in Ghana in the mid-1950s. This was short-lived and was followed in 1961 by the Ghana Musicians' Union. At this time, the socialist government of Doctor Nkrumah was encouraging unionisation. Government ministers Techie-Menson and E. K. Dadson were actually involved in the launching of the Musicians' Union. E. K. Dadson had been the lady impersonator and singer for the famous Axim Trio concert party in the 1930s, before going into politics and later business.

E. T. Mensah became the union's first chairman. The executive included top musical personalities like King Bruce of the Black Beats, Kofi Ghanaba (Guy Warren), Joe Kelly, Tommy Gripman, and Phillip Gbeho, who composed Ghana's national anthem.

This union, which catered to the dance-bands, was able to make significant headway. It forced Decca to double its royalties on each six-shilling record from two pence to four pence. Foreign artists were taxed. For instance, Louis Armstrong had to pay the union on his second trip to Ghana in 1962. At its height, the union membership was around two thousand and it became affiliated with the Ghana Trade Union Congress.

The concert parties and guitar-bands also set up a union. The National Entertainment Association was set up in 1960 by a popular magician called Kobina Segoe and twenty-eight founding concert bands.

Unfortunately both unions were dissolved after the anti-Nkrumah coup of 1966, as they had links with Nkrumah's Convention People's Party. There was even a ban on the movement of concert bands for a time. There were no music unions in Ghana until the Musicians' Union of Ghana (MUSIGA) was set up in 1974 by Faisal Helwani, Jerry Hansen of the Ramblers dance-band, Stan Plange of the Uhuru band, Don Quarcoo, King Bruce and Sammy Odoh of the Black Beats, and E. T. Mensah of the Tempos. Then, a couple of years later, the concert parties and guitar-bands organised themselves into the Ghana Cooperative Indigenous Musicians' Society (GHACIMS). The executive included top band leaders like E. K. Nyame, Doctor Gyasi, Kwaa Mensah, Nana Ampadu, Onyina, and Love Nortey.

In Nigeria the Musicians' Union (NUM) was formed in 1958 with Bobby Benson as its first president. The union was affiliated with the Nigerian Trade Union Congress. After a year Bobby Benson left to form a rival union with Victor Olaiya, so Chris Ajilo of the Afro-Cubanos band became president; the famous trumpeter Zeal Onyia, vice-president; Stan Plange, treasurer; and Amaefule Ikoro, secretary. One of the first things the NUM did was to organise a demonstration, as Stan Plange explains:

> It was in 1960 when the preparations for Nigeria's Independence were going on. The Nigerian government was intending to invite Edmundo Ros to come down and play at the National Independence Dance, as Princess Margaret was coming and we understood she liked Edmundo Ros. Victor Olaiya's band was to play second band. So the Nigerian Musicians' Union organised a demonstration to protest against the bringing of a foreign group. About eight or nine hundred of us marched with placards from the Empire Hotel, Idioro, to Government House to petition the Prime Minister Tafawa Balewa. Myself, Zeal, Chris, and Amaefule went inside and told him that the contract should be given to the union, who would then form a mass band and select musicians to form a national orchestra for the Independence Dance. He agreed and gave the contract to the union.

Stan Plange left Nigeria in 1961, and Zeal Onyia left for Germany in 1964. By the mid-1960s the NUM was defunct. But by this time drummer Bayo Martins had set up another union called the Musicians' Foundation. Stan Plange's comment on this problem of schisms is:

> You know, there's always been a split in the Nigerian Musicians' Union and I can't remember when there was one united union for as long as six months.

These splits persisted to the 1970s, with Victor Olaiya and I. K. Dairo of the Association of Nigerian Musicians on one side, and Bayo Martins, Bobby Benson, and Fela of the Musicians' Foundation on the other. The November 1974 issue of *Gong,* the Lagos music paper, notes:

> Nigerian musicians are at war with themselves. The two major bodies are at daggers drawn, each accusing the other of vices ranging from imposition and misrepresentation, to lack of organisation and ignorance.

The Nigerian Musicians' Union is today divided into four factions and the Music Foundation is defunct since Bayo Martins left the country for Germany. Just recently, though, a new constellation of artists has organised the Performing Artists Association of Nigeria (PMAN), patronised by many of Nigeria's top musicians like Sunny Ade, Ebeneezer Obey, Sonny Okosun, Christine Essien, Niko Mbarga, Victor Uwaifo, Bobby Benson (who died in 1983), and Laoulu Akins. PMAN was formed in 1981 and outdoored at Sunny Ade's Ariya Club. The main aim of this organisation is to put an end to pirating, which controls 60 percent of the Nigerian market. In fact, there has been so little control that pirate companies have openly given their names and addresses on the cassettes they copy—with musicians losing out all round. PMAN has obtained official recognition and is gaining wide support. According to the *Variety Entertainment* magazine of Nigeria (October 1982), even the chair of the Association of Nigerian Musicians, Eddie Okunta, has joined PMAN, claiming that the old association is dead.

PMAN, under the new leadership of Tony Okoroji, held a

peaceful demonstration in the streets of Lagos in 1988, to get the government to replace the copyright law of 1971. In December 1988 the Nigerian government issued Decree 47, which gives musicians 10 percent royalty on the producer price of a record or cassette and makes piracy (that was taking about 60 percent of all Nigerian music revenue) a criminal offence. There is a 1,000-naira fine for each pirated record/cassette. Copyright infringement through live performance nets a fine of 10,000 naira for individuals and 50,000 naira for corporate bodies, including radio and television.

In Ghana the economic decline in the music industry has forced musicians to come together, which in turn has strengthened the Musicians' Union. Today, the membership is around five thousand and includes not only dance-bands, but guitar-bands and cultural groups as well. MUSIGA has become the spearhead for Ghana's musicians and has been particularly active from 1979.

That year the union elected more dynamic leaders—Faisal Helwani, Eddie Quansah, C. K. Mann, Stan Plange, Tommy Darling, and Sammy Odoh. They immediately organised a vigil in Accra, attended by over ten thousand people. The next day nearly one thousand musicians marched through Accra to the seat of government at the Castle. Their demands were for official recognition

Interim executive of MUSIGA, 1979. Members include Sammy Odoh, C. K. Mann, Ami Johnson, King Bruce, Osei Tutu, John Collins, Sidiku Buari, Faisal Helwani, Koo Nimo, Ambulley, Joe Eyison, and Kwaa Mensah.

and a different approach to the music industry by the authorities. The union believes that music is a money-making commodity for the country, and therefore the government should encourage the building of multitrack studios and enforce copyright laws. Then Ghana could produce good quality home-grown material for the international market and obtain precious foreign exchange.

Two weeks after the musicians' march there was a coup in Ghana, led by young army officers. Part of their "house-cleaning" operation included sorting out some of the musicians' grievances. This acted as a shot in the arm for MUSIGA.

For two years after the young officers had handed back power there was civilian rule in Ghana. During this time MUSIGA expanded its membership to five thousand and Ghana hosted famous foreign musicians like Mick Fleetwood (of Fleetwood Mac), who together with MUSIGA and the Ghana Film Corporation made a film called *The Visitor*, and Brian Eno, who produced an album for the Accra-based Edikanfo band.

On December 31, 1981, J. J. Rawlings and the young officers overthrew the civilian government; once in power they imposed two years of curfew, which immediately curtailed the night-life scene. The new People's National Defence Council (PNDC) government, however, recognised the plight of the arts and entertainment business and undertook a series of remedies. In April 1982 the new People's Secretary (Minister) of Culture and Tourism, Asiedu Yirenkyi, launched the "cultural revolution," a program that included making traditional music and dance an integral part of the school curriculum, the recognition of the local Ghanaian comic theatre or concert party as a national art form, and the playing of more local music by the Ghana Broadcasting Corporation.

In addition, all the arts institutions in the country were rejuvenated and young men brought in to run them. The Ghana Film Corporation (and its recording studio) was to be managed by thirty-one-year-old Hurrana Attah. The three top directors of the Ghana Arts Council were transferred and the institution was to be managed by thirty-two-year-old Addrey Homeku. This shakeup of the Arts Council went even further a few years later, after Ben Mohammed Abdullah had taken over. The whole national organisation was decentralised into nine regional community centres.

It was during the PNDC period that MUSIGA finally obtained official recognition, and its membership expanded. For instance, in November 1983 an organisation affiliated with MUS-
IGA was set up. The Greater Accra Musicians Welfare Association
catered to old-time and retired musicians. A special branch of
MUSIGA was formed especially for highlife gospel-bands, dance-
bands used by the African Christian churches.

One of the most important things the PNDC has done since it
launched its cultural revolution programme is to bring out the new
copyright law (PNDC Law 110) in April 1985; it makes copyright
infringement a criminal rather than civil offence and also attempts
to protect folk dance and music by giving the government a 50
percent royalty share in traditional music if produced by non-
Ghanaians. At the same time, the Ghana Broadcasting Corporation has had to start paying out air-play royalties to local musicians
for the first time. Another positive result of this new copyright
law is that the cassette pirates have had to form an organisation (the
Ghana Recordists Association) that began paying taxes to the Ministry of Information's (later the National Commission on Culture's) Copyright Commission. The mobile discos, or "spinners,"
also have to pay a copyright tax.

A final boost to the Ghanaian music scene is coming from
abroad. Many musicians who, for economic reasons, left Ghana
are now returning or making regular visits back home, like the
"burgher" highlife musicians George Darko, Rex Ayanfi, Charles
Amoah, McGod, Kwadwo Antwi, and others who settled in West
Germany. Their funky style of highlife is now very popular in
Ghana and there have been many visits by their bands—all of
which is helping to stimulate the local music business. Even more
important are the Ghanaian musicians who have come back from
Europe to set up recording studios in Ghana; the most important
are Nat Fredua's Black Note Studio set up in 1986, Oko Ringo's
sixteen-track Walking Elephant Studio, set up in early 1988, and
Nana Boamah's Ark Studio set up in Tema in 1990. That year
another studio was set up by a Ghanaian ex-musician—the state-
of-the-art forty-track Overdrive Studio of Ralph Casely-Hayford
in Accra.

25 Running a Band and a Music Studio in Ghana

The Bokoor Band

After working sporadically for several years with the Jaguar Jokers and jamming with Sammy (Slim) Bentil, Andy Quist, and Glen Warren (son of Ghanaba) in an Achimota school band, I began running my own band in 1971. It was called Bokoor (the Spirit of Coolness) and I ran it together with Robert Beckley, a Ghanaian, and Peter Wilks, an English friend, when I was in my second and third years at Legon University. We were the second band of the famous Uhurus (Freedom) dance-band of Ghana and played everything from Hendrix and Santana to highlifes. The band finally folded when several of us who were at the university had to take exams.

For several years after that I played with a number of local bands, including Francis Kenya's Riches Big Sound (with whom I stayed in Madina near Accra for one year), Szaabu Sounds (together with Bob Pinado and Bob Fiscion, now both in Germany), the Bunzus (based at the Napoleon Club), and the Ga cultural group Abladei. I also recorded four songs for Phillips in 1974 with the palm-wine guitarist Koo Nimo and did several television ap-

Second Bunzus band at the Napoleon Club, 1974.

pearances with the Black Berets dance-band of the Recce Brigade of the army. This involved rehearsals at Burma Camp with army musicians wearing khaki uniforms and under strict military discipline. Even on stage there was no let up. Once when playing at the university Volta Hall, two of the Black Beret musicians, the drummer and keyboard player, switched roles without the permission of the sergeant major/band leader; as a result they spent three days in the glass-house (military prison) and were let out only when there was another gig.

In 1975 when I was living in Temple House in James Town, Accra, I formed the second Bokoor band initially as a cultural band (me on guitar and harmonica with plenty of percussion). I later expanded it to a full guitar-band with the addition of rhythm and bass guitars and trap-drums. We didn't play any Western music at all, but highlifes, congo jazz, Afro-beats, agbadzas, and pachangas; our shows also included traditional dancing, fire-eating, and snake-dancing by Gifty Naa Dodowa (later my wife), Brown Sugar, and Kpani "Gasper" Tetteh-Addy. Many musicians played

The Agbafoi cultural troupe, early 1970s.

with us at one time or another, including the late Ewe master-drummer Dan Bokovi Banini, Joe Kelly, Jr. (the son of a famous 1950s highlife trumpeter), Jones Attuquayefio (from the Agbafoi cultural troupe), Jerry James Lartey (who later formed Saka Saka), and another of the famous Ga Tetteh-Addy drumming family, Emmanuel. Incidentally, several members of that family, including Obo and Yacub, are in the United States running drumming groups like Obo Addy's Kukrudu in Portland, Oregon. Bokoor Band also briefly had two American musicians—Big Joe Galeota on trap-drums and Tony Green on guitar.

In fact, the band just seemed to grow and grow until it finally reached fourteen members after a show at the Ga fishing village of Botiano. When our bass player, Junior, didn't turn up, we tried to compensate by getting one of our rhythm guitarists, James Nanka-Bruce, to play only bass notes. But this didn't satisfy the

Core members of the Bokoor band, 1978/79. Standing, left to right: *Lamptey, Gifty, Bob Ajanka, Jones Attuquayefio*. Kneeling, left to right: *Junior, John Collins, James Nanka-Bruce*.

fishermen, who were on the verge of rioting. Gifty threw two python snakes into the crowd and did an impromptu act to bring the show to a successful conclusion. After that we always included two bass players in our group.

The band finally broke up in September 1979, largely due to the increasing economic problems and shortages in the country. I remember many times having to use pumice-stone to scrape the rust from our guitar strings, as we simply couldn't get new ones. The devaluation of the currency around 1977 hit us particularly hard. Our band had invested a lot of money with Grass Roots

*Gifty Naa Dodowa. (Courtesy
Charlie Pickup)*

*Gifty Naa Dodowa with two
pythons.*

Music Productions in organising a series of shows at the Sea View
Hotel in Accra, and this devaluation (or rather, sudden withdrawal
of a currency denomination by order of the head of state, Colonel
Akuffo) finished off the night-life scene for many months—and
our project with it. At the same time, the band had made some
recordings at the Ghana Films studio (with expert help from John
Kofi Archer and Mr. Kwakye) and was about to release an album
with Ambassador Records in Kumasi. This monetary adjustment,
among other things, delayed the pressing of the record for more

than a year. Only when Jones Attuquayefio and myself (after a dozen or so previously wasted trips to Kumasi) camped in the foyer of Ambassador Records with mat, cloth, water, food, and a charcoal stove were we able to get the company to produce the records. We got results, but had to make do with a thousand singles instead of albums because of the "devaluation"; singles were out of fashion in Ghana, and we lost heavily.

By coincidence the British-based Ghanaian master-drummer Ben Badoo was in town looking for a guitar-band to teach modern African music to West Indian unemployed youth at the Wolverhampton Council for Community Relations, where he had already set up a traditional dancing and drumming group called Lanzel (Unity). So Jones, Gifty, and myself spent a year in the English midlands teaching music. Initially they would not believe that there were electric guitars in Africa, or even electricity at all; only the slides of modern Lagos shown them by a Nigerian friend, Rufus Onishayomi, convinced them that electric bands were just as authentically African as were traditional drumming groups. These youths went on to form a band called the Twelve Tribesmen. Gifty, Jones, and myself, together with Nigerian/Brazilian guitarist Theo Pareira and Guyana drummer Dino Washington formed Bokoor number three and recorded a ska/highlife "crossover" twelve-inch single.

Bokoor Music Studio

The three of us returned to Ghana in 1981 and I brought with me a small portable studio (a TEAC 144 and later a 244) with which I planned to record our band when we had reformed it. The 1982 Rawlings overthrow of the civilian government and the resulting night curfew, however, convinced me that it would be impossible to run a band. I then began experimenting with the portastudio in my father's farmhouse (later called Bokoor House), which he had built from the pension he had received when retiring after thirty years at the University of Ghana's Philosophy Department. After a year of experimentation and using my old band equipment, I formally opened Bokoor Music Studio in 1983. Based on my experience as a musician and having worked in studios in Ghana and

Bokoor music and recording studio.

Recording session at the Bokoor music and recording studio.
(Courtesy Ton van der Lee)

Nigeria, I made two decisions about my own studio. One was to provide low-cost facilities to musicians. I built the studio with cheap local swish (mud) and did away with the usual air-conditioning. Second, I decided to have no clock on the premises and not charge by the hour. Instead, I would charge by the product (i.e., one album-length recording), which may take anywhere from two to four days, depending on the band. This together with the rustic surroundings provides a more relaxed recording atmosphere. Music and haste don't mix.

Bands and Musicians I Have Recorded

In the nine years that I've been running Bokoor Music Studio I've recorded about two hundred bands and hundreds of musicians of all sorts. The variety of Bokoor's recording activities says something about the vitality of Ghana's popular music scene in recent years.

On the traditional side I have recorded many pure drumming groups, one of the earliest being the group from Ofankor village, on whose land the studio and farm are situated. In 1984 I recorded the Guna Efee Noko band from Nungua, Accra, who that year won the Ghana Art Council's "Children's Cultural Group Competition"; the free session was part of my service for the institution, now called the Greater Accra Regional Community Centre. I did an outside recording of the drum ensemble at the School of Performing Arts in Legon, for the world-renowned Ghanaian musicologist Professor Nketia. Guitarist Edinam Ansah brought a Ewe Borborbor drumming group from the Volta Region of Ghana. Ansah, who had been with the Ghana Police Band and the First Battalion Army Band at Michelle Camp, had made several highlife recordings with me previously, including one released as an album in Holland on the Wawa label. Ewe master-drummer Michael Kojo Ganyoh has recorded in my studio and has been my own main drum teacher.

Many roots-type bands that use African percussion with acoustic guitar, like those of the famous palm-wine guitarists Kwaa Mensah and Koo Nimo, have recorded at Bokoor. One of my recordings of Koo Nimo was used on Sean Barlow's Afro-pop series for American Public Radio in the fall of 1988 and in the film about John Powell's intermediate "Swami Magazine" project in Kumasi (called *The Secret of Wealth: A Study of Grassroots Technology Transfer*). Two songs of Ghanaian Rastafarian Abdul Salaams Cultural Imani Band appeared on the *Guitar and Gun I* and *II* compilation albums I recorded and produced in the mid-1980s for Cherry Red's Africagram label in London.

I have also recorded many of my old friends from the bands of the Napoleon Club, where I worked as a musician in the mid-1970s: ex-Hedzolleh members Lash Laryea, who now runs a band called Amartey Hedzolleh; Oko Nortey, who has been bringing a string of local groups for me to record; and drummer Okyerema Asante (now working with Paul Simon in the States), who helped record some Pan-African songs with the Yananom band for producer Malcolm Ben. Other Napoleon Club musicians are Jerry James Lartey of Basa-Basa, who now runs a group called Saka Saka, and Chi-Kin-Chi of the Edinafo band who now is in Holland.

Among the many highlife and concert party bands that have come to my studio and appear on the *Guitar and Gun* compilation are Francis Kenya, Wofa Rockson (Koo Nimo's younger brother),

Francis Kenya with his manager. (Courtesy Ton van der Lee)

Kwesi Menu, Sloopy Mike Gyamfi's Adinkra Band, King Bruce's Black Beats, and Beach Scorpion (recently returned from eastern Nigeria and now working with American percussionist Joyce Gilbert and Ghanaian mandolin player Tornado Teike). One of my Adinkra recordings was featured on the BBC Channel 4 black music television series "Repercussions." Guitarist and singer Sloopy and drummer Captain Moro, who both played with one of Ghana's top guitar-bands run by Senior Eddie Donkor, are now in Amsterdam running a group called Sankofa. Other artists who have recorded at Bokoor are the funky or "burgher"-type highlife band of keyboard player Abbie Mensah, who used to play with A Band Named Bediako (that Bokoor Band often toured with in the late 1970s), the concert comedians Waterproof, Ruby Darling, and Super O.D., and the prison band with the apt name of Inside Out.

More experimental highlife bands are Kojo Dadson's Talents and Nokoko, whose leader Smart Pozo (Asmarte) was a member of the London-based Ghanaian Afro-rock group Boombaya, that also included guitarist Alfred Bannerman and drummer Kofi Adu.

I have also recorded many local pop-bands, such as the Classic Vibes reggae outfit (now based in Denmark) and Prince George's Anan's Grass Roots band, whose musicians (including Knox Lokko, Norbert, and Felix Dada, Charlotte Dada's brother) play everything from reggae and funk to soca and highlifes. On the non-pop end of the spectrum, Bokoor recorded the brass-band music of the John Tei School near Accra and the Pan African Orchestra of Nana Abiam, whose instruments include two wooden xylophones, ten bamboo flutes, three one-stringed gonje-fiddles, and a lot of percussion, including four massive Ashanti fontomfrom-drums.

Revofest

In November 1986 Mr. Kwakye of Ghana Film studio, Sammy Helwani of Studio One, and I recorded an event called "Revofest" (Revolution Festival), a twelve-hour presentation of a cross-section of Ghanaian bands organised for fund-raising purposes by the National Secretariat of the Committees for the Defense of the Revolution. Some thirty thousand people came to Revofest at the Accra football stadium to hear government and army bands such as the

Blay Ambulley.

Pink Five, the Police Band, the Prison's Band, the Sweet Beans (of the Cocoa Marketing Board), the Beautiful Creations, and the Sappers. Representing the Ga cultural groups were Wulomei, Naa Amanua's group, and Kyirem; highlife guitar-bands and artists included the African Brothers, A. B. Crentsil's Ahenfo, Koo Nimo, Onyina, Blay Ambulley, Paa Bobo, Joe Mensah, Abebe, Papa Yankson, Nokoko, the Kumapim Royals, and Safohene Djeni. The richly varied program also brought together the reggae groups of Felix Bell and Nframa, the gospel music of Ola Williams and Professor Abraham, as well as the female artists Lady Talata and Lady Lartey. For many people, a particularly memorable moment of the show was the introduction by the blind wandering minstrel Onipa Nua (Brother Man), who sang his own gravel-voiced version of James Brown's "Say It Loud," accompanying himself on a sardine can hand-piano; a moving rendition of "We Are the World" in various Ghanaian languages by sportsman turned musician Sidiku Buari; and an emotionally moving act by thirty-one-year-old disabled singer Pozo Hayes, which brought such a spontaneous rush forward by the audience that the stage nearly collapsed and stopped the show for a while. American audiences were able to share some of the excitement of Revofest when a selection from this marathon live recording was featured as one of the programs of the Afro-pop series on American Public Radio (program number 20).

Blind Musicians and Bands in Ghana

Several Ghanaian musicians are blind and face more than the usual hardships of touring musicians. In recording some of these musicians, I've talked with them about their unique experiences. Besides Onipa Nua, who played at Revofest, and Nana Kwese Amanko-Attah, who runs the Warriors highlife band, I have recorded an all-blind band from the Volta Region of Ghana called Markporlawo and led by Ewe singer Christian Dzizzan (two of these recordings are featured on *Guitar and Gun II*). Recently I worked with the Adom Professionals, a guitar-band and concert party from Nsawam, whose nine musicians came together at a school for the blind at Accropong. During the Bokoor recording session, a pale-coloured, dangerous-looking snake came into the studio and circled around the drums while we were in the middle of a song. I was the only sighted person in the room, so the musicians were unaware of it. I didn't want anyone to panic or frighten the snake, so I just kept going. After what seemed a long time, the snake reared its head, looked at us, and disappeared out of the door. Afterwards, when I told the musicians about our visitor, they said it was good to have left the snake alone as it was blessing us. Later I talked to the leader of the group, thirty-year-old Nti Agyeman, about the main problems facing them on tour.

Nti Agyeman: It's difficult because at the place we play we don't get accommodation afterwards. And when we don't rest we become exhausted and can't work as happily as we like. Sometimes we go on trek (tour) for up to forty days at a time.

Q: Do you think music's a good business for blind people to be in?

Nti Agyeman: Yes, and this is one of our prime aims in forming the band. You see, we wanted to create a chance for the blind in this country as in our days, when you completed school for the blind you either had to be a typist or crafts teacher. It is only quite recently that the government has made it possible for some blind people to go to the university and become lawyers. But formerly there were only

*The Adom Professionals, blind guitar-band from Ghana. The leader,
Nti Agyeman, is seated on the right.*

two channels of employment and we wanted to extend these to three. We also want to portray the capability of the disabled and blind people. You know, some people think that when you are blind or disabled you just become—excuse me to say—useless. Our second aim is to raise funds to assist other disabled persons and I would like to make this appeal to individuals and organisations throughout the world. When they get any disabled person in the family I beg them to send them to schools to learn something and become useful in the future. Also we want to go abroad to show people what we are doing here in Ghana and to let them know what the blind can do.

A Witness to Change

Since I started recording in 1982, the music scene has changed considerably as a result of the death of some major musicians as well as the growing importance of the church and women in the music business.

I first met Teddy Owusu, one of the greatest sax players in Ghana, in the mid-1970s on one of my trips to Nigeria with the Bunzus band. Teddy was in the habit of going everywhere, however far it was, on foot. We met him in Togo walking from Accra to Lagos, as Fela Anikulapo-Kuti wanted him to play for his group. I recall we had great difficulty persuading Teddy to get into our bus even though we were going to the same place and he knew we were all musicians. Teddy was a determined fellow and devoted to his music. I remember that in 1981/82 (several years before he died), when he was recording in my studio (actually in my kitchen, as that was where the studio was then) Teddy collapsed after a sax solo and continued to direct the session lying on his back in bed. Despite a serious illness and doctors' warnings, Teddy continued playing until his death.

When I first met Nii Koi, a wizard on Hawaiian guitar, he was already elderly; he had come to play with blind Christian Dzizzan's band; he plays the Hawaiian guitar on the two Mork-porlawo songs on *Guitar and Gun II*. Nii Koi died shortly after he brought his own band down to be recorded. Kwesi Abeka, pastor of the Christo Asafo church, was leader of that church's Genesis Gospel Singers, whose music is featured on the Cherry Red *Guitar and Gun I* and the *Ntutu* albums. By the time of his death in a car crash, Kwesi had become a very good friend.

Over the years, Samuel Paa Gyima, one of the top session guitarists in Ghana, played in several bands I've recorded, including Genesis, Adinkra, Francis Kenya's, and Kwese Menu's; he died in 1987. Another musician who had played with numerous groups was Dan Bokovi Banini, who played the bongos for many dancebands in the 1950s and 1960s and was also an active member of the musicians' union. I first met him when we were both members of the Bunzus, and he later joined my Bokoor Band as a percussionist. Dan was a great teacher of traditional African percussion; in this capacity he worked with Phillip Cobson's Aklowa organisation in London, and I remember seeing Dan play at the Albert Hall then. More recently he taught at the Kokrobiti drumming school near Accra, run by Mustapha Tetteh-Addy and his German wife. Dan recorded at my studio on numerous occasions and was one of my drum teachers. He died quite suddenly in 1989.

Even as musical styles and tastes change, these musicians will be remembered for their unique contributions to the development of Ghana's music and their influence on other musicians.

Gospel Highlife

From my studio vantage point, I can see how the music scene has changed since 1982, when the greatest proportion of bands that I recorded were highlife guitar- and concert party bands. By 1989/90 local gospel guitar-bands were in the forefront. They still play danceable highlifes, but with Christian lyrics, and in many cases employ the very same musicians who previously were with concert bands. The Separatist, Apostolic, and Spiritual Healing churches (like the Ethiopian and Zionist churches of southern Africa and the Aladura church of Nigeria) have for many years used drumming, clapping, and dancing in their services; in fact, this is one of the reasons why they broke away from the European churches, which viewed this type of worship as pagan. From the late 1970s the Ghanaian churches simply began to augment their drumming groups with guitars. In addition, the economic problems of the late 1970s and early 1980s in Ghana put many secular guitar- and concert bands out of business, and so their musicians drifted into the church bands that gave them an audience and patronage.

One such church is the Christo Asafo Mission, founded in 1971 after a visionary dream by the then twenty-five-year-old Prophet Kwadwo Safo (who had been a welder). The church now has fifteen thousand members. At first the members of this church clapped, danced, and sang in Twi (an Akan language). Since 1980 they have set up seven guitar-bands, including the Genesis Gospel Singer, Kuntum Thirteen, and Supreme Christian Singers (or Cal-

Prophet Kwadwo Safo of the Christo Asafo Mission, which uses seven guitar-bands in its mission outreach program.

vary Bells), all of whom I recorded and were featured on the *Guitar and Gun* albums. Kwesi Abeka of the Genesis band took me to the church's New Year celebration in 1984 as a guest of honour (together with Steve Obimpeh of the National Mobilisation Committee and Atto Austin, the minister of labour); during the celebration, the church donated food from its many farms to needy charities. Some time later, I asked Prophet Safo what made him decide to form so many bands and even stage religious musical plays.

Prophet Safo: I had a dream about music and woke up and started to buy instruments and straight away began to teach my people as I was able to control all the instruments and amplifiers by the dream. I even began to compose and arrange in my dreams as the music just used to come into my head.

Q: Why do you use highlifes and not European hymns?

Prophet Safo: Even the songs that Jesus and the disciples sang weren't European ones. If you look at Matthew 26–30 you will see that Jesus told the disciples at the Last Supper that they should all sing a hymn with him. Europeans would consider this a pagan song as they never met Christ. So there's nothing wrong with us using our highlifes.

Prophet Safo (wearing headband), demonstrating meals that can be prepared from local maize. His church is involved in many agricultural projects.

Some of the other many church bands that I have recorded are the Advent Heralds, the band of the Universal Prayer Fellowship Church (whose leader, the Reverend J. M. Odonkor, released an album in London), the King's Stewards, the Golden Gates, Sons and Daughters, the Gospel Sowers, James Antwi's band (an ex-Bokoor Band member), Compassion Inspiration (that featured Ray Ellis on keyboard), the Metallic Singers, the Blessed Elim Singers, the Saint Michael's group, El Shaddai, and the group of the Africanium church whose leader, the Reverend Damoah, was for a time a member of Flight Lieutenant Rawling's PNDC government. In addition, the concert party musician Francis Kenya, who left Ghana with his band in the early 1980s for the Côte d'Ivoire due to economic reasons, later set up a spiritual church in Abidjan, although he continued to run his band, which occasionally visits Ghana. In fact, there are now so many gospel guitar-bands in Ghana that in 1987 they set up their own National Association of Gospel Bands, which is affiliated with the Musicians' Union of Ghana (MUSIGA).

This move of Ghanaian popular music from the secular to the sacred is reminiscent to what happened in the United States sixty years ago. After the boom of blues music of the 1920s came the Great Depression, when many blues artists due to economic reasons began to operate in the Afro-American churches, where they created "hot gospel" out of a fusion of the blues and spirituals. In the 1960s this music moved out of the churches to become the "soul" music of James Brown, Aretha Franklin, Roberta Flack, and others.

The Growing Importance of Women Popular Artists

When I first began working as a musician in Ghana in the late 1960s, few women artists were active in the pop music scene. One of the first was Juliana Okine, who sang with E. T. Mensah's Tempos in the 1950s. In the 1960s Vida Rose ran a concert party. The concert parties generally employed men playing female parts (both for singing and acting) up to 1960, when the government formed the Worker's Brigade Concert Party that employed actresses. In 1969 Efua Sutherland of the University of Ghana launched her Kusum Agoromba concert party, which featured the actresses Esi

Kom and Adelaide Buabeng. Since then, many other concert actresses have become popular, such as Beatrice Kissi, Florence Mensah, Joyce Agyeman, and Mary Adjei of the Osofo Dadzie concert party, and Grace Omaboe (Mammy Dokonu) of the Obra group.

Only since the 1970s has a generation of female highlife singers come onto the local pop scene. Inspired by Western and black American women artists as well as by South Africa's Miriam Makeba, these include Lola Everett, Charlotte Dada (who worked with Pat Thomas), Ewe singer Efua Dokonu, and soprano sax player Eugenia Asabea Cropper (wife of Joe Mensah). A more recent addition is Lady Talata Heidi from northern Ghana, who had done session work in my studio and later recorded in Cotonu and released two albums.

This new prominence of women in Ghanaian popular music sped up in the 1980s due to the rise of gospel highlife. Previously the guitar and its music in Ghana (and West Africa generally) had been associated with drunkenness, loose living, and palm-wine bars; consequently it was frowned upon and put out of bounds by the families of young women. These days, however, parents can't stop their daughters from joining church choirs that are backed by highlife guitar-bands, and so there is an influx of church-trained women singers into the commercial popular music scene and recording studios.

Keeping West African Pop Roots Alive

One consequence of these changes in the music scene is that some of us have been convinced of the importance of preserving West Africa's pop music recordings. I am now in the process of helping set up Bokoor African Popular Music Archives. Over the last twenty years, I have accumulated a vast number of studio tapes and have collected old shellac 78 rpm records of West African popular music from the 1930s to 1960s. My record collections have been enthusiastically supported with the encouragement and donations of others who also believe in documenting our musical heritage— King Bruce, the late Kwaa Mensah, and Robert Sprigge, an Englishman who is a lecturer in the University of Ghana's History

Department and who used to play piano with the Red Spots high-life band in the 1950s. Other musicians, including E. T. Mensah and Koo Nimo, have helped with the project and I have had very special support from Beattie Casely-Hayford, who was the head of the Ghana Broadcasting Corporation for some years and ran a small "bush-type" recording studio back in the 1960s. For many years Beattie had wanted to establish an institute for highlife in Ghana, but his dream had not yet been realized when he died unexpectedly in 1989.

This is a particularly crucial time for such efforts due to the economic problems of Ghana, the exodus of local musicians, and the influx of mobile discos onto the dance floors. The live popular music scene in the country is declining and preserving this aspect of Ghanaian culture for future generations is parallel to the efforts of the university, arts councils, and other groups in preserving traditional music. I hope that the Bokoor African Popular Music Archives (BAPMAF) will be one of many organisations to preserve and teach highlife and other forms of Ghanaian and African popular music.

Cross-Overs

26 *Africa Goes West*

*M*ost people know that jazz, blues, and Latin-American music partly came from Africa, but do not realise that these dance-styles were not only taken back to Africa, where they became incorpo-

Ginger Johnson (on squeeze-drum) and his drummers playing with the Rolling Stones.

rated into the local music, but that these local fusions then crossed back over the Atlantic.

There are many early examples of these cross-overs of modern African music and its musicians. For instance, the Gold Coast Police Band introduced live highlife music to England in the late 1930s at the coronation of King George VI. Then, in the 1940s and 1950s, African musicians played with top American and British dance-bands and naturally pushed their own local music. Two of these were Ghanaian Caleb Quaye and Guy Warren. Warren played drums for Kenny Graham's Afro-cubists in London and then introduced Afro music to the States. Another was the late Ginger Johnson, a Nigerian drummer who played with the Edmundo Ros Band and later set up his own African drum orchestra and the Iroqo Club in London.

In today's pop world this process has gathered momentum and many African artists have a base in Europe and the States, visit these countries, and release records abroad.

27 The Original African Cross-Overs

Ghanaba and Kwesi Asare

Kofi Ghanaba (Guy Warren)

One of the earliest and most famous of the cross-over musicians is Ghanaian ace drummer Guy Warren, or Kofi Ghanaba as he is now called. In his early days he was influenced by jazz and took his Afro-jazz fusions to America in the 1950s, where they caught on with black Americans. He met and played with most of the top black jazz musicians in the States and influenced them to turn back to their African roots.

I first met Ghanaba in 1974 at his palatial home built from the royalties from his record releases. Being in advance of his times in every way, he was one of the first African musicians to get his songs copyrighted. Today he is a rather mysterious figure who likes being on his own and derives his spiritual powers from his drumming and his Buddhist faith.

Ghanaba was born in Accra in 1923 and from early on in life became interested in drums, both local percussion and jazz drumming.

We lived in downtown Accra where they had this bar that catered to seamen, prostitutes, and pimps. They had a combo there and we could hear them from where we were living. They played ragtimes. I learned to tap-dance and there was this great drummer who died, Harry Dodoo, a jazz drummer who used to juggle with the sticks and joke, just like Baby Dodds. He was my hero. Also, in my house, there were some Ewe people and every Saturday night they would hold a traditional drum session, for they are a very musical tribe. We used to have masquerade parades in Accra every Christmas and everybody would do a sort of poor man's quadrille to the sound of the bass drum, flute, and pati-drum.

For a time, Ghanaba was a member of the Accra Rhythmic Orchestra but found its music too "ballroomish." So, just after the Second World War, he joined the famous Tempos dance-band of E. T. Mensah. Ghanaba not only brought his excellent jazz drumming to this band, but he also introduced Afro-Cuban percussion instruments, since he had played with Kenny Graham's Afrocubists in London for a time.

But jazz was Ghanaba's first love. According to E. T., he was so fanantical about jazz, that when the Tempos were playing a highlife or foxtrot Ghanaba would only play half-heartedly, keeping all his energy back for the jazz numbers. Ghanaba developed a perfect American accent, which he explains, once got him into trouble at the European Club in Accra:

> During the intermission I went over to see a white guy. This guy's Canadian friend said, "What's an American nigger doing here?" He thought I was an American and I thought he was one. He pushed me and I saw red and thrashed his arse out. You see this was the sort of club where Africans were only seen padding about gently, dressed in white tunics and here I was beating this guy up. It was a sensation.

Ghanaba left the Tempos in 1950 and spent a few years in Liberia as a radio disc jockey. Then he made his way to America, where he met many of the greats, including singer Billie Holiday, Duke Ellington (whom Ghanaba calls "God's gift to musicians"), Count Basie ("a real gentleman"), Lester Young ("a gentle guy"), and Charlie Parker ("a drifter" to whom Ghanaba was particularly close). He went to the States with the intention of playing jazz. But it did not work out quite like that, for when he got there he realised

> I could never play like Gene Krupa, Max Roach, or Louis Bellson. They have a different culture. So I had to make a choice of being a poor imitation of Buddy Rich or playing something they couldn't. So I started to play African music with a little bit of jazz thrown in, not jazz with a little African thrown in. For it is African music that is the mother, not the other way around. But I had to find out the hard way!

It was in Chicago that he met his muse, to be "the African musician who reintroduced African music to America to get Americans to be aware of this cultural heritage of black people." It was from this time that he produced a series of revolutionary albums like *Africa Speaks, America Answers, Theme for African Drums, African Sounds, Third Phase,* and *Afro-Jazz*.

Ghanaba anticipated many of the Afro and root trends of the 1970s and the present generation of black musicians. In many ways he is their spiritual father and that is why Ghanaba is so critical of musicians who merely copy other people. He has gone through the whole process himself—of leaving home in search of a new sound and ending up coming back home.

Since the late 1960s he has been based in Ghana, and has been helping to develop the local music scene and collecting a vast archive of black music from all over the world. He also played at the meeting of black American and African musicians at the "Soul to Soul Concert" held in Accra in 1971.

His son, Glen Warren, is a well known drummer, and recently father and son released an album.

Ghanaba was far ahead of his time. The rise of African music to an international level, that he has struggled for all these years, is now well under way. The famous Afro-American jazz drummer, Max Roach, recognised Ghanaba's contribution to black music. In a letter written in 1973, he says,

> In this letter I would like to record that Ghanaba was so far ahead of what we were doing (in the fifties) that none of us understood

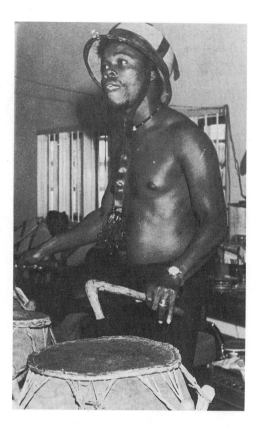

Glenn Warren.

what he was saying—that in order for Afro-American music to be stronger, it must cross-fertilise with its African origins. Ghanaba's conception, like that of Marcus Garvey, George Washington Carver etc., was beyond our grasp. We ignored him. Seventeen years later Black music in America has turned to Africa for inspiration and rejuvenation and the African sounds of Ghanaba are now being played all over the United States, wherever Afro-American music is played.

Ghanaba is still very active. On July 14, 1988, he and Nigerian drummers Bayo Martins and Remi Kabaka played an extraordinary percussion session together at the W. E. B. DuBois Memorial Centre in Accra, during a three-day "Focus on Nigeria" event during which the Nigerian high commissioner in Ghana presented

Jam session with drummer Bayo Martins (left) and Kofi Ghanaba (right). (Courtesy Yemo Nunu)

Nigerian cultural material to the centre as a Nigerian contribution to the archival documentation project of the DuBois Centre.

The highlight of the event was a drum workshop, "The Powers of Drums in the Society," introduced by a lecture from Bayo Martins, who is now living in Germany. Fifty-two-year-old Bayo Martins worked with the late Nigerian dance-band leader Bobby Benson in the 1950s and later went on to study at the Central School of Dance Music in London and the School of Radio and Television Journalism in Berkeshire. While in England he formed the Bayo Martins Band Africana. On returning to Nigeria he helped set up the Nigerian Navy Band and also, together with Bobby Benson and Fela, was an executive of the Musicians' Foundation of Nigeria.

In his lecture Bayo Martins first talked about the general impact of music on society, in the realm of politics, communication, religion, medicine, and meditation, summing up by stating that "a

*Kofi Ghanaba and family with drummer Remi Kabaka (*standing, second left*) and friends. (Courtesy Yemo Nunu)*

society without music is a society without soul and may be regarded as dead." Then turning to the topic of drums in particular he said that these have both the power to rouse people to a frenzy as well as sedate them and that the hostility of Europeans to African drums during the days of slavery and colonialism was a result of this instrument being used to stir up and coordinate revolts.

> What causes the drums to be so revered in Africa and so dreaded by others elsewhere? What is the source of powers the drums are believed to possess? How do they influence the mind? Could this influence stem from a number of elements rather than just one source? As a drummer myself I can testify to the mysticism of the drums. There is obviously something in the drums which can be properly termed "power," and this power has a way of affecting people which is universal. For anywhere the drums are played or displayed, whether they are made of hollowed wood covered in hide or of chrome, people—black and white—become excited.

One element in the explanation of the power of drums and music that Bayo Martins gave was that "of all the arts, the art of music has in particular been considered divine because it is the exact miniature of the law working through the whole universe. If we study ourselves, for example, we discover that the beat of the heart, the inhaling and exhaling of the breath are all the workings of rhythms and life depends on the rhythmic working of the whole mechanism of the body."

Martins concluded his lecture by stating that "the drums with its distinct rhythms is the only instrument on the continent that has maintained its true African character, despite years of foreign adulteration . . . and African drumming should be taught and performed in all African schools . . . for a musical mind is a sound mind."

Martins' talk was followed by musical action, the first being a short musical interlude from Nana Danso Abiam's group that consisted of one-stringed gonje-fiddles, the apremprensemma (giant thumb-piano), small thumb-piano, atentebens (bamboo flutes developed by Ephraim Amu), and assorted percussion. And this was immediately followed by the three drum maestros from Nigeria and Ghana.

Ghanaba came on stage to join the two Nigerians, coated in white clay, wearing dark glasses and a white cloth. In spite of his 65 years he looked as fit as a fiddle. He was accompanied by his two daughters, Midie and Mawuko (likewise covered in clay), a man carrying a rifle, and Nigerian talking-drum (odonno) player Ayanbode Oluwole. Ghanaba sat down at his amazing array of Ashanti fontomfrom-drums, accompanied by Bayo Martins on congas. On trap-drums was Remi Kabaka, who over the years has played with many famous names, like Paul McCartney, Steve Winwood, Mick Jagger, Hugh Masekela, Fela, the Afro-rock band Osibisa, and Ginger Baker. In fact Remi traveled across the Sahara Desert with this English rock drummer in 1971/72, when Ginger was on his way to help set up the ARC sixteen-track recording studio in Lagos, the whole journey being filmed for the BBC television documentary "Across the Sahara."

These three master drummers then proceeded to weave a complex tapestry of sounds as they explored common features of the

12/8 rhythmic patterns of Nigeria's konkon beat and Ghana's adowa and agbadza beats. It was a perfect sonic combination with Remi's light and crisp jazz-kit, the spacey and mellow tones of Bayo Martins' congas, and the deep thunder of Ghanaba's fontomfrom-drums. To two of these massive hand-carved drums Ghanaba had attached foot-pedals, so sometimes he would play flute or wave the Ghanaian flag around his head while maintaining the intricate cross-beat with his feet. It was a brilliant dialogue among three master percussionists with each giving the others plenty of room to solo. Whenever Ghanaba's solos took performers and audience alike into out-of-this-world rhythmic dimensions, Remi and Martins were always there to catch the rhythm and bring it back to earth again. This amazing Nigerian/Ghanaian drum communion ended abruptly with a rifle shot from the man who had been standing behind Ghanaba throughout the performance.

And then, just as Ghanaba was drummed in, so he was drummed out by Ayanbode. The drum workshop was truly a salute to this creative Ghanaian drummer who has done so much for African music at home and abroad.

Kwesi Asare—Ghana's Drum Ambassador

Kwesi Asare Asuo Gyebi has unostentatiously been spreading African rhythms abroad for years: to jazz musicians in the late 1950s and 1960s; among West Indian and British youth since the late 1970s; and now in the United States, where in 1987 he was awarded the title of "cultural ambassador" by America's oldest black newspaper, the *Philadelphia Tribune,* founded in 1881.

Kwesi was born in Larteh, a hill-top town in southern Ghana in 1931. On his Guan maternal side he is the grandson (or, more precisely, the grand-nephew) of Nana Oporabea, life president of the Psychic and Traditional Healers Association of Ghana and high priestess of the Larteh Akonedi Shrine (which has branches in New York and Washington, D.C.).

This most important Ghanaian traditional religious centre is in fact today a composite of four spirit cults, each with its own rituals, shrines, and music. The oldest of them is the Akonedi spirit

Kwesi Asare.

shrine founded in the last century by an ancestor of Kwesi's called Nana Adwo Komfo. Junior to this is the Asuo Gyebi spirit (from which Kwesi gets his name), which is embodied in a stone with a hole in it; Kwesi's maternal uncle, Yaw Akyea, the master-drummer for the then Akonedi high priestess Nana Okomfo Ansa, discovered the stone seventy years ago in a forest. The two other spirits of the Larteh shrine are Asi Ktewaa and Adade Kofi, the latter being introduced by Kwesi's grandfather, Kwerku Ahia. And as each of these four religious cults have their own special dances, songs, drums, and rhythms, Kwesi was brought up in the right environment to be groomed as a master-drummer.

In spite of his rich background, Kwesi left Ghana in 1955 to study motor-mechanics in the northern British town of Manchester. He soon gravitated back to music and learned to play alto sax. From then on he worked in a factory but spent all his spare time playing with a succession of Afro-American jazz giants who came on tour of Britain.

In 1958 he met and jammed with Duke Ellington, and the following year began a long relationship with Count Basie. Kwesi and the band's guitarist, the late Freddie Green, began working out Afro-rhythms for this large swing group; Green had advised Kwesi not to copy Basie's music but rather to use what Basie had taught him to play his own African music. With this good advice Kwesi stuck to his drums and in the 1960s played percussion with a number of black American musicians, including singer Sarah Vaughan; pianist Thelonius Monk, who stayed with Kwesi whenever he was playing in Manchester; and the multi-instrumentalist Roland Kirk, who played with Kwesi at the Club 43. Kwesi explains that he was able to play with these top American musicians because "when I came to England I studied Western music and could hear that blues, jazz, and soul grew out of African music. They go side-by-side, so I can play drums with anybody."

In the late 1970s and with a growing British interest in roots music, Kwesi began teaching African drumming to the Afro-Caribbean community in Manchester. And in fact this is when I first met him; for in 1979/80 I and two Ghanaian members of my Bokoor Band were teaching unemployed West Indian youths African guitar-band music at the Wolverhampton Centre for Community Relations, and Kwesi often came down to help us out.

Finally in 1982, with the help of the North-West Arts Council, Kwesi set up his own band called the Kantamanto Kruti Ayisi Cultural Group (Twi for "my word is my bond") made up of unemployed West Indian youths from Manchester's Moss Side. This group, consisting of five men and four women, began playing all over Britain—at the Royal Festival Hall and Almeida Theatre in London, the Arnofini Theatre in Bristol, and the International Jazz Festival in Hayfield.

In 1987 Kwesi went to the United States, where he spent six months in Philadelphia. He taught African music at schools, academies, and art institutions. He and the famous Afro-American jazz drummer Edgar Bateman gave a series of workshops entitled "African Rhythms and American Music" at Coltrane House, dedicated to the Afro-American sax virtuoso John Coltrane. (Coltrane, who died at age 40 in 1967, had lived in the house, which is now a cultural centre and museum run by his cousin Mary Alexander.)

Kwesi also accompanied the poet Elizabeth Suber Bennett (who subsequently became his manager) on talking-drums at the Afro-American Historical and Cultural Museum.

In spite of his heavy teaching schedule, Kwesi still had time to jam in Philadelphia with trombonist Al Grey at Jewel's Lounge, with Count Basie's band at the Trocadero Club, and several times with the Sun Ra Arkestra at the New York Cafe Club. Indeed, Philadelphians liked Kwesi so much and were so inspired by his wise and sensitive teaching approach that he was invited there again. This modest master-drummer explains the magic of his international success in this way:

> You can't be selfish when you're playing. You have to be sincere. If you have ego problems you have no chance. Don't think about yourself, "Look at me, watch me." That's no good. You have to be honest and put all your heart to it. Don't be afraid of learning. Don't be afraid of asking someone who knows more than you. Don't be shy. If you know you don't know but won't ask, you are being insincere and full of ego. . . . When you're playing you're gaining sound, then you create more sound and rhythm—but not all at once. So try to hear other things. Listen a lot, listen, listen.

28   Roots, Rasta, Reggae

Stepping-Stones back to Africa

On the West, "progress" is no longer taken for granted. On the one hand, it is no longer automatic because of limited resources and the claims of the underdeveloped world to basic human rights and to a fair division of the world's resources. On the other hand, the negative effects of progress through overmechanisation cannot be turned off. These negative effects include technological determinism, squandering of resources, industrial serfdom, and redundancy. This has led to a basic questioning of the tenets of technological civilisation and a reevaluation of cultural traditions. An example of this quest is the immense success of Afro-American Alex Haley's book *Roots,* which traces his ancestors all the way back to Africa and looks at what happened in the New World.

Roots in the Caribbean

The biggest upsurge of the "back to Africa" identity and heritage theme has come from the Caribbean, with its reggae music, preaching the doom and downfall of Babylon, that is, Western civilisation. Reggae is the most recent of a number of Jamaican dance-styles following the calypsos and mento of the colonial peri-od. The first of these new styles was ska or blue beat, fast dance music in which the rhythm of calypso was combined with black American rhythm and blues but with the beat turned inside out. The biggest commercial success of this music was Millicent Small's "My Boy Lollipop," Chris Blackwell's first Island Record success, released in the early 1960s. By the mid-1960s this tune had become so well known that Millie made two tours of Africa.

Ska was followed in the late 1960s by a slowing down of the beat to rock steady, played by bands like the Heptones and artists like Ken Boothe.

Around 1970 the tempo sped up a little into reggae. Main art-ists were Desmond Dekker, Jimmy Cliff, Toots and the Maytals, Peter Tosh, and Bob Marley and the Wailers. This music has dom-inated the world music market.

Linked with the waxing of reggae music was the surfacing of the Jamaican millenarian cult, Rastafarianism, a cult of protest against discrimination. The collapse of the overcomplex Western world is forecast and followers are urged to return to their roots and a simpler way of life. This Ethiopian Christian church is based on the beliefs of Jamaican Marcus Garvey, who in the 1920s pre-dicted that a King of kings would be crowned in Africa. This would be the signal for the downfall of the West and the repatria-tion of blacks to Africa.

This prediction seemed to come true when Haile Selassie was made Emperor, King of kings, and the Lion of Judah in 1930, and later when the Italian colonialists were defeated. The word "Ras-tafarian" comes from the royal title of Haile Selassie, Ras Tafari. It was also widely believed that Selassie was the leader of a secret society called the Nyabingi. Members of this society had long matted hair, used ganja as a sacrament, and were dedicated to over-throwing white and black oppressors. The dreadlocks of the Rastas were copied from these "nyamen," as the West Indians call them.

By the 1950s there were Rasta communities all over Jamaica and their spiritual music, dance, and chants were played on hand-drums and rumba boxes. The Rastas reached a state of possession through their music and through "trumping" (rhythmic deep breathing). Disorientation of the everyday perceptions leads to heightened perception and to transformation.

It is the religious music of Rasta that has so deeply influenced reggae, turning it into the apocalyptic roots reggae of Bob Marley and the Wailers.

Rasta Spreads to Europe

In spite of all opposition, reggae music and the Rastafarian faith have not only flourished in their birthplace, but in Europe as well, the very heart of Babylon, where the first Industrial Revolution took place. In Britain, where many West Indians were invited to settle in the 1950s with the hope of a bright future, these immigrants saw their children condemned to unemployed life in city ghettos like Saint Paul's in Bristol, Notting Hill in London, and Toxteth in Liverpool—the very places where the youth, spearheaded by blacks, have gone on the offensive against the police. At the Notting Hill Jamaican Carnival in London, attracting a half-million tourists, violent clashes between youths and the police occurred several times, although recent carnivals have been peaceful. The disillusionment with British life-style and establishment is expressed by the poet Linton Kwesi Johnson, born in Jamaica but brought up in Brixton. He has gone back to the African tradition of combining poetry, music, and dance with social and political commentary. In poems like "Dread inna Inglan," he has become a spokesman for frustrated youth.

Today in the United Kingdom not only West Indian youths, but people in general, are becoming more interested in Africa. Information is provided by institutes such as Aklowa House run by the Ghanaian Felix Cobbson, the Iroqo Club of the late Ginger Johnson of Nigeria, and the Africa Centre run by the OAU (Organisation of African Unity). As a result, in the last few years, a number of bands and dance groups playing Afro-Caribbean music have been set up jointly by West Indians and Africans.

Steel and Skin was set up in the mid-1970s by Jamaican-born Peter Blackman. This London group combines the music of Ca-

Steel and Skin.

ribbean steel drums with African hand-drums and wooden xylophone, and features traditional African dances.

Lanzel (Unity) was set up in 1978 by an African master-drummer together with some unemployed West Indian youths, who were members of a black self-help organisation called Harambee. There are many other mixed bands, like Ekome, Mystic and the Israelites, Kutamba, Black Velvet, Matta Fancanta, Maas Movers, and the Ujaama Players. Ekome (Unity) was formed in Saint Paul's, Bristol, in 1977 by Barrington Anderson and his sister Angela, after a series of Steel and Skin workshops.

Afro-Caribbean group, Ekome.

Originally Ekome was formed by unemployed West Indian youths, but later Ghanaian dancers and drummers came to help them, making them into one of the best Afro-Caribbean groups in the country (they've appeared on television with Pattie Boulaye). Since 1982 Ekome has been holding its own arts festival in Bristol and has also launched an educational programme for school-children. Barrington and company have also helped set up Afro-Caribbean bands elsewhere, like Uzuri Binti from Swindon, the Cardiff Afro-Caribbean Dance Group, Kwame Nkrumah from Gloucester, and the African Arts Project at Derby. Ekome has gone electric and has added a full-scale dance-band to its cultural group, which plays West Indian and African music and features the famous Jamaican trombonist Vinnie Gordon.

Just as with West Indians, these groups are becoming popular with the white youth, as many of the Afro-Caribbean bands are teaching African drumming and dancing in the primary schools.

So whites have begun to play African music. The Ojah band contains musicians from England and Africa. Then there is German drum-freak Jojo Wolfe and Ghanaian guitarist Kris Bediako, creating their klogo-motion, based on the kpanlogo rhythm of the Gas of Ghana. Also from London is Dagarti, a band with musicians from as far afield as Africa, the West Indies, England, Australia, and New Zealand.

Even some of the African musicians who came to the West to play pop and jazz are being infected by the roots movement. Gaspar Lawal went to England in the 1960s and played with top rock bands there such as the Rolling Stones and Airforce. In 1980 Gaspar released his *Ajomase* album, which prominently features traditional African percussion and the kora, a harp-lute.

So whether it's the Afro-American roots-jazz musicians like Sun Ra and Taj Mahal, the rasta and reggae music of the West Indies, or the mixed Afro-Caribbean bands of Europe, all eyes and ears are now on Africa.

It is not at all surprising, then, that West Indian music, particularly reggae, has crossed back over to Africa and top stars like Jimmy Cliff, Eddy Grant, and the late Bob Marley have made tours there.

Reggae in Africa

Reggae is having an immense impact on the modern African music scene and has been copied by many local musicians there. This process has led to the emergence of African reggae, which is feeding back into the international reggae scene.

The most internationally well-known Afro-reggae stars are Nigeria's Sunny Okosun (who released "Papa's Land" and "Fire in Soweto") and Alpha Blondy of the Côte d'Ivoire. But there are many others.

In Nigeria, Victor Uwaifo has been experimenting with Jamaican music for a number of years in such songs as "When the Sun Shines" and "Five Day a Week Love." Bongos Ikwue has also been playing reggae numbers. More recently Victor Essiet and Peggy Umanah of the Mandators had two hit reggae albums in Nigeria, *Crisis* (1987) and *Rat Race* (1988). And Nigeria's current top reggae woman, Evi Edna Ogholi-Ogosi, has released three albums since 1987—*My Kind of Music, On the Move,* and *Happy Birthday*—and she is popular in Ghana as well. In fact, six of her nine-piece band are from a Ghanaian group called Big Eye. The most recent Nigerian reggae releases are Ras Kimono's *Under Pressure* and Majek Fashek's *Prisoner of Conscience*. Majek was influenced by both Bob Marley and Steel Pulse, who visited Nigeria in the early 1980s.

One of Ghana's top guitar-bands, the African Brothers, in their release *None But You* have fused local highlifes with reggae— as have the City Boys, Kumapim Royals, Grass Roots, and Salam's Cultural Imani group, to name but a few. Other groups such as the Classic Handels, the Classic Vibes (who moved to Europe in the mid-1980s), and Felix Bell concentrate on reggae numbers.

Liberian singer Miatta Fahnbulleh's "Koko-rioko" is a reggae/traditional song that she has released as a twelve-inch single. Also released as a twelve-inch disco record is an Afro-reggae by a Nigerian band called Cloud Seven, simultaneously released by Otis Brothers in Africa and Europe. Gaspar Lawal's roots album *Ajomase* contains a reggae track entitled "Kita Kita."

One of the most successful blends of reggae and African music has been the brainchild of Rokafil Jazz from eastern Nigeria, which used a reggae-type bass line in its smash hit "Sweet Mother."

So with reggae music looking to Africa for inspiration, and African musicians playing local versions of reggae, it is no wonder that the resulting Afro-reggae fusion is breaking all national boundaries and drawing the pop scenes of Europe, the New World, and Africa closer together.

29   *Africa and New Wave*

*N*ew wave and punk music have turned toward Africa for inspiration. Perhaps the West has run out of ideas or wants to get back to a balanced body music again. Maybe it is just the general disillusionment with Western civilisation's unemployment, pollution, the arms race, and creative disintegration.

New wave and punk originally emerged in the mid-1970s as a reaction to the optimism of 1960s rock, with its gurus, superstars, and stoned-out, passive audiences.

Punk brought this rarefied music down to earth, and got the fans on their feet, dancing to live and immediate music. They did this by getting back to the origins of rock, the rock and roll and skiffle of the 1950s. Rock and roll itself is a copy of black rhythm and blues, and therefore the punks were copying a copy of black music.

Two-Tone

Unemployment and decay are particularly evident in Britain's industrial Midlands, where new wave's shift to black roots came about. It started in 1978 when the two-tone phenomenon was launched by the Coventry-based band, the Specials. This mixed black and white band fused white punk lyrics with black ska and reggae music. Many groups followed suit, such as the Beat, Madness, Body Snatchers, Selecter, Swinging Cats, and UB40.

As Selecter's Neal Davies says, "This world tries to separate everything, but two-tone means nonseparation and bringing together, seeing things in their entirety. Thus, two-tone is proving that black and white can work together harmoniously in Britain."

This black and white fusion reflects a growing interest in Afro-Caribbean and African music. For instance, Dave Steele of the Beat called his music "psychedelic calypso." The band's black saxist, Saxa, specialised in tangos, mambas, and cha-cha-chas. The Beat's two guitarists used the African technique of cross-rhythms and inside rhythms. According to Dave Wakelin, the band's white guitarist, "Andy, the Jamaican guitarist, and I get cross-rhythms going—me going down while he's going up—and these create a third rhythm of their own."

Vaughan Tru of the Swinging Cats moved his two-tone sound from ska to the bossa nova. In 1980 the Piranhas group got as far as number 5 in the British Top Twenty with their punk version of the South African jive "Tom Harke." Many English kids began to whistle this catchy tune without realising it was from Africa. The Specials and Bombay Duck started using African-type clip rhythms in some of their songs in 1980.

This trend in new wave continued. Adam and the Ants and Bow-wow-wow used Burundi drumming from East Africa in some of their hits and John Lydon's band, Public Image, used North African drums. When I visited the home of Ian Dury of the Blockheads, I discovered that he was building up a collection of Fela Anikulapo-Kuti's albums.

One reviewer of the Police said that this band had "an African feeling, being ardent exploiters of gaps in music, always emphasising the bits around the beat, rather than the beat itself." Selector actually had two African members: Ghanaian-born guitarist Compton Amanor and vocalist Pauline Black, who is half-Nigerian.

This move toward Africa has been recognised by one of new wave's leading lights, English musician Brian Eno, who is based in New York. In a three-page interview in *New Musical Express* in 1980, Brian explained that he became a fan of highlife and Fela's Afro-beat because he considered them "perfect for dancing to, as they leave holes in all the right places." At the end of 1980, he visited Ghana for three weeks and worked with African musicians there.

What the new wave musicians and fans appreciate is that music must be danced to and that Africa is pop's supreme source of dance music. Instead of the deafening and overwhelming sounds of heavy metal rock and extreme forms of punk, people are now looking for music with holes and space inside. Space within the criss-crossing rhythms gives everyone a chance to create and swing around in that space. Many music fans are fed up with the follow-the-leader approach of watching superstars ego-tripping. Instead of watching passively, they want to get up and participate. They want a balanced music rather than wild, loud noise. Punk started off as pure noise, but two-tone was a move toward a balance.

It is no wonder that many new wave stars such as Brian Eno, Malcolm McClaren, David Byrne, Stewart Copeland, and Sting began turning toward African music in the 1980s. African music is body music, compelling everybody to participate. African music has been a balancing factor behind the scenes in Western popular music ever since ragtime, as African music has space inside for all.

30   *Black and White*

So much has been happening recently in the African music scene of Europe and America that I will finish off this musical cross-over section of the book with a brief look at the African music bands in the West, country by country. Some are composed solely of Africans, some are mixed, and a few are completely white.

Britain

Britain is a major focus for African music at the moment, especially since the World Festival of Music and Dance (WOMAD), held in 1982 at Shepton Mallet in the west of England, at which many African and Afro bands played, like the Konte Family, a griot group from Gambia who had just released an album on Virgin called *Mandinka Music*. From East Africa came the Master Drummers of Burundi, who were featured on a Joni Mitchell album in 1975 called *The Hissing of the Summer Lawns*. Another traditional African group that played at WOMAD was the Cultural Group from the Dagomba area of northern Ghana.

Highlife superstar Prince Niko from eastern Nigeria was also there, backed by the London-based Ivory Coasters. This band was formed in 1980 by saxophonist Stuart Boardman and guitarists David Draper and Musi Musawi. Musi, from Cameroons, later left to form the Banana Bunch and then the Bushmasters. The Ivory Coasters, with its brand of soukous or congolese music, was very popular, with Dave and Stuart backed by Martin McManus

Master-drummers of Burundi.

on percussion, Dave Kenard on drums, Martin Robinson on bass, and George Howder and Claude Deppa (South African) on trombone and trumpet, respectively.

Gaspar Lawal also played at WOMAD, with his Drum Oro Band, as did mixed African/West Indian bands like Steel and Skin, Aklowa, and Ekome.

British pop-bands with an Afro feel also played at the festival, like the Beat with their African-like cross-rhythms created out of a blend of rock and ska. Then there was King Trigger from Bristol, who play a jungle beat. XTC from Swindon released a song on the WOMAD album called "It's Nearly Africa." This double album, *Music and Rhythm* (released by WEA), contains many songs from the artists who played at the festival, plus top stars who have been bitten by the African bug, like Brian Eno, David Byrne, Peter Gabriel, and Pete Townshend.

British-based Ivory Coasters. (Courtesy Duffy Weir)

Gaspar Lawal.

Ekome.

Orchestra Jazira.

One of the most successful London-based African bands is Orchestra Jazira, which operates from Dalston in North London, where it is associated with the Jenako Arts Centre run by Richard Austin.

This band comprises eleven musicians—six Africans and five whites. Isaac Tagoe and George Fiawoo on percussion came from the London-based Ghanaian cultural group run by Felix Cobbson (Aklowa). Also from Ghana are bassist Opata Azu and Kwarkwo Oteng on keyboard. From Sierra Leone there's Follo Graff on rhythm guitar. Martin Nii Moi is one of the more recent members. For many years, he played with the Ghanaian army dance-band, the Black Berets (a band in which we both played together in the mid-1970s). English members of Jazira include Nigel Watson on drums, who used to be with the Holloway All Stars, and Ben Mandelson on lead guitar, who helped compile the *Sounds D'Afrique* album for Island Records. Jazira's front line is an all-female one with Jane Shorrer (ex-Thompson Twins) on tenor sax, and on alto sax Nicky Scott Francis, who has played with South African Julian Bahula and with a feminist band called Jam Today. Finally there's the trombonist "Fish," a musician, juggler, and street performer who played with the women's collective theatre known as Cunning Stunts. Jazira has released one disco 45 called

Love/Dedevi (Earthworks label) and with its fusion of black and white, male and female has built up a large fan club of dancers. But I'll let the bassist Opata have the last say about the group:

> We can play many types of music but it's now time for African music to come forward. African music is peace and love and it is international. We are English and African and we want the African to realise that the time for fighting is over—it is time to unite. We want Jazira to be a symbol of our unity.

Also managed by Jenako Arts is the Sierra Leonean band the Super Combo. This group was originally formed in 1975 and had six hits with funky meringues in Sierra Leone. Then disaster hit in London when all their equipment was stolen and they faded out of sight for many years. Now, with the growing interest in African music in London, they have re-formed. The lineup of the group is guitars (Emil Ogoo and Len Jones), drums (Sidiku Foster), percussion (Akie Kamara), bass (Lonnie Williams), and vocals (Otis Thompson).

Also based in London are the Highlife Internationals, led by guitarist Kwabena Oduro Kwarteng, who spent six years with the Ranchis Band of Ghana before going to Britain in 1976. Fellow Ghanaians Ashilley and Herman Asafo-Adjei are on percussion and bass, respectively. Then from South Africa comes saxophonist Frank Williams and drummer Tzu Tzu Mihaly and from Britain Stuart Harman on trumpet. Highlife Internationals have signed up to do an album with Stern's African Record Centre (Britain's oldest African record shop).

Alpha Waves is another popular London-based Ghanaian highlife band, led by ace saxophonist Ray Allen. Ray was first with the Uhurus dance-band of Ghana until 1970, when he came to Britain and played with Traffic, Eddie Quansah, and Hi-Tension. Willi Stallibras is the guitarist and he once played for Chilli Willi and the Red Hot Peppers and later Ojah. Ghanaian Kofi Adu is the drummer (he also played for Pigbag, which he told me he joined because Pigbag's own drummer couldn't stand flying to gigs!).

Also Ghanaian-led is the Afro-rock group Kabbala, formed in 1980 by trombonist Mike Osapanyin and his younger brother

Alpha Waves.

Isaac Dankwa Osapanyin (percussion). Bass player Herman Asafo-Adjei is from Ghana, and from Nigeria comes James Mene, the drummer.

One of the group's newest members is Osei Tutu, who until recently was the leader of the Edikanfo band. Edikanfo was the resident group at the Napoleon night-club in Accra, which had some production help from Brian Eno for their album released in 1981 on Brian's EG label. The only white member of Kabbala is the saxophone player, who is an Australian woman, Louise Elliot. White women playing what are usually considered to be male instruments seem to be common with the British African bands, and may have something to do with the fact that horns in African music are played in a receptive and feminine way. Instead of blasting out reels of solos, the African horn section punctuates the music and responds to the voices and other instruments, integrating the music rather than dominating it.

A disco 45 by Kabbala called *Ashewo Ara* (Afro-rock) *Voltain Dance* (Rock-Agbadza) got into the British disco charts in 1983.

Mike Osapanyin.

Then there's a London-based group led by Liberian vocalist Corinna Flamma. In 1969 she and her three sisters had a West African hit with their *Bassa Love* release. Then in 1983, with a little help from Nigeria's Gaspar Lawal and Mike Odumosu, she released a single in Britain called "Put Your Spirit Up," a fusion of new wave and African music.

A popular six-piece South African/white band resident in London is Jazz Afrika, led by Julian Bahula. The two other African members are guitarist Lucky Panku and pianist Mervyn Africa. Alan Jackson is on drums, Michael Nielson is on flute and sax, and on double-bass is Roberto Bellatalla.

English pop bands such as Pigbag, Bow-wow-wow, Rip Rig, and Panic have also been influenced by African music. Another is the Cardiff-based band, Weekend, led by bassist Alison Statton (originally with the Young Marble Giants). Highlife, congo jazz, and kwela influences are very noticeable on Weekend's album *La*

Variété. Jimmy the Hoover has also been influenced by the African beat.

Since 1983, when Sunny Ade hit the international scene, a constant stream of African bands have toured Britain, including Nigerian Fela; Eric Agyeman, Smart Nkansah, and A. B. Crentsil from Ghana; Kanda Bongo Man and the late Franco from Zaire; Johnny Clegg's multiracial South African bands Juluka and Savuka; Zimbabwe's Thomas Mapfumo; and Angola's twenty-five-piece band Semba Tropicana.

There are also some new African bands operating permanently in Britain, such as Sierra Leonean Abdul Tee-Jay's Rokoto band and Somo Somo run by the Zairian guitarist Fan Fan, who was for a time with Franco's OK Jazz. Then there are the South African all-woman Shikishi group; the Bhundu (Bush) Boys, a four-piece guitar-band from Zimbabwe; and Taxi Pata Pata, formed in 1986 by Zairian singer N'Simba Foguis and which includes musicians from Zimbabwe, Ghana, Sierra Leone, and Britain.

North America

The United States

The United States is the home of many South African expatriate musicians like Hugh Masekela and Miriam Makeba. In New York, with its African population estimated at fifty thousand, there is a lively African music scene at clubs like Club Afrique and the Fez Ballroom. Resident bands in the city are the African Connection made up of Sierra Leonean and Liberian musicians, and a Liberian band called OAU, which had a Pan-African hit record.

The Mandingo Griot Society is based in Los Angeles and was formed by Gambian kora player Foday Musa Suso and white American percussionist Adam Rudolph, who has played with the Detroit contemporary Jazz Quintet, Eternal Wind, and Streetdance. The two met at the Institute of African Studies at the University of Ghana, and went to America in 1977 to form the Mandingo Griot Society. There they teamed up with three Afro-American musicians: Joseph Thomas on bass guitar; John Markus on lead/rhythm (both played with Earth Wind and Fire, Sun Ra, and Peter Tosh); Hamid Drake on drums (who has toured Africa with black American jazz trumpeter Don Cherry).

The Mandingo Griot Society have brought out two albums on the Flying Fish label, the first one featuring Don Cherry. Suso also provided some of the griot music for the popular television series "Roots," based on the novel by Alex Haley.

It would be impossible to give a full list of all the other African bands operating in the States, so I'll mention a few that I know personally. Two have been created by members of the famous Ghanaian Tetteh-Addy drumming family. Obo Tetteh-Addy runs his eight-piece Kukrudu in Portland, Oregon, which is made up of Ghanaian and black and white Americans. Yacub Tetteh-Addy runs Odadaa (a traditional Ga rhythm) in Washington, D.C. In New Haven Mikata (All of Us) was formed by percussionist Richard Hill in 1979, after he had spent a couple of years in Ghana. Paul Hall and Synia are the dancer-singers, Jeff McQuillan is on bass, Asher Delerme on percussion, Alan Mesquido on alto sax, and George Alford on trumpet, with drummer Ned Grant and guitarist Kenny Blackwell.

In Buffalo, New York, there are several Afro-bands. The oldest is the Outer Circle Orchestra, which was formed in the mid-1970s by Charles Keil (who wrote *Urban Blues*) after he returned from Nigeria, where he studied traditional Tiv music and modern Yoruba juju music for some years (in fact, there was a juju band in Nigeria called the Inner Circle Orchestra). When he returned, he became a professor at the University of Buffalo's American Studies Department and it is from the drumming classes he started there that the band originated. Some of the band's present lineup are Spencer Bolden, Martin Dalmasi, Herbert Tillman, and Andy Byron on percussion, Oren Hollasch on trombone, Senegalese singer Malik Sow, and Charlie on bass guitar. In fact, dozens of musicians have passed through this group, including New York avant-garde jazzman Elliot Sharp and Jerry Augustyniak, the drummer with 10,000 Maniacs.

Two spinoffs from Keil's drum classes and Outer Circle Orchestra are the all-female drum quartet called Street Rhythms, led by Cyndi Cox and flutist Kilissa McGoldrick; and Azucar, formed in 1989 with Mark Dickey on keyboard, percussionist Charlie

Isso, guitarist Ed Handman, and Senegalese drummer Mbaye Rama Diagne.

To add to this African underswell, two new developments have occurred in recent years. In 1988 the first nationwide programme devoted to African popular music began—National Public Radio's Afro-pop series produced by Sean Barlow and hosted by Cameroonian George Collinet. In fact, I was involved in the musical recording and mixing of program number 20 called "Revofest," which was of a live show at Accra's football stadium in 1986.

The other new development is that some of the top bands in the States have become interested in African music. The Grateful Dead now opens its shows with the sixty-year-old New York-based Nigerian master-drummer Babatunde Olatunji and "deadheads" love it. The Talking Heads' album *Naked* uses African and Afro-Caribbean musical ideas. But most important was Paul Simon's 1986 *Graceland* album, which sold 10 million copies and in which he worked with a number of South African musicians and bands, such as Shirinda and the Gaza Sisters, the Zulu vocal group led by Joseph Shabalala called Ladysmith Black Mambazo, the Boyoyo Boys sax and accordion band, and guitarist Chikapa Phiri of the Stimela Band. The album was followed by a Graceland tour, in which the musicians in the album were joined by two of South Africa's top musicians, Miriam Makeba and Hugh Masekela, then exiled. In addition, there were two West African musicians included in the tour. Master-drummer Okyerema Asante had come to the States in the early 1970s as part of the Ghanaian Afro-rock/beat-band Hedzolleh brought over by Hugh Masekela; since then Okyerema has worked with many American artists such as Lonnie Smith, the Crusaders, Fleetwood Mac, Herbie Hancock, Roy Ayers, and Third World. The other West African was percussionist Francis Fuster from Sierra Leone, who had been the original conga player for Geraldo Pino's soul-oriented Heartbeats, set up in Freetown in 1961. Later on Fuster formed his own band in Lagos called Baranta, which I once had the pleasure of jamming with in the mid-1970s. Continuing his experimentations with African music, in 1990 Paul Simon based one track of his *Rhythms of the Saints* on the old Ghanaian highlife tune "Yaa Amponsah"— for which he employed two West African guitarists.

Canada

African music seems to have caught on in Canada as it has in North America generally since Paul Simon's *Graceland* album. In my recent trips to Canada I discovered that literally dozens of African musicians and bands were visiting or resident there.

Just before my first trip, the Ninth Annual International Jazz Festival was held in Montreal in July (1988) at which three Senegalese bands played: Doudou N' Diaye Rose, Toure Kunda, and Youssou N'Dour. Then from Gambia there was Mamma Tongue, from Mali Salif Keita (of Les Ambassadeurs fame) and Johnny Clegg's multiracial South African Savuka group that later returned to Canada as part of the North American tour they were doing with pop star George Michael.

I arrived in Canada in August 1988 to give a talk on highlife music at the Toronto World of Music, Art and Dance (WOMAD)

Rex Gyamfi.

Festival. WOMAD fosters Third World music and was originally founded in 1982 in Britain by Peter Gabriel. At this week-long event held at Toronto's Harbourfront many of the 250 artists who performed were from Africa, including the Shikisha female dance trio from South Africa, Mohama Konate's traditional Farafisa group from Burkina Faso, Shalambe from Zambia, Malian guitarist Ali Farka Toure, and the Tanzanian soukous group Orchestra Super Matima led by the colourful Remmy Ongala. Also from Africa, although not residing there, was the U.K.-based Zimbabwean guitar-band the Bhundu Boys and the German-based Ghanaian musician Rex Gyamfi, who is one of the pioneers of funk-influenced highlife. And there were African musicians resident in Toronto as well, like Gambian kora player Jali Lamine Suso, Ghanaian highlife singer Pat Thomas, and Africanada, a group of West Indian dancers led by Ghanaian Vida Hynes (it was Vida and her husband Julian who arranged my first trip to Canada). For one of its shows at WOMAD, Africanada was backed by Nexus, a mostly white Toronto African drumming ensemble led by Bob Becker, who in November of that year played with minimalist composer Steve Reich at London's South Bank.

In fact, Toronto has become Canada's main centre for African music—and particularly Ghanaian music, for it has the second largest number of resident Ghanaians (between five thousand and eight thousand) of any North American city after New York. As a result there are several Ghanaian and Ghanaian-influenced bands operating there who play at African music venues like the downtown Bamboo Club.

Besides Pat Thomas and Africanada, there is the Wanna Wazuri band run by Ghanaian keyboard player Alfred Schall, Nakupenda led by vocalist Nana Yaw Boakye, and Bishop Okele's mainly white group, the Officials. There are a number of all-white bands in town playing Ghanaian and African music, like Todd Fraracci and Patsy Stevens' Rayo Taxi, Orchestra Pavalo, and the League of Nations. And in the few months that I was in Toronto in 1988 several bands came from Ghana to perform. A. B. Crentsil's Ahenfo came twice and Jewel Ackah and his Butterfly Band came during a North American tour. Jewel was accompanied by his amazing twelve-year-old vocalist son and by his manager, John

Jewel Ackah.

Kofi Archer of Ghana Films. Although not directly from Ghana, but led by Ghanaian bassist Herman Asafo-Adjei and ex-Osibisa guitarist Alfred Kari Bannerman, the London-based Native Spirit band also made one of its numerous visits to Canada. And their drummer Kofi Baker, was none other than rock-drummer Ginger Baker's son, following his father's interest in African music. (In 1989 Native Spirit settled in Toronto.)

To cater to all this Ghanaian music, Ghanaian record companies have lately been established in Toronto. Alfred Schall's Wazuri label has recorded and released three albums: two of his own group and A. B. Crentsil's popular *Toronto by Night* album, which was released in 1985 and was the first Canadian-Ghanaian production. Another company called Royal Albert has produced the *Happy Birthday* album by Pope Flynn and *Highlife in Canada* by the prolific A. B. Crentsil. Then there is Rex Gyamfi's album *Awa Waa Tuu*, released by yet another Ghanaian record company called Nubian that is managed by Stanley Ansong, who also runs *African Letter*, one of Toronto's two black newspapers. By far the largest Ghanaian record company in Toronto is Highlife World/Afro-nova, managed by Sam Mensah and Thaddy Ulzen (who also run a weekly African programme on Toronto's CKLN FM station). Albums released by them include Thomas Frempong's *Aye Yi,* Pat Thomas's *Highlife Greats,* Jewel Ackah's *Electric Highlife* and *Oh Jesus,* Asare Bediako's *Lovers Highlife,* and Herman Asafo-Adjei's *Native Spirit.*

So Toronto is now producing a new blend of highlife music. Most important for this development is the ability of the different Ghanaian musicians abroad to work together and pool their resources to create a distinct modern sound that appeals to fans at home and abroad. And this seems to be the pattern in the highlife that's beginning to emerge from Canada; for at the WOMAD Festival Pat Thomas, Rex Gyamfi, Ghanaian master-drummer Gideon Foli Alorwoye (based in Chicago), and the Africanada group worked together on stage to give a session of highlife music and dance that went down well with the audience of three or four thousand. On his latest album *Saturday Night,* Alfred Schall worked with a number of Ghanaian musicians, including Pope Flynn, Nana Yaw Boakye, A. B. Crentsil, Alfred Kari Bannerman, and Rex Gyamfi.

Continental Europe

France

In Europe the main centre of African music is undoubtedly France, the focus of the French-speaking African record industry and the home of many top African artists, like South Africa's Bongi Makeba, blind guitarist/poet Pierre Akendengue from Gabon, and musician/writer Francis Bebey from the Cameroons. Cameroonian music is called makossa, a funked-up version of the traditional abele wedding parade music and tribal bolo-bo beat. Many Paris-based artists have had success with this music: Manu Dibango of "Soul Makossa" fame; bassist Vicky Edema, with his *Thank You Mama* album; and vocalist Rachel who, backed by musicians like Jojo Kouch, Lobe Valery, and Mango, stole the show at the Festival des Tropiques in 1982. At the Casino de Paris you can hear such bands as the eight-piece group M'bamina, which plays

Zairian rumba-rock, and Agbavia, led by Kito de Silva of the Republic of Benin, which plays highlife and salsa.

Other top African musicians in Paris are Sam Mangwana (after leaving Abidjan), Kanda Bongo Man, and his ex-guitarist Diblo Dibala, who has formed his own soukous (i.e., rumba rock) group called Loketo. In 1988 there were two massive African hits in France, "Ye Ke Ye Ke" by Malian kora player Mory Kante, and an album by Johnny Clegg's new band, Savuka.

In addition, Paris has become the centre of a fusion between African soukous and makossa and the zouk music of the French Antilles (played by bands like Kassav) being put together by Zairian musicians Souzy Kasseya, Kanda Bongo Man, guitarists Diblo Dibala and Ringo Star, Bopol, and M'Pongo Love, Cameroonians such as Moni Bile, Toto Guillaume, and Alhadji Toure, and Daouda from the Côte d'Ivoire.

Belgium

In Belgium, the interest in African music grows out of its historical ties with Central Africa. For example, the annual Sfinks (sphinx) Festival in 1982 featured artists such as Manu Dibango, Toto Guillaume, Lazare Kenmegre, and Francis Bebey from the Cameroons, and Bovick from Zaire. Belgium was the European base for the late Grand Master Franco of OK Jazz.

A result of this has been that some Belgian pop groups have gone African. African Queen from Brussels is English musician Sarah Osborne playing with four Belgians and Roland Binde from Zaire. They've all been influenced by Fela, who played in Brussels in 1981.

In other European countries like Germany, Scandinavia, and The Netherlands, African sounds are also catching on, particularly since the tours there by Fela and Sunny Ade.

Germany

In Germany griot music has become popular, and successful albums of this music have been produced, like the 1982 release of Bubacar Jammeh. Ghanaian highlife artists like Pat Thomas are also doing well, and in 1983 George Darko had a hit with a disco-highlife album. Another group operating in Germany is Kapingbdi from Liberia, led by Kojo Samuels and horn player Maisha, which plays highlifes, Afro-beats, and traditional Liberian music.

Another type of African music popular in Germany is the disco/funk style of highlife known as "burgher" (i.e., Hamburg) highlife, as it is a product of Ghanaian musicians resident in Hamburg and elsewhere in Germany, such as George Darko, Rex Gyamfi, Lee Duodo, Allan Cosmos Adu, Charles Amoah, and McGod. Not surprisingly, burgher highlife is also popular in Ghana and it is the first time in the hundred-year-old history of highlife that a major style of the music has evolved outside of West Africa.

The burgher phenomenon began in 1982, when guitarist George Darko (influenced by George Benson's playing) released the hit album *Akoo Te Brofo* (Parrot Speaks European), in which he combined the traditional Yaa Amponsah type of highlife with a touch of jazz, a lot of funk, and polyphonic keyboard effects played by Bob Fiscion—whom, coincidentally, in 1973/74 I was in a Accra band with, called Szaabo Soundz—together with Nana Fredua (who now runs the Black Note recording studio in Accra), Leslie Tex (now a preacher), and Bob Pinado, who is another Ghanaian musician in Germany.

Since 1982 George Darko has released more burgher albums, such as *Highlife Times, Moni Palaver,* and *Odo Soronko.* His original vocalist Lee Duodu has gone on to form his own funk highlife band called Kantata.

Scandinavia

In 1983, the Anglo-African Jazira band made its first tour of Scandinavia, where there were already a number of similar mixed bands such as the Danish group Kutarshi (Hausa for "wake up") and Amandu Jaar in Sweden.

Kutarshi's lineup includes artists from Ghana, Togo, Sierra Leone, South Africa, and Denmark. Delip Apo, the leader, is from northern Ghana. Before coming to Europe, he played with many West African bands. In Ghana he's played with the Vis-à-Vis pop-band and guitar-bands like Gyasi's, Okukuseku's, Akawaboah's, and Frempong's; in Sierra Leone with the Afro-Nationals and the

Delip Apo and his Afro-Danish group.

Godfathers; in Liberia with Afrodelics; and in the Côte d'Ivoire
with the Superstars.

Since then, more mixed bands have appeared in Scandinavia
like Zebra, composed of three Danish musicians, a singer from
Tanzania called N'Guza, and two Ghanaians—drummer Henry
Zyi Soloman (Solo), who used to be with Classic Vibes, and Ewe
master-drummer Akakpolee Afadi. The three Danes were in fact
in Ghana in the mid-1980s studying local music. These were
bassist Christian Glahn, keyboard player Christer Moller, and sax-

ist Mike Nielsen. And on this visit Mike played on an album by
Pat Thomas.

More extraordinary than the mixed bands in Britain, Denmark, and Sweden are a number of other African pop-bands in
Scandinavia whose composition is practically all white. In
Copenhagen, an African pop-band called Doctor Livingstone and
the Presumers is made up of ten Danish musicians. Also in
Copenhagen is the Africapa band, all of whose musicians except
one is white (the exception being a Ghanaian). The band was led
until recently by guitarist Frank Bojestraum, who was in Ghana in
1987 for the Accra conference of the International Association for
the Study of Popular Music (IASPM). In the town of Aarhus there
is an all-white band called the Highlife N'Gogo Orchestra that
boasts fourteen members.

Similarly, in Gothenberg in Sweden, there is an eleven-piece
all-white African band called Mama Malumma, several of whose
musicians (Hans Edberg, Anders Lindstrom, and Jesper Landhaal)
have visited Ghana.

So in Scandinavia one finds a strong mirror-image of what
goes on with many copyright bands in Africa. While in Africa the
musicians huddle around a record player learning the latest copyright hits from Europe and the States, in more northerly climes
white musicians sit huddled around learning African music in parrot fashion. It is most certainly an odd sight seeing all-white bands
playing African music and singing in Swahili, Lingala, and Twi.
But even though they may not understand what they're singing
about, the rhythms are genuine enough. And it all helps spread the
African music message abroad.

The Netherlands

After the independence of Surinam many Surinam people settled in The Netherlands. Their musical taste and the long-standing
interest in jazz in The Netherlands provided a receptive public for
African popular music.

After leaving Osibisa and producing the funk-band Hi-Tension, Ghanaian percussionist Kofi Ayivor settled in The Netherlands with his Surinamese wife. Then there are the Gambian musicians who make up Ifang Bondi (to prove oneself), which plays

Afro-mendengue music. This group, formed in 1967, was originally known as the Super Eagles of Gambia, and I remember seeing them in Ghana around 1970. At the time they were playing soukous and were well known as the first African band to introduce the wah-wah pedal and fuzz-box. Since then they've gone back to their roots and now play a funky sort of griot music.

Another way the African-feel is slipping into the Dutch pop mainstream is through the white ska music of groups like Doe Maar (Do Your Own Thing) and Mark Foggo and the Secret Meeting. These bands are modeled on British two-tone bands like the Beat, UB40, and the Specials, and like them have crossed punk-rock with reggae-ska, creating African-like crisscross rhythms. Their lyrics are heavily political, again like those of British two-tone. Two of Doe Maar's biggest hits in Holland in 1982/83 were "De Bomb," about the nuclear bomb, and "Pa." According to Stan Rijven, a music reporter for a newspaper in the city of Trouw, the reason for Doe Maar's huge success in The Netherlands is that ska is the best vehicle for singing in the Dutch language. In other words, ska and Dutch go together like Italian and opera.

One of the top African bands in Amsterdam at the moment is Sloopy Mike Gyamfi's Sankofa band, formed in 1987. Sloopy was born in Ghana in 1956 and for five years was a member of Eddie Donkor's second band, the Simple Seven. In the early 1980s Sloopy formed his own band, Adinkra (the name of a type of Akan cloth print); they recorded at my Bokoor Studios and one song from those sessions was released on the *Guitar and Gun II* album by Cherry Red label in London in 1985. An Adinkra appearance (recorded at Bokoor) was aired in the BBC black music television series "Repercussions." In the mid-1980s Sloopy left Ghana for Holland and for a time was guitarist/vocalist for fellow Ghanaian Charles Tetteh's Amsterdam-based band, Kumbi Saleh (the name of the capital of ancient medieval Ghana). He then formed Sankofa (Go Back and Retrieve), which plays a type of highlife Sloopy calls "brightlife." Captain Moro, the ex-drummer of Eddie Donkor's Simple Seven, joined him, as did Sloopy's brother Seth Darko for a while. Seth had played with the Odomankoma concert party and the Rural Soundz (of the Ghana

Seth Darko, Sloopy Mike Gyamfi's brother.

Department of Rural Development) for some years, before moving to Togo to play guitar for the Christ Apostolic band of the Ibo United Church of Christ and the pop-band Cloud Seven. He was also a session musician at the Top Rank studio in Aba in eastern Nigeria.

World Music

Since the mid-1980s African popular music has become part of "world music" or "world beat," which also includes non-mainstream black music of the New World such as the Brazilian samba, Trinidad soca, the zouk music of Martinique and Guadeloupe, and the folk music of Bulgaria, Vietnam, Indonesia, Cajun people, Portugal, Afghanistan, and elsewhere. Pioneering this development have been independent record labels in North America such as Shanachie, Celluloid, Original Music, African World, and Makossa, as well as the older folk labels Nonesuch and

Folkways. In Britain a World Music label was set up in 1987 by twelve independent labels, including Sterns African Records, Rogue, Cooking Vinyl, Earthworks, Globestyle, Hannibal, Oval, Triple Earth, Topic, WOMAD, the British National Sound Archives, and World Circuit. World music is also being released by big companies such as WEA, Virgin, Polygram, and Mango. Mango was set up in the late 1980s by Island Records, which, after the death of Bob Marley, was the first big record company to turn to African music in 1982/83.

Radio, television, and other media are following the world beat trend. In the States there is the National Public Radio Afropop series. In Britain there are programs hosted by John Peel, Andy Kershaw, and Oval Records owner Charlie Gillett, who wrote the pioneering book on rock history called *The Sounds of the City*. Also, American and European pop stars like Bob Geldof, David Byrne, Michael Jackson, Quincy Jones, Lionel Ritchie, UB40, Paul Simon, George Harrison, and Peter Gabriel have been working with African and Third World artists and/or using world media linkups to obtain funds for famine relief, the anti–apartheid struggle, and other human rights and ecological movements. These efforts resulted in concerts such as Band-aid and the Nelson Mandela concert at Wimbley Stadium in 1988, as well as the song "We Are the World."

The recent reclassifying of what was known as African or Afro-pop as world music, however, has a double edge to it. On the positive side, it stresses the idea of African music being global and cosmopolitan, rather than primitive and folk/ethnic. But at the same time the term removes the African connection. Whereas people should be made even more aware of the importance of African music, and that just as practically the whole of Western pop music has rested for a hundred years on the shoulders of the black music of the Americas—from ragtime to rock and rumba to reggae—so is world music being carried on the shoulders of African popular music. And this trend started with the Island Records *Sounds Afrique* album of soukous music that fuses African music with the Cuban rumba, and their albums of Sunny Ade's juju music (Yoruba dance music with a touch of the samba). It should be remembered that just as African dance and music were taken by slaves to the New World, the black music of the diaspora has returned home.

Of course there have been previous African pop crazes in the West, such as the South African kwela and "penny-whistle" hits of the 1950s, the township jazz of Hugh Masekela, Abdullah Ibrahim (Dollar Brand), and Miriam Makeba (helped by Harry Belafonte) in the 1960s, and the Afro-rock and Afro-soul of Osibisa and Manu Dibango in the 1970s. But these never went global, as did African music in the 1980s. Now that it has—and is being taken up by the commercial music industry, pop pundits, radio DJs and television/film companies—the African name is dropped and Africa's popular music is categorised with relatively exotic folk music styles that have never had the international impact of either black New World or African music, which had to make their way through both slavery and colonialism.

To be quite blunt, the black musics of the Americas and Africa are the nearest thing this planet has to a global twentieth-century sound and lingua franca. No other folk music, nor for that matter European (and usually state-subsidised) classical music, has done this. So the terms "world music" or "world beat" are fine as long they are not used to obscure the fact that black diasporic and African dance music has become the mainstream style for both the Old and the New World, East and West, North and South—and practically all other popular music-styles are feeding into, mixing with, or flowing out from African-American and African music.

About the Author

John Collins knows Africa from the inside. He was brought up there as a child and went to a university in Ghana. Since 1969, he has been playing and recording with many of the top West African musicians and bands featured in *West African Pop Roots*. John has published his research into African music in books, articles, and broadcasts. He has contributed to journals such as *West Africa Magazine, Afrique, Africa Journal, Africa Now, Music Express* (Lagos), *Africa Music* (Lagos), *African Arts* (USA), *Latina and Noise* (Japan), and *Black Echoes* (UK). In 1975 John formed his own guitar-band, Bokoor, and has released records in West Africa and Europe. He now runs Bokoor Music Studio at Ofankor, eight miles north of Accra, and is in the process of helping to set up a Ghanaian/African popular music archive there. In 1991 he was appointed to the Ghana National Folkloric Copyright Administration's board of trustees.

Acknowledgments

Warm thanks and appreciation are due to the numerous musicians, researchers, and friends who have provided information for this book: Bob Vans (comedian with Ghana Arts Council); Frank Drake; Max Steuer and Christine Allen; Robert and Basia Andrews; Dr. J. L. Harrison; Tony Amadi (African Music); Colin and Ronnie Ayers; Colin Lodge; Stuart Sutton-Jones; Jones Attuquayefio; Roderick Ebanks (Institute of Jamaica); Hilton Fyle (disc jockey); Brian Eno; Jumma Santos (Taj Mahal band); Richard Hill; members of Osibisa; Randy Weston; Paul Richards; Eddie Meadows; Peter Kunzler; Nii Nortey; Godwin Avenorgbor (Ghana Broadcasting); Fred Gales; Francis Goby; Bob Bundy; Juliet Highet; Anton Corbijn; Stan Rijven; Ian Watts; Jason Berry; Yebuah Mensah (Accra Orchestra); E. T. Mensah (Tempos); Kofi Ghanaba (Guy Warren); Joe Kelly (Tempos); Horace Djoleto (Tempos); Amoo Dodoo (Tempos); Jacob Awuletey (Tempos); M. Williams (Williams and Marbel); Professor Opoku (Institute of African Studies, Legon); K. P. Amponsah (Koo Nimo); Robert Sprigge (History Department, Legon); Squire Addo (Jazz Kings); Kweikumah Stevens (Red Spots); Dr. Wiredu (Philosophy Department, Legon); E. F. Collins (Philosophy Department, Legon); J. K. Addo (Casino Orchestra); A. A. Mensah (musicologist); Efua Sutherland (Institute of African Studies, Legon); Dr. K. N. Bame (Institute of African Studies, Legon); Professor Nketia (Institute of African Studies, Legon); Martin Owusu (English Department, University of Cape Coast); F. A. Torto (Excelsior Orchestra); Victor Olaiya (Cool Cats); members of the Jaguar Jokers; Y. B. Bampoe (Opiah); Mr. Baidoo; K. M. Hammond; Bob Johnson (Axim Trio); Francis Kenya (Riches Big Sound); Bob Cole (comedian); Ajax Bukana (comedian); Mark Anthony (artist); Kwaa Mensah (concert party); E. K. Nyame (Akan Trio); James Moxon (publishing); Ebeneezer Obey (juju musician); Johnny Opoku Acheampong; Charlie, Carol, Omar, and Marimba Easmon; Cliff Eck (Bunzus); Eddie Omari Agyepong (Bunzus); Nii Ashitey (Wulomei); Faisal Helwani ("F" Promotions); Jerry James Lartey (Basa-Basa); Nii Ayitey II (Basa Basa); Bob Pinado; Fela Anikulapo-Kuti and J. K. Braimah (Africa 70); Samuel Oju King (Echoes); Ignace de Souza (Black Santiagos); Segun Bucknor (Assembly); Joni Haastrup (Mono-Mono); Victor Uwaifo (Melody Maestros); Stan Plange (Uhurus); Osei Bonsu Senior (African Beats); Roy Chicago (highlife band); Big Joe Oladele (Granadians); Angus Ukoli; Dean Okoro/Disi; Remi Akano (music reporter, Lagos); Albert Jones (Heartbeats '72); Daniel and Moses Banini (drummers); Michael Ganyhoh (master-drummer); Lincoln Deku; EMI archives; David Coplan; Peter Drury; Peter Wilks; Charlie Pickup; John Chernoff; Misseli Botiano (Afrique); Kofi Ayivor; Victor Amarfio; Sammy Odoh; members of the Ghana Musicians' Union; Akie Deen; James Armstrong; Jak Kilby; Stern's African Record Centre; Ronnie Graham; Robert Urbanus; Wouter Rosingh; Brother Sam, Stagger, Aaron, and members of the Harambee Two black self-help organisation; Dinah Reindolf (Ghana Arts Council); Willie Anku; Mike Popham; Jilian Jackman; Daryl Curtis; Florence Akst (BBC); Patrick Collins; Nora, Ellen, and Panyin; Simon and Larry Harrison; Diane Roy; Laura and Kevin Sala; Gill Garb; Dovey Soklu; Dennis Beesley; Duncan Carmichael and family; Flemming Harrev; Bayo Martins; Eddie Bru-Mindah; Ms. Chapman-Nyaho; Gifty Naa Dodowa; Julian and Vida Hynes; Cathy and David Locke; Eddie Quansah; Apostle Akwesi Abeka; Reverend J. M. Odonkor; Eddie Ansah; Chris Waterman; Wolfgang and Jutta Bender; Thierry and Regina Secretan; Christian Glahn; King Bruce; Robert, Jimmy, and Dawn Beckley; Charles and Angie Keil; Jan van Bella; Beattie and Pinnock Casely-Hayford; Charlie Isso; Patsy and Todd Fraracci; Kwese Asare; Hamish Ramsay and family; and Ghassan, Morwan, Osama, Nada, and the Kalmoni family.

Index